Praise for *Marriage That Works*

"At Focus on the Family, we hear from couples every day who are struggling in their relationships and desperately seeking healing in their marriages. Through personal and pastoral experience—along with a keen understanding of biblical teaching—Chip Ingram casts a vision for marriage as God intends it. Better yet, he shows readers how to achieve the kind of marriage they've always dreamed of."

Jim Daly, president, Focus on the Family

"This is not just another book on marriage. Chip cuts through political correctness to get to the heart of Christlikeness by challenging both men and women to greater sacrifice in their relationship with one another."

Kyle Idleman, author, *not a fan.* and *Don't Give Up*

"If you are looking for a practical, biblically based picture of marriage, you need look no further. Chip Ingram has nailed it. I highly recommend *Marriage That Works*."

Gary D. Chapman, PhD, author, *The 5 Love Languages*

Praise for *Why I Believe*

"Chip Ingram has a way of taking complex and intimidating material and making it accessible and applicable to everyone."

Kyle Idleman, pastor, author of *Grace Is Greater*

"We all need straight answers to the questions we ask about God, faith, and the Bible ˰˰˰ ˰ ˰˰ ˰ ˰˰˰ ˰ our

D1367013

hearts and minds around the most important issues we face and offers authentic and transparent answers."

Jack Graham, pastor of Prestonwood
Baptist Church, Plano, TX

Praise for *The Real God*

"Chip Ingram provides wonderful insight to help you see God's character as presented in Scripture. In these pages, he offers practical biblical help to live out the implications of a refreshed and renewed perspective of God. The principles in this book will inspire, encourage, and empower you to become more like Jesus Christ."

Rick Warren, founding pastor, Saddleback Church

Praise for *Good to Great in God's Eyes*

"The principles that my good friend Chip Ingram outlines in this book will inspire, encourage, and enable any sincere reader to maximize their God-given potential for the glory of God and for the good of others. Read this only if you want your life to matter."

Tony Evans, PhD, senior pastor,
Oak Cliff Bible Fellowship

I CHOOSE PEACE

I CHOOSE PEACE

HOW TO QUIET YOUR HEART
IN AN ANXIOUS WORLD

CHIPINGRAM

BakerBooks

a division of Baker Publishing Group
Grand Rapids, Michigan

© 2021 by Chip Ingram

Published by Baker Books
a division of Baker Publishing Group
PO Box 6287, Grand Rapids, MI 49516-6287
www.bakerbooks.com

Printed in the United States of America

Library of Congress Cataloging-in-Publication Data
Names: Ingram, Chip, 1954– author.
Title: I choose peace : how to quiet your heart in an anxious world / Chip Ingram.
Description: Grand Rapids, Michigan : Baker Books, a division of Baker Publishing
    Group, [2021] | Includes bibliographical references.
Identifiers: LCCN 2020042357 | ISBN 9780801093821 (cloth) | ISBN 9781540901286
    (paperback)
Subjects: LCSH: Peace—Religious aspects—Christianity. | Anxiety—Religious
    aspects—Christianity. | Stress management—Religious Aspects—Christianity. |
    Bible. Philippians, IV—Criticism, interpretation, etc.
Classification: LCC BV4908.5 .I54 2021 | DDC 248.8/6—dc23
LC record available at https://lccn.loc.gov/2020042357

21 22 23 24 25 26 27   7 6 5 4 3 2 1

In keeping with biblical principles of creation stewardship, Baker Publishing Group advocates the responsible use of our natural resources. As a member of the Green Press Initiative, our company uses recycled paper when possible. The text paper of this book is composed in part of post-consumer waste.

To the Venture Church family—
elders who became fast friends
and modeled these truths,
staff who practiced them with me,
and a congregation who loved and supported
Theresa and me for nearly a decade.
May the *shalom* of God be in you
and with you all the days of your precious lives.

CONTENTS

INTRODUCTION

Jesus and His disciples were crossing the Sea of Galilee in a small fishing boat one day when a violent storm swept over the water. Waves crashed over the side of the boat, and the disciples were terrified. They cried out to Jesus for help, but somehow, some way, He was still asleep in the stern. They were overwhelmed with fear for their lives; He was taking a nap. And when they woke Him up and accusingly asked, "Don't you care if we drown?" (Mark 4:38), He didn't thank them for alerting Him to the problem. He simply calmed the storm and asked why they were so faithless and afraid. In circumstances that would make most people panic, Jesus had astonishing, supernatural peace.

If you are a believer and follower of Jesus, you have peace too. Maybe that's news to you. Perhaps you've been struggling and straining to find peace in the midst of tumultuous circumstances and personal crises. Maybe, after discovering that being a Christian doesn't pluck anyone out of all life's problems, you've wondered where that elusive peace is. You know it's a promise in Scripture. You just don't know why you aren't experiencing it. And you might argue with someone who tells you that you already have it.

But I'm telling you anyway. You already have it. Jesus actually gave *His* peace to all His followers the night before His crucifixion. "Peace I leave with you; my peace I give you. I do not give to you as the world gives. Do not let your hearts be troubled and do not be afraid" (John 14:27). So you don't have the kind of peace the world tries to give. You have the peace that Jesus gives—the same peace He had that day in the back of the boat while a storm raged around Him.

So why don't all Christians experience this supernatural peace? Because we must willfully, purposefully choose to walk in the peace He gave us. It isn't automatic. Even though we already have it, we tend to pursue peace on the world's terms. The world offers it to us if and when we are successful, accomplished, pretty, rich, famous, or secure. It holds out an ideal that most people can never attain, and those who do attain that find out it isn't all it's cracked up to be. It promises peace but can't deliver. And in the process, it robs us of the peace we've already been given.

This book will help you overcome the various challenges and lies that rob us of Jesus's peace. We will discover the biblical truths and principles that allow us to experience deep, lasting peace in the midst of relational conflict, anxious moments, the brokenness of this world, difficult circumstances, a materialistic culture, tests of faith, and all the uncertain times we experience in the chaos of life. We will look at the theological basis for experiencing supernatural peace, but the focus is not on theory. It's on actually experiencing it. By the end of the book, you will have numerous practical steps you can take to experience the fullness of the peace Jesus has promised.

This book is not written in a vacuum, an ivory tower, or a pulpit. It comes from decades of experience, much of it hard earned, and observations about how God works. Many of its illustrations come from the hardest times of my life. It was written during a pandemic that threatened the global economy and changed the way we live. And all the adversity, challenges, and crisis situations of life do nothing to change the truths and practices we find in God's Word. In fact, they confirm them. These principles of peace apply in the best and worst of times because they aren't dependent on the times. They are rooted in the nature and character of God Himself.

That means we can have the kind of peace that is available twenty-four hours a day, seven days a week, 365 days a year. It is never beyond our reach if we know how to reach it and take the steps God has given us to experience it. That's my prayer for you in the pages that follow—that you will anchor yourself far deeper than the chaotic circumstances and values of this world and live high above them. And that every day for the rest of your life, your heart, mind, and soul will be filled with the peace that passes all human understanding.

CHAPTER 1

Choose Peace
in Relational Conflict

I didn't grow up following Jesus. I went to church, but I never encountered God there and met a lot of people who talked one way and lived another. I didn't know if God existed and really didn't care. I didn't think I needed Him.

Life has a way of pointing out your needs over time, and I had plenty of them. And God has a way of bringing people into your life who can show you what He is like and how He meets those needs. Right after I graduated from high school, I met some people whose lives were radically different from mine. They shared God's love with me and invited me into a personal relationship with Him. They told me Jesus died in my place to break down all the walls between me and God so I could have peace with Him. It was all very new, and I was very skeptical, but I turned from my self-will and sin and asked Jesus to come into my life.

As a new believer, I was given a Bible that was written in easy-to-understand language. No one told me I had to read it, but I couldn't put it down. I even hid it under my pillow; I didn't want my parents to think I'd become a Jesus Freak. But there were some things I couldn't hide. I changed. My insecurities had driven me to be a type A overachiever who just had to date the right girl, get the right scholarship, and accomplish whatever would make me a "somebody." But when my new relationship with God made me a somebody, there was nobody left to impress. He had taken up residence inside me. I had peace.

My father was an alcoholic and a retired Marine (not an ex-Marine, as I was once bluntly corrected). When I came home from college after my first year, he asked what was going on with me.

"What do you mean?" I asked.

"You're different," he said. "Really different."

"What's different about me?"

"There's peace in your life. How'd you get it?"

I was hardly a theologian at the time. It was all very new. So I gave him the best answer I could. "I have no idea. All I can tell you is I have a personal relationship with God and have been reading the New Testament."

"Where do you get one of those?"

I told him, and he started getting up early every morning to read the Bible. Eventually he came to grips with some of his issues and turned his life over to Christ. He began to change too.

Peace is part of the package when we enter into a relationship with God in Christ. It's not always a smooth path—Dad and I both had plenty of ups and downs along the way—but it's ours for the taking. Yet we have to choose it. Peace is a gift and a choice.

> **Peace is a gift and a choice.**

Over the years, I've learned how to determine whether I receive or reject that gift. I've managed to figure out some unfortunate ways to quench God's peace so I don't actually experience it. I know how to worry, stress out, focus on the future, and get into conflict with other people, including my own wife and children, and I've seen the peace dissipate pretty quickly. But I also know by now how to be intentional about it. It's possible to train our hearts and minds to shift our focus and experience the peace we've been given. We really can choose to live in peace and experience God's restoration in our lives.

What Is the Source of Your Peace?

People tend to search for peace from one of three sources. One is *inward*. Advocates of this approach will tell you that you just need to look within. It's already there; you just need to find it. You can do that through meditation, relaxation, centering, and whatever else it takes to find harmony with the cosmos. But it's not "out there" somewhere, and you can't depend on circumstances and other people to give it to you. You have to discover it yourself, somewhere deep inside.

There's some truth to that approach. Circumstances and other people really don't provide peace, and there is some value in going deep within. But what source are you going to find there? Meditation and relaxation are means in a process, not sources. The search within would have to lead to something reliable and true.

Another source people commonly appeal to is *outward*. We are told to achieve, to conquer our fears, to control our emotions and our environment, to perform in ways that lead to lasting peace. It's out there, and we are to discover it by accomplishing something that brings us peace—getting into a good school and making good grades, finding the right person to be with, finding a meaningful and profitable career track, having a nice home and driving a nice car, creating a secure income. The idea is that if we achieve, conquer, and perform, our desires and circumstances will align, and we'll have the peace we're looking for.

The problem with this approach is that the peace that is out there is always just out of reach. There's never enough achievement and success to make life truly peaceful. There's always a situation or two that need to be fixed. There's never quite enough money to completely satisfy us. American oil tycoon J. Paul Getty was the richest person in the world, at one point bringing in $20 million a day, and he was consumed with keeping it going and getting more. He was divorced five times and alienated from his children, often prioritizing money over their health and welfare. Near the end of his life, he said he would gladly give his millions away for just one lasting marital success. He had spent his life accumulating more and more and still had no peace. No matter how much he tried to buy it, it just wasn't "out there."

Eastern traditions tend to emphasize the inward source of peace, while Western traditions have gravitated toward the outward source. And some of these approaches are not inherently wrong in themselves. There's nothing wrong with breathing deeply, relaxing, and centering, on one hand, or earning money, making good grades, and searching for the right relationships on the other. Those can be great skills to have. But they are methods and endeavors that work much better as by-products or outcomes of peace, not the source of it. They can't ground us in reality, and they aren't dependable.

The dependable approach, the one that grounds us in truth, is *upward*. Peace is a person, not a condition (Ephesians 2:14). Jesus said He doesn't give the kind of peace the world gives. He gives His own peace (John 14:27). We trust in Him, depend on Him, and abide in Him. We cultivate faith, love, and obedience to His ways, and He gives His peace to us. We don't discover it within or reach for it outside of ourselves. We receive it by faith.

> **Peace is a person, not a condition.**

When I turned from my sin and invited Christ to forgive me and come into my life, He took up residence in me and sealed me with His Spirit. I didn't know such monumental events happened at the time, but I can look back and see that they did. The Holy Spirit lives inside of those who believe, and through Him we experience God's sovereignty over a chaotic world, the goodness of His nature, and the peace and calm of knowing Him. In fact, peace is one of the fruits of the Spirit (Galatians 5:22). Regardless of whether circumstances go up or down, relationships are good or bad, or the stock market rises or falls, we can have a supernatural peace that transcends human understanding (Philippians 4:7). He will keep us in perfect peace as our minds are stayed on Him (Isaiah 26:3).

God's Peace: *Shalom*

Dictionary definitions of *peace* often describe it as the absence of something—the absence of disturbance and hostility, of internal and external strife, of conflict between people or nations. In other words, it's the calm between the storms, those times of getting along or being at rest that are so often disrupted by crises and turmoil. In fact, many people have a hard time describing peace without focusing on what it is not. But God's definition of peace is different. It's something we can choose, embrace, and enjoy. We don't run away from turmoil to find it. We enter into it. Rather than the absence of some conflict or stress, it's the presence of something God gives.

The Hebrew word for this peace is *shalom*. It's a familiar term for many, and *peace* is the best one-word translation we have for it. But the English word *peace* doesn't nearly capture the meaning of the Hebrew expression. *Shalom* is much bigger. It's a rich, full concept that covers every area of our lives.

There are four aspects of the biblical use of *shalom*: (1) complete wholeness and health; (2) harmony in relationships; (3) success and progress in our purpose; and (4) victory over enemies. So in contrast to the world's peace, God's peace includes our mind, body, and emotions. It covers our marriages and children, relationships with neighbors and coworkers, and fellowship with other members of the body of Christ. Our alignment with God, His purpose for our lives, and the ability to live in His will are all involved—no matter how many ups and downs we go through in following Him and walking out His plans. And this *shalom* encompasses confidence that He is protecting us, providing for us, helping us overcome difficult problems and adversaries, and giving us victories in life's challenges.

We will face those challenges, sometimes long-lasting ones, in every one of these aspects of *shalom*. Some people spend nearly their whole lives wondering if they are in the right job or the right place or if they are with the right person. Many of us live with the dreaded fear of missing out, that FOMO that keeps us thinking of alternatives almost constantly. At some point we will have conflict with somebody, face challenges that seem insurmountable, struggle with physical and emotional issues, and search for God's will for our lives. But we can trust that God will lead us toward *shalom* in every area of our lives as His stated purpose for each of us. He wants us to have peace in all its fullness.

Jesus is the Prince of Peace (Isaiah 9:6), literally the Prince of *Shalom*. The night before His crucifixion, He told His followers that He was giving them His *shalom*. "Peace I leave with you; my peace I give you. I do not give to you as the world gives. Do not let your hearts be troubled and do not be afraid" (John 14:27). That's more than a promise of a calm demeanor in a moment of crisis. *Shalom* is a comprehensive expression of God's will for us in every situation we face.

> *Shalom* is a comprehensive expression of God's will for us in every situation we face.

"Do not let your hearts be troubled and do not be afraid." What a great line for us—an assurance of the peace of God in any area where we feel unsettled. When you're watching the news and feel threatened by a rapidly spreading disease or an economic downturn; when you're worried about your future, whether you will ever find the right job, get married, have children, and have good, satisfying relationships through it all; when you're looking around you and seeing all the things people are dealing with in this world, you need that kind of assurance. The good news is that God gives it to us.

That doesn't mean everything will always work out just the way we want it to. It does mean, however, that we can live our entire lives as followers of Christ with supernatural peace. Some people go through their whole lives with that kind of peace available to them and never choose it. They are robbed of something that was theirs for the taking. The purpose of this book—and God's purpose for our lives—is to give us the understanding and the tools to avoid that tragedy.

In the first five chapters, we're going to look at five things that rob us of our peace. Paul covers them in Philippians 4, and the first is conflict in a relationship. Some of us get along with nearly everybody, while others have a hard time getting along with anybody. But all of us have someone in our lives with whom we would like to have a better relationship. If you had to come up with a person who is at odds with you (or you with them), whether in your family or somewhere else in your social network, whether now or buried in the distant past, who would it be? Maybe you can think of several, but my guess is one person came to mind first. Who is that?

Whoever that is—an old friend, an in-law, an ex-spouse, a contentious coworker—you can't experience your God-given *shalom* if you push it down and cover it up, or if you always think the problem is all the other person's fault and none of your own. Whatever lack of relationship health you don't deal with, whatever poison or bitterness eats away at you will affect you somehow. It may color your healthy relationships in negative ways, unsettle your emotions, or manifest in physical issues like indigestion and migraines. Whatever the case, you need to be at peace in your relationships, at least as far as it depends on you. Full reconciliation may not always be possible, but it is possible to know you've done everything you can do and be content with that. In the following pages, we are going to walk through a biblical process for getting peace when you have relational conflict.

Dealing with Relational Conflict

● *The Context*

When Paul wrote Philippians, he was in confinement in Rome—probably under house arrest awaiting a trial for

23

crimes he didn't commit. He deeply loved the church at Philippi, where he had also been in prison, though just for one very dramatic night. God had done amazing things in this church, and Paul thought of it fondly. It was one of the bright spots of his ministry.

But there were a few problems in Philippi, and when we read between the lines of his letter, we can see that some people may have been drifting away from God and forgetting the importance and the power of the gospel in their lives. There was also apparently some relational conflict, some sort of personality clash or competitive spirit between some of the members. So Paul wrote to remind them of his love, to encourage them to stand firm, to urge them to plant their feet in the kingdom of heaven where their true citizenship was, and to give them hope in the midst of the mess of this world.

He ends chapter 3 with these reminders and a call to live out their new, heavenly life on earth. And in that context, he turns his attention to the two people who need to remember that heavenly citizenship in the midst of their relationship. These two women might have expected a stern rebuke, a command to get with the program and behave, but that's not the heart behind Paul's words. He was encouraging them to remember who they were, who God is, and how their hope applies to life in this world. Listen to his tender but strong words to each of them.

"Therefore, my brothers and sisters, you whom I love and long for, my joy and crown, stand firm in the Lord in this way, dear friends!" (Philippians 4:1). Those are not the words of an angry leader. They are the words of an encouraging friend. These people are his *joy* and his *crown* whom he *loves* and *longs for*. He is telling them that when they don't live in the peace God provides, it breaks his heart. He wants them to stand firm in the hope they have been given.

● *The Plea*

Then Paul issues a direct plea for unity and request for counsel:

> I plead with Euodia and I plead with Syntyche to be of the same mind in the Lord. Yes, and I ask you, my true companion, help these women since they have contended at my side in the cause of the gospel, along with Clement and the rest of my co-workers, whose names are in the book of life. (Philippians 4:2–3)

These are two good women. Paul is not looking for fault here. No one is "the bad guy." From the context, we can tell that this is not a moral or a doctrinal issue. Perhaps they disagree about how the church ought to function, or maybe their personalities just rub each other the wrong way. We don't know. But we do know that Paul sees them as strong and faithful members of this church who have been greatly used by God. They have contended with him, "at [his] side" as his right and left hands, in the growing of this church. They have been instrumental in the strength of this church through its beginnings and its opposition and challenges. Their names are written in the Book of Life. For whatever reason, they aren't getting along now. And, as in any family or small group, conflict between two people affects the others.

So Paul pleads with these women to agree, literally to have the same mind. He also asks a "true companion" to help them—to intervene in the situation and give them counsel. Sometimes two people can't resolve their own differences. They need help. There's nothing wrong with that. It's how the body of Christ works to bring unity and peace.

The phrase "true companion," or "loyal yokefellow" in some translations, is the Greek *syzygos*, which describes a strong bond between two parties—in marriage, labor (like two oxen bound together), or with a very close companion. Here it could refer to one of Paul's partners in ministry—an idea that has led to plenty of speculation about this person's identity—or it could be read as a proper name. In any case, the meaning fits very nicely with the point of Paul's plea, which is aimed at getting people to walk together in peace and harmony. The small church, which likely met in someone's home at this point, had a problem. Conflict, resentment, competitiveness, and whatever other dynamics that were involved were affecting the whole group. Paul recognized someone there who probably had the gift of exhortation and wise counsel, and he wanted that person to sit down with these women and help.

● The Commands

Next Paul gives two commands. The first deals with this church's relational focus. It's easy in the midst of a conflict to focus on the problem, specifically on the other person's faults, motives, offenses, and attitudes. We replay events and conversations in our minds, fixate on whatever part of the relationship is bad (even if most of it is good), and begin to demonize the other person. We harden our hearts, nurse our wounds, and cultivate our anger. And anger that simmers long enough begins to boil over. Our focus makes the problem worse. So Paul tells them to change their focus.

"Rejoice in the Lord always. I will say it again: Rejoice!" (Philippians 4:4). We may read these words as a nice encouragement, but in context, it's a command. Paul is telling them to get their eyes off horizontal relationships among human beings and put them on their vertical relationship with God. This command is not just for the two women at odds with each other; it's for the whole church. He doesn't want them to take sides, to try to figure out who's right and wrong or how this power struggle is going to play out. That's our tendency, isn't it? We develop cliques and factions, and small conflicts turn into big ones. We find people who agree with us, and the stakes get higher. If we want to have peace, we have to shift our focus from people to God.

If we want to have peace, we have to shift our focus from people to God.

Try going to a coffee shop sometime and listen to everybody's conversations. Pretend like you're doing something on your phone or your laptop but tune in to what's going on around you. "I don't know what he's thinking, but . . ." "He plays golf three times a week and expects me to take care of the kids!" "I can't believe my roommate; I don't know how much longer I can do this." "My supervisor must be on drugs." What are these people doing? Gathering people to their cause, building up their side, stirring up animosity against someone else. It's like pouring gasoline on a fire. You can't imagine that these conversations are actually making anything better.

What would make things better is a change in focus. Turning our attention to God, rejoicing in all that He has done, celebrating the life and promises He has given us—that radical shift in attitude quenches a lot of fires. Some things are much more important than making sure we are happy in a situation and getting the respect we think we deserve. Recognizing the bigger issues makes our other issues look a lot smaller.

Recognizing the bigger issues makes our other issues look a lot smaller.

Then Paul gives a second command: "Let your gentleness be evident to all. The Lord is near" (Philippians 4:5). These believers have a personal responsibility to each other. Instead of putting the blame on the other person, they are to have enough humility to take the lead in resolving the problem. Why? Because the Lord is near.

The Lord's nearness could be taken in two ways: either that He is close by and available, watching us in our conflicts and offering solutions for them; or that He is coming back soon, which is consistent with Paul's words at the end of chapter 3. Whether the focus of this passage is Jesus's availability or our accountability in light of His return, the application is the same. Life is short. We will all face Him soon enough. It's important to live with that perspective.

That implies living with a sense of *gentleness*. No single English word translates this Greek concept well, but it includes tolerance, forbearance, geniality, generosity, kindness, and humility. One commentator calls it "sweet reasonableness."[1] Paul is essentially telling them to be willing not to get their way in the relationship for the sake of the reputation of Christ and His people. In other words, we don't have to be proved right. We don't have to establish the fact that we are only 5 percent at fault. We can go ahead and own 51 percent and get the ball moving because it's more important for things to be right than for us to be right. That takes a lot of humility. And Paul says to make it "evident" to all.

> **It's more important for things to be right than for us to be right.**

Five Ways to Defuse Relational Conflict

Relationships matter to God. We don't just choose peace for our own sakes, although we greatly benefit from doing so. We choose peace because God seeks reconciliation with everyone, and we are being conformed to His image. It's a reflection of His nature. So resolving conflict has a lot to do with following Him well.

Reconciliation isn't easy when we think we know how the other person is going to respond. We often adopt a "why try?" attitude. But we try for the same reasons Paul urged Euodia and Syntyche to resolve their differences and because God says to make every effort. So if your network of relationships is ruptured, especially in a relationship with a family member or other member of the body of Christ, seek peace as diligently as you can. Be very intentional and persistent in following these steps toward restoration.

1. Resolve to stop procrastinating. Make a commitment to address the problem. Whichever relationship first came to mind when we started this chapter, think of a specific step you can take toward reconciliation. Maybe it begins with a conversation, an appointment with a counselor, or even a prayer for God to help you as you walk this out. Whatever moves you in that direction, be decisive about it and commit to it.

Why is it so important to stop procrastinating? Because a lack of peace in your relationships adds stress to your life and affects your physical and emotional health. You may not feel it happening—sometimes the stress is very subtle—but the harmful effects are doing something to you beneath the surface. Many people who wrestle with addictions aren't primarily facing a problem with food, shopping, porn, alcohol, or drugs. They are covering up the pain of a broken relationship and a wounded heart. When you lack peace, you try to calm an unsettled soul with all sorts of short-term remedies that mask the pain but heal nothing. And the fixes that give you artificial peace keep demanding more and more of you. You have to address the problem at its core.

You have to address the problem at its core.

Through Paul's pen, God instructs us to do just that. "Be careful to do what is right in the eyes of everyone. If it is possible, as far as it depends on you, live at peace with everyone" (Romans 12:17–18). *Everyone* means everyone—Christians, non-Christians, family members, coworkers, supervisors, neighbors, everyone. The term for "be careful to do" means "to consider." It's an accounting term, a reckoning, a thoughtful appraisal of the situation. That approach takes us out of all the "he did this" and "she did that" reasonings that go on in our minds. It enables us to see from someone else's perspective and try to understand why they think they are right. Perhaps it helps us recognize that they are gifted in different ways or have a different background that informs their perspective. It puts us in a position to quit being defensive and think objectively. Understanding the situation is the necessary first step toward any kind of resolution, restitution, healing, or forgiveness.

2. Reevaluate your expectations. Some of us got the idea somewhere in our spiritual development that Christians should never argue—that if we are really being spiritual, our relationships will always be harmonious. That means if we have a falling out with someone, that person must be unspiritual, disobedient—maybe even just bad.

In Philippians 4, there isn't a bad person creating problems for the church. We see two women who have contended for the faith and whose names are written in the Book of Life—and, as Paul may be thinking, are going to have to spend an eternity together and might as well start getting along now. But at the moment, even though they are committed Christians and God has worked through each of them, not everything is wonderful between them. That happens. We can't expect that Christians will never make mistakes, offend anyone, or speak thoughtless words. We can't assume Christian relationships are always smooth.

Sometimes we're shocked by what other Christians do—how Christian businesspeople work, how Christian leaders lead, how Christian families get dysfunctional like other families do. Some Christians are "rescuers" who just want everything to get fixed, and others are "warriors" who just want people to recognize how wrong they are and own their stuff. We expect other people to behave in certain ways, and we're shocked or disappointed when they don't. Whatever solution you tend to play out in your imagination—other people coming to grips with their mistakes and confessing how wrong they were, or some great revelation that makes it all a huge misunderstanding—things probably aren't going to happen that way. We'll never find genuine reconciliation or experience genuine peace until we get past those unbiblical and unrealistic expectations.

Conflict is real, and Christians aren't immune to it. Paul could testify to that himself. He and Barnabas had a strong relationship that went back to Paul's earliest days as a believer, when only Barnabas trusted his conversion and helped him out. Years later, they were sent out together on a missionary journey—Paul with his gift of communicating the gospel and Barnabas, the "son of encouragement," planting numerous churches and spreading the gospel far and wide. But when the time came for a second journey, they had "such a sharp disagreement that they parted company" (Acts 15:39). Barnabas wanted to include a young believer named John Mark, who had quit on the first journey and went home, and Paul didn't want to go through that again. So Paul took Silas because he felt like he could trust him, Barnabas took John Mark probably because he thought it would be good for him, and they went their separate ways.

We don't know all the details of that story, but we know that for an encouraging, generous personality like Barnabas to part company with a high-powered, driven personality like Paul—after they had worked so closely, been so fruitful, and ministered to each other in times of great need—it had to be an extremely contentious situation. This wasn't a case of two men weighing the pros and cons and deciding that perhaps it would be in their mutual interests to split this into two trips rather than one. Apparently, they blew up at each other. They each had certain expectations of the other that weren't met.

People have different styles, philosophies, and personalities. Sometimes they disagree, not over some crucial doctrinal or moral issue but simply over the way to do things. There's nothing wrong with agreeing to go separate ways. But it isn't right or healthy for the relationship to end in anger, resentment, bitterness, and brokenness.

3. Get competent outside help. Sometimes God will put it on your heart to seek restoration in a relationship, yet everything you try seems to make it worse. This can be especially painful in a close, long-term relationship with a spouse or other family member, but it's also frustrating with friends, coworkers, small-group members, a business relationship, or anywhere else you experience ongoing friction. In any relationship, there's no shame in asking for help.

In most relationships, that can be as simple as having a trusted friend to mediate or offer counsel. In the really big relationships like marriage and family, it may mean getting professional help. That's really difficult for many people, especially men. Some of us avoid the touchy-feely stuff or think counseling is for people with "real problems," which of course is never us. Usually those expressions are just another way of saying we feel really threatened in that area and don't want to look too closely at our own lives. We run from the tools that could help us the most because they might be painful to use.

In any relationship, there's no shame in asking for help.

That's where I was early in my marriage. I was in seminary, learning to preach the Word of God to others, and I couldn't even get along with my own wife. We didn't have much income, and professional help can be expensive, even at a student rate. But the bigger issue for me was a stubborn, arrogant pride. It was extremely difficult for me to admit that Theresa and I might need some help. I struggled to overcome my inward resistance and swallow my pride, finally realizing it was the only way to improve my marriage.

We had another little bump five years later, and this time it wasn't as big a deal. By this point, I'd learned that humility is the channel grace flows through. We had been talking for hours and realized we weren't making any progress, so we decided to go talk with someone we trusted who could look at it objectively from a biblical point of view. It was amazing, and it helped us find some resolution.

When you get help from someone objective—not your friend or the other person's friend, but someone who will treat you equally—you'll probably hear some things you don't want to hear. You'll learn something about yourself. Both of you will walk away having decided not to demand that the other person change for the relationship to be what it needs to be. You can't control the other person, but you can be responsible for yourself. And if you choose to work on your own issues, whether the other person responds or not, you're well on the way to improving your relationship and ultimately to restoration.

> **Humility is the channel grace flows through.**

4. Refuse to allow one relationship to ruin your life. Human beings have lots of ways to get offended, and some of them are legitimate. It happens in churches a lot. You lead a Bible study but have to be away for a week, and the next year the leadership asks the person who filled in for you to lead the study this time. Or someone moves the flowers you arranged for a funeral, puts you in a different spot on a ministry team, or disrupts the routine you've gotten used to over the last two decades. Offenses turn into animosities, and animosities hold us captive. We have to get free from them.

A young woman came up to me in tears after a service years ago and talked about how her dad left when she was fourteen. Understandably, this was a traumatic experience for her, the kind that can leave deep wounds for a long time. She'd had no relationship with him since that time, and she was captive to her pain. Her wounds were completely legitimate, but I had to ask her if she was going to give him that kind of power. The broken relationship clearly wasn't her fault, but it had still left her hurting. Could she forgive him and leave that pain in the past? It's a hard thing to do, but it's the only way to be free.

Offenses turn into animosities, and animosities hold us captive.

Many people have a relationship like that—with an ex-spouse, an alienated child, a friend or business partner who betrayed us. We'll talk about how to start a conversation in those situations without letting it blow up in your face, but there's something else that has to come first. You have to make a decision not to let that one relationship ruin your life. The other person may not respond well when you take a step toward reconciliation, but having done all you can to fix things, you can step back and be at peace. "If it is possible, as far as it depends on you, live at peace with everyone" (Romans 12:18). Sadly, it's not always possible. But once we've done all we can, we can then "let it go" and be at peace.

Years ago I went through one of the hardest times of my life. I felt like I'd been betrayed. I'm sure my perspective was only partly true, but I was so angry I couldn't sleep. My stomach would churn if I didn't distract myself with music in the car. I kept reliving scenes with certain people and the things they had said and done. It was eating away at me.

One day a friend who was helping me through this told me to "get vertical." That wasn't news to me, but I needed the reminder. I'd been a pastor for years and knew what to do, but it felt impossible to do it. It was good to be pushed in that direction.

Then this friend asked if I would do him a favor.

"Sure," I said.

"I can see that you've gotten some raw deals here. But I want you to meet me here next week at this time, okay?"

"Yeah, okay."

"And I want you to pray for seven days. I want you to list all the mistakes throughout this whole situation as God reveals them to you. In addition, think of all the specific ways you sinned against the people you can't stop thinking about."

This was my friend, a godly guy I trusted, but he didn't seem very friendly right then. But I did what he said, and I remember coming back and sitting in the same place, leaning forward with tears in my eyes, and telling him how I had pushed all those people's buttons. I listed all my leadership mistakes. And even though it was hard to confess some things as sin, I wrote down what God showed me and gave him the list.

You have to make a decision not to let that one relationship ruin your life.

It's amazing how often we demand justice in our relationships with other people but expect mercy in our relationship with God. That was a turning point in my life because I realized I couldn't ask God to give me mercy for all the things I had done and justice for all the things that had been done to me. And in that process, I was able to let it all go. Nothing got fixed, and no circumstances changed. The people I was angry with may have never seen things any differently than they did before. But I could let it go and be at peace.

You can refuse to let a broken relationship ruin your life.

That's how it may be for you. The situation may not be fixed, the relationship may not be restored, you may never shake hands or hug each other again, and there may be no bow to tie up the package neatly. But you can agree to disagree, you can forgive, and you can move forward. You can refuse to let a broken relationship ruin your life.

5. Remember that a right response is more important than being right. I recently had an intense conversation with a young man and realized I'd just poured cold water on his confidence. I regretted it immediately. I went home and went to bed, and that night I found myself in one of those situations when God wakes you up and suddenly makes things clear. *What am I going to do?* I wondered. Human nature always wants to defend itself, of course, so I started to rehearse all the reasons and justifications for saying what I said: *He needs to grow up. Learning to lead means telling people hard things. He'll get over it. I'm older and wiser . . .* And God said, "I'll take care of all that. What about your part?" I knew I had to deal with some things.

Own your part and then some. If you're like me at all, you're guiltier and more messed up than you think. Your perspective doesn't quite go as far as it should toward objectivity.

If you think a conflict is 25 percent your fault, just assume it's probably 50 or 60 percent. That's how it works with me, and I'm pretty sure I'm not alone.

I realized the only thing I could do to make things right was to tell him I was sorry. I typed up an email apologizing for saying certain things, being defensive and too intense, and so on. I just needed to repent. I saw the same

Own your part and then some.

guy a couple of days later, and he was so supportive and loving. "I got your email," he said. "You're forgiven." And I was at peace again.

That's normal. This is how it should be. If you want to accomplish something with your life, have a good marriage, have a great relationship with your kids, and work with other people to do something important, there are going to be sparks at certain points along the way. Count on it. And count on being uncomfortable with it. That's just the way it is. But you can deal with it in ways that don't throw gasoline on the fire. You can speak the truth and cover it in love. You can resolve conflict and restore relationships. You can choose peace.

These five steps offer a biblical template for the kind of reconciliation that reflects God's love and prioritizes His peace in our lives. You can find a lot of other relationship advice out there, some of it helpful and some of it not, but one resource I've found very useful for myself and others I've counseled is a book called *Crucial Conversations*.[2] Several people recommended it to me, and it's a great tool for saying hard things in a loving, nonthreatening way. The important thing is to make a commitment to choose peace in your relationships and take initiative to get there. Let love be your motivation, and let God be your guide.

One of the most important things you can do as a next step is to ask Jesus to lead you. Take a few minutes to reflect on the state of your relational health. Pray that He would show you what He wants you to do. Ask Him to put His finger on anything that needs your attention, any broken or damaged relationship that would benefit from your steps toward reconciliation and restoration. And trust Him to walk with you every step of the way.

Let love be your motivation, and let God be your guide.

QUESTIONS FOR DISCUSSION AND REFLECTION

1. On a scale of 1–10, how would you rank the level of stress and concern you are currently experiencing from any problem relationship?

2. Why does relational conflict rob us of peace? What price are you paying to allow this to continue?

3. What specific steps does Paul give to help us resolve relational conflict? Which ones would be most challenging for you? Why?

4. Is there a relationship in your life that calls for you to follow this pattern? When and how will you follow God's plan for peace (as far as it depends on you)?

5. Who could help you turn your good intention into action this week?

CHAPTER 2

Choose Peace
in Anxious Moments

Horatio Spafford was an attorney in Chicago when the Great Chicago Fire destroyed much of the city in 1871. He lost most of his investments in that fire, and it took a while to get on his feet again. He thought it would be good to get away for a vacation, and his friend D. L. Moody was planning to preach in England, so he arranged to take his wife and four daughters to Europe.

Not long before the trip, he had to deal with some zoning issues with one of his properties, so he sent his wife and daughters ahead and promised to join them soon. But he received a distressing telegram from his wife during their journey: "Saved alone." Their ship had collided with another, and all his daughters died in the shipwreck.

On his way to meet his wife in England, the captain of Spafford's ship pointed out the place where the ships had collided and his daughters had died. As Spafford looked out over the ocean and saw the billowing waves, his pain still fresh from his tragic losses, he was moved to write a hymn. "When peace like a river attendeth my way, when sorrows like sea billows roll," it began. It is still widely sung in churches today. "It Is Well with My Soul" is a touching and profound testimony of the peace we can experience even in our most distressing moments.

It's hard to imagine a song of such tremendous peace being written in the face of such heart-wrenching circumstances. Yet that's exactly the kind of peace Jesus promised the night before His crucifixion, knowing His followers were going to be thrown into anxious, tumultuous, painfully trying times the next day. "I have told you these things, so that in me you may have peace," He told them. "Take heart! I have overcome the world" (John 16:33). Trials will come, but they can't destroy us. We can overcome them and have peace in the process.

Trials will come, but they can't destroy us.

Spafford is just one person among millions who have experienced God's peace that passes human understanding. He may have had more anxious and tragic moments than most of us do, but we all have them. We lose loved ones, face uncertain futures, deal with alarming or devastating news, and encounter frustrating and futile experiences. We go through sudden twists and turns in our personal lives and in world events—a pandemic that disrupts our financial, work, and social lives; a volatile economy; wars and natural disasters; the death of a loved one; or any number of other tragic circumstances. Many people go through them all with high stress, raw nerves, and deep-seated anxieties. But we don't have to. Like Horatio Spafford, we can choose peace even in the midst of our most difficult times.

Understanding Our Anxiety

What is anxiety? The books define it as uneasiness, apprehension, dread, concern, tension, restlessness, and worry, and tell us that people get anxious when facing misfortune, danger, or doom. But that doesn't really explain very much, does it? That describes where what many of us experience throughout each week.

The New Testament word for *anxiety* means to "care for" or "take thought." Sometimes it's positive, but usually it refers to an inability to get our minds off of something, perhaps even an obsession. In German, it comes from the word for choking or strangling, which feels very appropriate for us at times. At its heart, the New Testament word suggests pulling us in two different directions and causing enormous stress on our emotions.

Our anxiety can come from several causes. The most common is probably a fear of the future. We are well aware of all the bad things that can and do happen: health problems, financial crises, abandonment, divorce, rejection, problems with our kids, pandemics, terrorist attacks, failures in any area of life, and a multitude of other possibilities both private and public. We hope for the best, but we often worry about the worst. Anxiety becomes a part of our lives.

Anxiety can also be caused by conflict in the present—stresses in marriage, with kids, at work, with neighbors, with in-laws, and so on. And some wrestle with anxiety about the past—regrets that pop up at any given moment, those things we wish had never happened and hope no one ever finds out about. Those of us who came to Christ after years of living without Him can recall plenty of mistakes we made beforehand, but those aside, we are all aware that mistakes don't end at conversion. There are things we can't change about our past, and when memories of them surface—along with a heavy sigh and a softly muttered "I blew it"—they produce anxiety. It can be overwhelming. A drink or a pill can't fix it. Anxiety can ruin our lives.

Anxiety can ruin our lives.

Anxiety has horrible effects. A textbook on psychological disorders identifies numerous spiritual, mental, and emotional by-products of anxious thoughts. It can make people hyperalert, irritable, fidgety, and overdependent. It can cause insomnia, fainting, excessive perspiration, muscle tension, headaches (including migraines), quivering voices, hyperventilation, abdominal pain, nausea, diarrhea, and high blood pressure.[1] That's a pretty scary list, and it makes me want to get rid of anxiety as quickly as I can.

How to Overcome Anxiety

How do you deal with your anxiety when you wake up in the middle of the night and can't get your fears about the future out of your mind long enough to go back to sleep? What do you do when your stomach keeps churning and your neck is perpetually tight because you can't handle the stress? It's one thing to identify anxiety, another to figure out what to do with it. We have to be able to change our thought patterns.

You do not have to live with anxiety. It is possible to have complete peace in the midst of difficult, uncertain, troubling times. We know this is true because Jesus promised that we could. And His Word gives us the tools to do it.

We have to be able to change our thought patterns.

Imagine a kid coming home from school Friday afternoon and pitching his bookbag into the corner of his room. "No homework! It's the weekend!" He isn't thinking about the homework that will be coming in the future or the assignments from earlier in the week. He has taken his load off and set his mind free, at least for the next few days.

That's the picture Peter gives us. "Cast all your anxiety on him because he cares for you" (1 Peter 5:7). It's like taking off a heavy burden and throwing it into the arms of someone who can handle it easily. Those problems, struggles, and fears are no longer yours. You're free from the responsibility. You entrust them to the hands of someone else—a personal God who is in control, who has no lack of wisdom, who is all-powerful, and who sees the future perfectly. And He is not begrudging about taking care of you. You are the object of His affection. You can release everything to Him and know He is always going to handle it with your best interests in mind.

So the key to overcoming anxiety is releasing the things that cause it—not the situations themselves, of course, but the weight of them, the fears and stresses and regrets that contribute to an anxious life. We give our past, present, and future to the God who sees and redeems all of it and who works everything together for the good of those who love Him (Romans 8:28). We will never encounter a single moment in which the grace for dealing with that moment is lacking. We can trust God to be with us and carry us through all of life. He knows how to handle everything.

> **We will never encounter a single moment in which the grace for dealing with that moment is lacking.**

Dealing with Your Anxieties

Paul gives us a specific game plan for dealing with anxiety whenever it comes knocking on the door of our mind and heart. He shows us how to cast our cares on the Lord, as Peter instructed, and how to receive peace in their place. Every time anxiety surfaces within us, we can run into the Father's arms and have His peace instead.

Do not be anxious about anything, but in every situation, by prayer and petition, with thanksgiving, present your requests to God. And the peace of God, which transcends all understanding, will guard your hearts and your minds in Christ Jesus. (Philippians 4:6–7)

If we look at the mechanics of the original text, we notice some pretty interesting things in the way certain words are emphasized. The first instruction here is literally, "Nothing be anxious about." It's a negative command, and it's worded strongly to emphasize *nothing*. Stop being anxious. Quit worrying. This is not a small issue. It can eat up your soul, distort your emotions, undermine your relationships, and choke the life out of you. Stop it.

God and His inspired writers in Scripture don't give us commands without providing the power and the tools to obey them. So Paul continues with a positive command: "But in everything." He gives us four specific words to do in "everything"—in every situation and especially in every anxiety-producing circumstance: *prayer, petition, thanksgiving, requests*.

The New Testament uses four different words for prayer, and all of them are in this verse. The point? Whenever anxiety knocks on the door of your heart, let prayer answer it. That's your primary response.

But this is not just prayer in general. By using this range of words, Paul gives us some very specific ways to pray that address those waking hours in the middle of the night, that churning stomach, those mental projections into an upsetting future concerning your health, your job, your kids, your marriage, or whatever else you tend to worry about. When your mind starts to go down that well-worn track, these prayers will turn it back in the right direction and quiet those fears.

That's the promise—that when you offer your prayers and petitions with thanksgiving in your heart, making your requests known to God, His peace will enter in and guard your heart and mind. It will shift the focus of your thoughts onto truth.

The word *guard* means that when you pray like this, the Holy Spirit monitors and protects the deepest parts of your thought life and warns you when something is wrong. He acts like the red light on your dashboard that tells you to look under the hood. When you lose your peace, you have turned your focus from Christ to something else, and He becomes an arbitrator or monitor warning you to get back into that place of abiding in Him. He keeps you in peace.

That's an overview of the grammar and mechanics of these verses and the words they use, but we need to go deeper in learning how to apply them because that's where our anxieties live—in the depths of our hearts and minds. Let's go back and look at these instructions a little more closely.

Applying the Commands to Your Life

We've seen that Paul issues both a negative and a positive command. The negative command is not just an encouraging pat on the back that tells us worry is unnecessary. It's actually a command: *stop worrying about anything.* Then the positive command is just as insistent and powerful: *pray about everything*. These are two sides of the same coin, a behavior to stop and a behavior to begin, a way to reverse the current of your thoughts, turning them in the opposite direction of where you have always taken them.

That may feel like forcing a river to flow upstream. That's because many of us have practiced being anxious most of our lives. We learned from our parents; our peers; the media that bombards us every day with the terrible, tragic, fearful news going on in our world; and our culture in general. Almost everyone is well trained in anxiety, and almost everyone has certain ways of coping with it, medically or with distractions that cover it up.

Many of us have practiced being anxious most of our lives.

So we live in a society of escape—through TV, shopping, a glass of wine, prescriptions, work, food, sex, and myriad other ways to mask, cover, distract, and medicate. There is nothing wrong with any of these things in their proper place, of course; entertainment, food and drink, medications, and all the rest are normal and often necessary for daily life. There are healthy ways to engage with them. But they aren't good substitutes for emotional health. They create the illusion of peace for a moment but never actually give us peace. There's a vast difference between relief and restoration. Some of these things give us a sense of control when life feels out of control, and some just change the way we feel for a time—usually a very short time. We address our anxiety in all sorts of ways, and most of them aren't very helpful.

My personal false mechanisms for appeasing my anxiety are sports and work. Somehow watching other people play games makes me feel better for a while. Sometimes I'll immerse myself in some project that occupies my mind and prevents it from going to anxious places. You'll never hear me preach or write about the evils of sports and work because both of those are perfectly normal and good activities. But when they are substitutes for prayer and the peace of God, there's a problem. When we're trying to get our minds off of a gnawing anxiety, we are just relieving a symptom.

We live in a society of escape.

We aren't actually changing anything, and the anxiety almost always comes back later, sometimes much stronger. Distracting our minds and silencing our hearts is not at all the same as letting the peace of Christ rule in our hearts and minds.

The command to pray about everything is a great way to address our anxieties, but it's important to notice that Paul is talking about some very specific kinds of prayer in this passage. There's nothing wrong with a desperate plea to God in an anxious moment—*Oh God, help me, please, help me, God.* You've been there, I'm sure. We all face challenging crises, and a believer's instinct as God's child is to cry out to Him. But I think God wants to teach us how we can pray purposefully and effectively. Otherwise, we pick up those backpacks filled with burdens as soon as the crisis passes and start carrying them again until the next crisis comes. So Paul identifies some specific ways to pray that will enable us to cast our burdens on God and let His peace come in.

How We Pray: Four Very Important Words

Our prayers are characterized by four words in the New Testament, all of them included in Philippians 4:6. If we understand the meaning of these four specific words and put them into practice, anxiety will begin to dissipate from our hearts and minds, and God's peace will begin to rule there.

● *Prayer*

Proseuche is the most common word in the New Testament for prayer. It involves turning our thoughts and feelings upward the moment we feel anxious, shifting our focus to God. It includes pausing, recognizing what's going on, worshiping and adoring God for who He is, and acknowledging that He is greater than our struggles.

I have to admit, I've had more than a few struggles with anxiety over the years. I tend to juggle more balls than I can handle and try to accomplish more than I'm actually capable of doing. Sometimes when I wake up, the first thought in my mind is about the day's to-do list—meetings, projects, events to prepare for, responsibilities with family members, and tons of other things that just have to get done. And then I check my phone or email and see that the Dow has dropped, a problem at work has come up, and something I didn't anticipate needs to be dealt with right away. If you're like me, you know how that kind of start to your day can set you up for disaster. What I've learned to do to combat mornings like this is to begin by spiritually, mentally, and emotionally bringing my life and everything in it to God.

The first thing you need to do every morning is pray—say the Lord's Prayer, recite Psalm 23, or find some other verse or prayer that immediately prioritizes your relationship with God and puts your focus on Him. I've learned that if I don't see life through God's lens, I'm going to be in big trouble. Life will bring challenges that I'm not prepared for. Even the ones I already have are more than I can handle. I have to start out with something that casts current and potential burdens on Him.

Jesus began the model prayer with the words "Our Father." In the midst of the world's craziness and messes, we can acknowledge that the One who is sovereign, who sent His Son to die for our sins, who is all-wise, all-knowing, and all-powerful, is our Father in heaven, our Papa who loves us beyond our wildest imaginations. We can trust Him. He won't lie to us, His intentions toward us are always good, and He's in control of everything.

So I've developed the habit of praying while I'm still lying in bed, slowly going through Psalm 23 or the Lord's Prayer, worshiping my Father who loves me. Then when I get up, I don't check my email. I have my coffee, I let the dog out, and I stand on the patio and look up. Out loud, I say something like this: "Almighty, ever-living Creator, little people like me have stared at the stars in this sky for thousands and thousands of years, and this is only a tiny fraction of the ones You've created—a few among the two hundred billion stars in this little galaxy, with another couple hundred billion galaxies beyond. At this moment, on this day, I am the object of Your affection. I'm going to go in and talk to You and listen to what You want to say to me in Your Word. I don't know what's going to happen or how to pull off anything I need to do, but I'm going into this day with You, the Creator of the world, at my back and Your Holy Spirit at my side."

If you get a clear, high view of God like that every morning, your day is off to a great start. Your God gets really big and your problems get really small very quickly. Our anxieties make problems big and God small, and this kind of prayer returns us to the right perspective. Human nature and anxious thoughts focus in on the problem areas of our lives. If our marriage is 90 percent good, we tend to obsess about the 10 percent that isn't. If work is going really well except for that one supervisor who keeps causing problems, we can't stop thinking about the supervisor. If our kids are doing pretty well in most areas of their studies but get a bad grade in one class, we zoom in on the grade that needs to be improved. We soon see all of life through these negative, it's-gotta-be-fixed lenses, and our emotions and physiology fall in line with them. We think this is reality, what our world really looks like. But it isn't. Prayer restores our focus on who and what is actually real.

> **When anxiety knocks at the door of your heart, let prayer answer it.**

When anxiety knocks at the door of your heart, let prayer answer it. Right from the start, acknowledge that your Father is the God who can deal with the situation, whatever it happens to be. He can heal cancers or carry you through seasons of grief. He can handle your unemployment and find you a new job—probably His purpose all along, even if the process felt traumatic to you. He can get into the heart of the child who isn't following Him, and He may have ways of doing it that you haven't even considered yet. Look at the universe He created and recognize whom you're praying to. Nothing is too difficult for Him (Jeremiah 32:27). Nothing going on in your life is bigger than He is.

Most of us know that intellectually. But we don't experience it until we worship Him. We have to pause, reflect, and pray for it to begin to sink into our hearts. The first word Paul uses for prayer takes us to that place of worship and adoration that gives us a true perspective.

● Petition

The second most common word in the New Testament for prayer focuses on need. It's a prayer that expresses need before we ask, a sense that we're unable to handle what we're facing. We know we have limitations, and we know God doesn't. Our impulse to petition Him comes from this acute awareness that we need Him.

That's where many of our anxieties come from, in fact. We face a problem or concern, and we immediately wonder how we're going to respond, what we're going to do to fix it, how we will be able to cope. The more we think those thoughts, the more overwhelmed we begin to feel. Our sense of need just grows and grows.

If the first kind of prayer turns us in the direction of adoration, this one turns us toward confession. *God, I can't handle this situation. I don't know what to do. I have tried everything under the sun. Unless You intervene, I don't know how I'll get by* . . . It doesn't matter whether this is about a marriage crisis, a rebellious child, a difficult boss, a financial disaster, or anywhere else you feel like you're in over your head. Certain situations in life will drive us to our knees, and we feel like we have no other option than to plead for help. That's more than okay. Paul actually recommends this kind of prayer for just these anxiety-producing moments.

These situations bring us to a place of humility and dependency. We can't cast our cares on God while we're still holding on to them, somehow thinking we might still be able to handle them with our hard work, ingenuity, personality, and creativity. We like to be problem-solvers. But when we encounter problems we can't solve, we have to humble ourselves and acknowledge our dependence on God. Our petitions grow out of that attitude.

> **We can't cast our cares on God while we're still holding on to them.**

When we bring our petitions to God, we are essentially saying, "Lord, I know You care for me. I can't handle this, but You can." That confession—that focus on our needs—positions us to ask Him for help.

● *Thanksgiving*

This is an interesting compound word in Greek. It comes from several roots that together include the ideas of rejoicing, being glad, showing favor, and having grace. Gratitude is not just an expression of prayer, it's an attitude that should liberally season every other kind of prayer. It's a focus on and appreciation for what God has done.

This is a natural outcome of the first two types of prayer we looked at. When I'm looking up at the stars and worshiping God, or I'm confessing how incapable I am of handling the challenges I'm facing, He very often reminds me of how good He has been in the past—how Theresa and I have made it through so many things in four decades of marriage, how my son was in ICU and got well, or the impossible situations I've been in that turned out not to be impossible when God got involved. And I say, "Thank You." He has been faithful. That awareness needs to saturate all our prayers.

If your mind wanders when you pray, if you have trouble concentrating and staying focused, you may find that your prayers and petitions aren't really getting rid of your anxiety. You spend time talking to God, but your mind is here and there and everywhere, and by the time you're done, the anxieties are exactly where they were before. I can certainly relate to that. But I've learned that anxiety can't coexist with thankfulness. The two really just don't go together. Your petitions, as important as they are, are still very often focused on your problems and needs. Thanksgiving is focused on the good things God has filled your life with. In the fullness of biblical prayer, when we add gratitude to our prayers and petitions, anxiety eventually gives way.

Anxiety can't coexist with thankfulness.

For example, I sometimes have trouble concentrating during difficult times. I pray, remind myself of who God is, confess what I am not able to do, and ask for a renewed mind and forgiveness for self-focus. But I still may be looking at things through a negative lens and having negative emotions. Sometimes my mind wanders—you've probably experienced how unfocused we can be when we're praying and get distracted with pressing thoughts—so I've learned to make a list. I keep a journal and write down things I'm thankful for, then I go through them one by one.

Nothing is too big or small to put on this list. I've thanked God for times of rest, laughing with Theresa, hearing her say she felt better physically than she had in a long time, enjoying many of the gifts He has put in my life, appreciating that I haven't had to take anti-inflammatories for my surgically repaired back in several days, the encouragement He has given me, the opportunities to help other people I meet, and on and on with everything that comes to mind. In spite of all the unpleasantness and difficulties of many aspects of life, in spite of personal shortcomings and mistakes as a husband, father, leader, and friend, I can thank God for loving me, delighting in me, having mercy on me and my family, and giving me a fruitful ministry. He isn't shocked by the fact that I don't measure up, by my limitations, or by my need of His mercy and grace every moment of every day.

By the time I get through recognizing all those things I'm thankful for—His provision, protection, guidance, and grace—I am at peace. Anxiety is gone. I'm not worried about not measuring up, being overwhelmed, and not being able to handle the difficulties well. Just being honest about those things prompts gratitude. I have great needs, but I also have a great God. And thanking Him helps me experience His presence, where no anxiety can stand.

Requests

This last word is powerful. What do you do in light of your adoration, confession, and thanksgiving? After you have worshiped God for who He is, seen your need, and focused on what He has already done, what's next? You outline your needs and make requests.

This is where we get specific. Many people don't experience God's peace and power because they pray general prayers—that God would help them grow spiritually, bless their family, help their children, and work things out for a good day. That's like Theresa sending me to the store and telling me to buy some good food she knows how to cook and that everyone will like. She just wouldn't do that. She would give me a list, take a picture of the label, remind me it has to be organic or the sixteen-ounce size or low-sodium—everything down to the detail. We go to the store to get specific things.

Or imagine asking a ten-year-old what he or she wants for Christmas and hearing, "Oh, I don't know. Just some good stuff. You know what's best." That's not usually how it works, is it? Even at a young age, we have a strong sense of what we need and want, and we don't hesitate to ask for it.

God is much more than a store or a Santa Claus, and we don't ever want to treat Him like a heavenly vending machine. But He is our source for everything, and He does encourage us to make specific requests. I write specific things in my journal and put a check-box next to them, just like a grocery list. When I pray, I give them to the God who is all-wise, all-powerful, and all-loving. I turn my cares, concerns, and anxieties into requests. When He answers, I check them off. As I write this, I have a list that is just a few weeks old, but only two unchecked boxes remain. I'm experiencing that God is showing up. He's alive in my life. He's alive in yours too, but if you aren't asking specifically and in some way tracking the answers, you may not be aware of it.

We are invited to pray for definite things. *God, I ask You specifically to move in my supervisor's heart to give me favor with him and for me to make a significant contribution in this meeting. Lord, I'm asking You for "x" amount of dollars because this is what is happening in our family situation, and this is what we need to deal with it. God, I am asking You for the best doctor in this region. Help me find the right one. Will You set up the right contacts so we can deal with this cancer?*

Once you've worshiped God for who He is, acknowledged your need, and thanked Him for how He has been gracious to you, you can tell Him what you want. Give Him the "grocery list." Some people do only that, and they come across as demanding and entitled. But your previous three kinds of prayer have worked the right attitude into your heart, and you are invited to come boldly to God and ask. You're His son or daughter, and He wants to help you.

I try to turn all my anxieties into prayers. When an anxious thought comes, I try to see it not as a threat or stressor but as a prayer prompt. Writing them down and checking them off helps me in the mental process of giving it to God, and I know I can trust Him to handle it in just the right way. Some requests take time, but it isn't because God is hard of hearing or slow about His answers. He's a master of timing. But I can see over time that He is alive in my life. He shows up in amazing ways. If you pray specifically and track your prayers, you'll see Him showing up in your life too.

You are invited to come boldly to God and ask.

If you've had children, you've probably had the experience of your child having a bad dream, running into your bedroom, and asking to get in the bed with you. You open the covers and let them in, and thirty seconds later they are sound asleep and breathing deeply. Why? They have gotten close to the one who loves them, is in control, and can protect them. They have found refuge in a safe place.

That's what the God of the universe is inviting you, His child, to do. He wants you to stop fretting, stop trying to figure out how you can solve everything, and get close to Him. He wants you to see His arms around you and begin breathing deeply and resting soundly again. He wants you to pray this kind of prayer—adoration, confession, thanksgiving, and supplication—and run into His arms.

Why We Pray: The Promise of Peace

Philippians 4:7 promises that "the peace of God, which transcends all understanding, will guard your hearts and your minds in Christ Jesus." This would be an empty promise if the prayers of the previous verse were not powerful in transforming us and the circumstances around us. But because these kinds of prayers lead to this kind of peace, we can draw some very important, logical conclusions:

1. Peace and anxiety cannot coexist.
2. Anxiety and biblical prayer cannot coexist.

This is the promise of these two verses and the reason we pray. Anxiety really does give way to the peace of God.

One way to put the step-by-step process of this chapter into memorable form is to think of ACTS. *A* is the adoration of our prayer; *C* is the confession implied in our petition; *T* is thanksgiving; and *S* is our supplication, the requests we actually ask for. As soon as anxiety knocks at your door, remember ACTS and run into your Father's arms—again and again and again.

Don't be alarmed if this takes some practice. You don't go out on a golf course two or three times a year and expect to make par on every hole or go bowling for the first time in ten years and expect to score a 300. This is not magic. It's a

A-Adoration

C-Confession

T-Thanksgiving

S-Supplication

spiritual mindset and practice we have to learn to develop in our lives. We do find some immediate relief, but we also get better at it over time.

We have all developed lifelong patterns in our thought life and habitual responses to the anxieties we feel. Many of us have unintentionally cultivated some very dysfunctional, painful, damaging ways of dealing with worries and stress that are bad for ourselves, our relationship with God, our family members and friends, and our work. If that's true for you, this is going to take some persistence. Thought patterns don't change immediately; in fact, they usually take at least three weeks to begin to change, and even then, the old neural pathways battle against the new neural pathways for supremacy. So you'll have to go into training and be tenacious about it.

You'll have to go into training and be tenacious about change.

If you're in the middle of a stressful situation and need to walk through this process of prayer, it's okay to take a break. I've been in anxious situations and not known what to do next, and I've just excused myself to step out of the room so I could have a few minutes with God. I ask Him to help me remember the steps, I acknowledge His abilities and my limitations, thank Him throughout the whole conversation, and tell Him I need His wisdom, power, and love in that moment. He gives His peace even in times like that. He is more than willing to meet us in our times of need.

Remember, biblical prayer is God's antidote to anxiety. It's simple and profound. Whenever you feel anxious, even in the coming hours, days, and weeks, remember ACTS. When anxiety pounds on the door of your heart, let prayer answer it as you run into your Father's arms.

This promise is for those who have entered into a relationship with Jesus. If God is not yet your Father—if you haven't yet become His child by faith—this won't work. If that describes you, the first prayer is easy: choose today to ask Him in. Receive Him by faith. It's the biggest, most effective anxiety-relieving prayer you could ever pray. When you turn from your self-will and sin and ask Him to forgive you and take up residence inside you, your peace begins. And for the rest of your life, no matter how many stressful situations you find yourself in, you will have everything

Biblical prayer is God's antidote to anxiety.

you need for the peace of God to guard your heart and mind in Christ. All His children are welcome at any moment to run into His arms to find peace.

QUESTIONS FOR DISCUSSION AND REFLECTION

1. When do you tend to be anxious? What situations or people bring out your stress? How can you prepare spiritually to handle those stresses?

2. What issues in your life are "strangling" and "stressing" you mentally and emotionally? What would your life be like if you cast those cares on God and released them?

3. In what ways will you put the message of this chapter into practice? Who will help/encourage you in your battle to overcome anxiety?

4. Do you know of someone in your network of relationships who would benefit from this pattern of prayer? How can you share this with someone else who struggles with anxiety and needs your help?

CHAPTER 3

Choose Peace
in a Broken World

What is your greatest fear right now? I'm not talking about passing thoughts or today's momentary troubles. Those come and go without causing too much stress in our hearts and minds. I'm asking what you fear most in this season of life. Are you afraid of the future? Something bad happening to one of your kids? The economy? Never getting married? A health issue? The direction of the world? Several of those or something like them may surface in your worries at times, but most people have one in particular that weighs on them consistently. What ties your stomach in knots or raises your heart rate when you think about it? What keeps you awake at night or makes it to the top of your prayer list every time you pray?

Now think about what it would be like to overcome that fear—not necessarily to make the situation go away, but to be able to think about it without any worry or anxiety. Imagine how different your life would be. What would it feel like to be free?

It would take some effort, of course. Lasting change in anything, including our spiritual lives, isn't easy. But it is possible. We've seen that in Jesus's promise to His disciples to give them His peace (John 14:27). It's also in Isaiah's prophecy that God will keep in perfect peace those whose minds are steadfastly trusting in Him (Isaiah 26:3). The most common command in all of Scripture is to not be afraid—often followed with, "Because I am with you." We apparently have to be told this very often, with many promises and reassurances. But because we are told so persistently and repeatedly, we know it's possible. It's something God enables us to do.

How do we experience God's power and presence to the degree that our awareness of Him undoes our fear in the midst of storms? How do we get free from the fear that seems to enslave so many of us? In order to answer those questions, we first need to understand how God has wired us—how our mind and emotions work together. That will tell us a lot about how to deal with living fearlessly in a broken world.

A study conducted at the University of Tennessee several years ago divided participants into two groups—one that listened to a radio program with benign news for five minutes every day for twelve years, and another that listened to a program with negative news for the same time. The group listening to negative news heard about earthquakes, crimes, abductions, riots, scams, murders, and all the other things the rest of us hear about from time to time, but they were required to hear concentrated segments of it every day. After twelve years, the two groups were evaluated. The people who listened to the negative news were more depressed, pessimistic, and afraid than the other group, and they were less likely to trust and help others.[1]

That's not particularly surprising, of course; it confirms what many of us would have suspected. But the fact that this exposure to negative news was only five minutes a day over and above what people normally hear rather than a three-hour scary movie every day is sobering. It tells us that even small adjustments to our mental and emotional diet can have major effects.

The familiar phrase, "You are what you eat," is not just true about our physical bodies, is it? If we eat lots of sweets and fats, we end up a lot larger and less healthy than if we eat lots of fruits and vegetables. But we are what we eat psychologically too. Science and Scripture fully agree on this point: Whatever we keep taking in will work its way into our hearts and minds and have substantial impact on what we think and how we feel.

We can't eliminate the bad things that happen in the world. A lot of challenging circumstances are going on out there at any given moment. That's reality. But how we handle them makes a difference. If we keep feeding our fears, they will grow stronger. We have to learn to starve our fear and feed our faith.

The Truth about Our Thoughts and Feelings

Science and Scripture are in sync on the effects of our thinking on the rest of our lives. Studies like the one mentioned above confirm many truths from the Bible, including these three:

1. We are the products of our thought lives. You are who you are today because of the things you've thought in the past. Those things shaped your opinions, attitudes, decisions, and beliefs. "As he thinketh in his heart, so is he," says the old King James translation of Proverbs 23:7. You live out the thoughts you entertain. You follow the form shaped in your heart. Or, as is often said, you become what you behold.

2. Our emotions flow from our thoughts. Whatever you think triggers feelings about that thought. Sometimes this process is hardly noticeable; you can find yourself feeling a certain way without realizing how you got there. But your thoughts shape your emotions, and you make decisions based on the emotions that have followed your thoughts. Romans 8:6 tells us that "the mind governed by the flesh is death, but the mind governed by the Spirit is life and peace." When the Holy Spirit shapes our thoughts, our hearts are at peace.

3. What we allow into our minds is the most important decision we make each day. If your thoughts shape who you are and how you feel, then what you feed your thoughts with becomes an extremely important series of choices. For better or worse, what you watch, listen to, read, say, and think about are life changing. Your eyes and ears are the gateways of your soul, and whatever enters in will seep down and color your perspective of everything. Over time, those seemingly minor choices add up to a personality, a philosophy of life, a belief system, or however else you might describe your mental and emotional makeup.

When the Holy Spirit shapes our thoughts, our hearts are at peace.

That ought to give every parent pause. You have an obligation to care for not only your own mental and emotional state but also that of your children. If you have kids in your house, you need to find loving and respectful ways to be a gatekeeper for their eyes and ears. It isn't easy today with the access children have to videos and music through their phones, laptops, and other devices. But there's a world out there competing to capture your children's hearts, and they don't suspect a thing. They tend to let anything in when they are young, and even when they are older and more discerning, they can get caught in tempting and deceptive images and ideas. They need you to train them in filtering out the harmful influences that will affect their personalities, perspectives, and beliefs.

These three truths have obvious relevance to our fears. If we are the product of our thoughts, our emotions flow from our thoughts, and our mental and emotional intake is such an important decision each moment of the day, we very clearly have the ability to feed our fears or starve them. They are the product of what we've been fed, and that's an area where we have a lot of control. So we have to change our psychological "diet" in order to weaken fear and strengthen faith.

How Can We Choose Peace in a Broken World?

When Paul wrote his letter to the Philippians, he had been going through some very challenging experiences for several years. He had been arrested on false charges, confined for at least a couple of years, brought before local rulers, taken on a ship to Rome, and then placed under house arrest awaiting an official trial. That's where he was at the time of this letter, yet he had peace. And he wanted the Philippians to have the same kind of peace in the circumstances they were facing.

The Roman world was filled with violence and injustice, and Christians often felt those injustices acutely. They were very aware that they lived in a broken world. We can relate—perhaps not to the same kinds of injustices they experienced, but certainly to that strong awareness of the brokenness all around us. So Paul's words are as relevant to us as they were to the people of Philippi two millennia ago, and they assure us that we can have peace in an uncertain world. They also tell us how.

> Finally, brothers and sisters, whatever is true, whatever is noble, whatever is right, whatever is pure, whatever is lovely, whatever is admirable—if anything is excellent or praiseworthy—think about such things. (Philippians 4:8)

This is our mental agenda, the things we should fill our minds with all the time. Paul is saying that of all the different ways to think about life, this is God's way. We are to let our minds dwell on these things, to ponder, meditate, review, and become saturated in them.

But he immediately follows this command with a second one: "Whatever you have learned or received or heard from me, or seen in me—put it into practice" (Philippians 4:9). He reminds them of the things they learned when he was with them—the things they hungered for, took in, and actually applied. They heard him talk and watched him live, and he now calls them to follow that lifestyle. This is how Paul nurtured his own thought life.

And then comes the promise: "And the God of peace will be with you" (v. 9). In other words, the God of *shalom*, the Father of blessing and favor, the one who protects and provides and wants to give us the best in life, will do more than give us peace. He will be with us.

> **Command #1:** Think about these things.
>
> **Command #2:** Put this into practice.
>
> **The Promise:** The God of peace will be with you.

We are all a product of our thoughts, yet most of us can be extremely casual with what we allow into our minds. We are shaping our character, decisions, perspectives, beliefs, and emotions without really paying attention to what we are shaping them with. That's a serious problem.

So let's look at the words Paul uses to describe a godly, healthy thought life. For each one, I want us to look at a definition and a question that will help us discern what we are feeding our minds. If you were to ask these questions for ninety days before you let anything through your eyes and ears into your heart and mind, or before you let the harmful thoughts and feelings that are already in there grow deeper and stronger roots, you would be shocked at the improvement in your emotional health. The lies, fears, insecurities, and everything else that disturbs your soul would stop undermining your faith and disrupting your peace. Your life will change dramatically.

The first command in these two verses tells us to think about these things—to dwell on them, contemplate them deeply, meditate on them, talk about them, ponder them, and let them sink in. The word is *logizomai*, literally to reckon, consider, keep a mental record, and to reason about. We get *logic* from this word, not because it implies unemotional, detached rationalism but because it suggests our normal process of reasoning and deducing. That's how we discern good and evil and decide what we're going to fix our minds on and what we'll filter out. Paul tells us to line up that mental process with reality and use it to our advantage.

● Whatever Is True

We are constantly confronted with lies. Some of them come from outside of us; others are thoughts, perceptions, and impressions we have developed deep inside over the years. Sometimes they are overt; others are subtle and hard to put a finger on. We are constantly exposed to misleading thoughts and become so accustomed to them that we rarely stop to ask if they are actually true.

I woke up one morning recently with a negative attitude. I don't know where it came from. I just saw everything through a negative lens. So I put this verse into practice. I prayed slowly through Psalm 23 and began to see things a little more positively—until I remembered that I needed to do my back exercises, which I don't exactly enjoy. As that bad attitude was creeping back in, I decided to say out loud every verse that came to mind during my exercises. I quoted passage after passage, which I can count on as truth, and then started declaring things about myself that I know to be true: *I'm a son of the living God. I have an inheritance in Him. He is preparing a place for me in heaven. He has given me spiritual gifts and has filled my heart with His peace. He has blessed me with a wonderful wife and children who love me.* On and on, I declared these things out loud, and little by little I was filled with gratitude. My negative emotions faded away.

We tend to believe a lot of lies and premises from early in life. In *The 4:8 Principle,* a book focused entirely on this one verse from the Bible, Tommy Newberry lists many of the things we unconsciously tell ourselves that produce negative emotions, including anxiety and fear.[2] We make inner vows or assumptions: *I'll never be happy again, things probably won't work out for me, bad things always happen to me, I'm not worthy of being loved, I just have to accept my limitations, I never say the right thing, I'm not attractive, funny, interesting, smart . . .* You get the idea. Each of us has something like this going on inside us, and we may not even realize it. It's our "normal." But it isn't true.

Since you're the product of your thought life, these kinds of inner assumptions tend to prove true over time. We live out the things we believe. If we want anything to change in our lives, we have to learn to think differently.

If this sounds like positive thinking, you're right. It is—at least in the sense that God's truth about you is very positive, and He tells you to agree with it and let your mind dwell on it. But it isn't *only* positive thinking. Usually when people criticize that concept, they assume it means talking ourselves into something that isn't true. But in this case, we're talking ourselves into something that *is* true. We're leaving behind the lies that have done nothing but harm us and embracing what God says. And He is very positive about His love for you and who you are in Him.

If we want anything to change in our lives, we have to learn to think differently.

Some of the lies we believe are hard to pinpoint because they are mixed with truth—for example, the idea that our children's education and career choices are evidence of whether we succeeded or failed as parents. Are you really a failure if your son or daughter doesn't get into the best school and become a doctor or lawyer? Does your reputation really depend on such things? These thoughts come from insecurity and produce anxiety. They also create pressure on your children and other people around you and produce unhealthy, dysfunctional side effects. They are good aspirations attached to faulty reasoning. Wanting your children to do well is a desire based on truth. Defining success for them and tying it to your own self-perception is a lie.

Another lie is the idea that you will never be happy unless
. . . you get married, own your own home, have the right job,
or whatever else you want to finish the
sentence with. This is not a true premise. **The lies we**
You may long for one of these things, and **believe are**
there's nothing wrong with having the
desire, but the idea that you will be mis- **hard to pinpoint**
erable and unfulfilled without it is a lie. **because they**

This is what we call "premise thinking"— **are mixed**
the idea that some activity, success, event, **with truth.**
or person will make things right for you.
If this happens, then you'll be happy. Otherwise, you won't.
That's a false belief.

These desires are not bad, of course, but there's a big difference between thinking it would be nice for them to be
satisfied and thinking that satisfying them is necessary for
you to have value or be fulfilled as a person. None of these
things are promised in Scripture as the key to fulfillment or
a statement of your value as a human being. Your value is
not dependent on grades, athletic success, career advancement, a marriage and family situation, a home, a lifestyle,
or anything other than God's view of you. You are loved by
Him, adopted into His family, sealed with His Spirit, and
given a purpose of glorifying Him with your life. That's the
truth. Any deviation from that truth is a lie.

When we dwell on what is true, we are choosing to focus on
objective reality according to God. We reject distortions, de-
viations, and deceptions. We refuse to embrace illusions that
promise peace and happiness but can't ultimately deliver.

We think about and meditate on the reality of what God says.

The question to ask on this point when you're discerning what to let into your mind is very straightforward: *Is this true or false?* That is not at all the same as asking whether something *looks* true or false. It's a question that digs down into the truth or falsehood of our perspectives.

Your emotions, after all, are not necessarily responses to reality. They are responses to your *perception* of reality. The people who listened to negative news in the study mentioned above developed a different perception of reality over time than their counterparts who listened to benign news. They more often assumed that other people wanted to harm them, that disaster was more likely to happen, or that disease was more likely to affect them. Their perceptions lined up with stories of what had actually happened in the world but didn't fit the likelihood or statistical probabilities of what might happen. Their sense of reality was skewed toward the negative.

All of us have experienced this distinction between reality and perception. You might see something that looks like a snake, and instantly you freeze: your heart rate accelerates, your stomach tightens, and you experience a jolt of adrenaline. Then you look closer and discover it was just a coiled rope or twisted branch, and everything in you calms back down. You just experienced an emotional response to your perception, not to what actually existed. But the emotions were exactly the same as if you had really seen a snake.

Human beings engage in a lot of "snake" thinking—fears, worries, anxieties, dread, and panic that profoundly affect our emotional state even when based on something that isn't actually true. In every situation in life, ask yourself, *Is this true or false?* Then let your mind dwell on whatever is true.

● *Whatever Is Noble*

This word, often translated *honorable*, means sober, serious, worthy of respect, inspiring awe. It refers to those things in our lives that reflect the weight and importance of our purpose. Nothing is wrong with getting excited about a basketball game, awards programs, a fantasy football league, or a great new movie. But these are peripheral to our lives. The world is full of trivia, and in the midst of it all, we have been given a serious, sobering mission full of eternal meaning and significance. We have been rescued from eternal condemnation through the amazing gift of the sacrifice of God's Son on a cross. We are loved unconditionally, live under the umbrella of His favor, and walk out His amazing plan for our lives. We are God's workmanship (Ephesians 2:10), His artistry and poetry, designed for a purpose He specifically ordained for us from before the foundation of the world. That's a big deal. It's honorable and noble.

Are you fulfilling that purpose? That's a weighty issue. You are living in a small window of time but have been created for eternity. Heaven and hell are real. You are called to live simultaneously in overflowing joy and in the sobering reality of your calling. You don't need to focus on that all the time and carry a serious expression on your face into every joyful situation, but do not buy into the fast-paced, pleasure-above-all culture we live in. The writer of Ecclesiastes says there is far more wisdom at a funeral than at a party (7:2). Let those deep thoughts shape your perspective.

Theresa once asked me what I'm most afraid of. I said, "Squandering the life God has given me and falling short of His purpose for me."

"Why?" she asked.

"Because at least by the world's standards, I'm more successful than I thought I would be, and God has given us more than I dreamed of. But that can create a lifestyle and comfort level that work against the kind of focus and sacrifice I need to have in taking up my cross and following Him. I don't want to slip into a status-quo life that everyone else thinks is wonderful, but I and the Lord both know better."

That's a noble thought, and I've had to be intentional about keeping it in front of me. It doesn't just happen when we let our minds wander. We have to choose to fix our minds on whatever is honorable.

So ask this question about the things you let into your mind: *Does this honor or dishonor God?* That's a broad question that applies to His nature and character, His purposes and calling for our lives, and the eternity He has set before us. When you're watching or listening to something, when you're engaged in a relationship or an activity, does it honor Him? Is it noble? Is it a gray area that isn't necessarily evil but also not particularly uplifting? Or does it clearly glorify

Him and align with His ways? Let your mind think about the things that are noble and honorable.

● Whatever Is Right

This word is also translated as *righteous*. In the New Testament, it refers to God's actions and His character and describes the life of Jesus. It pictures doing the right thing when tempted. Another way we might interpret it is living with integrity.

God's character creates a standard, and integrity for a Christian means aligning with that standard. It is not outside of Him as a universal norm or ideal that even He conforms to. It's the ideal that is in Him and that the rest of the universe should conform to.

The question you need to ask here is, *Is this right or wrong?* Is it the whole truth or a partial truth? Am I doing my taxes this way because it's what everyone else does or because it's the right thing to do? Am I fudging on this because I know I can get away with it or can justify it as ethical by my own definition? Is this a lack of integrity? Am I treating people right or defrauding someone? Is it okay to live with someone I'm "practically married" to? Does this video game honor life and love or do fictional people get blown up and mutilated by the fingers and thumbs of my kids? Are we just doing something recreational, or is it one of those many shades of gray?

These aren't always easy questions to answer. Some of them really are borderline issues that might be truly ethical and right from our own perspective but shady or wrong from someone else's. The Bible doesn't always give us black-and-white answers for everything. But it does tell us a lot about God's nature and character, and it calls us to conform to His ways. Use that as your standard. Then let your mind dwell on the things that are right.

● *Whatever Is Pure*

This word comes from the same root as *holy*—being "set apart" for a special purpose. It suggests being innocent, free from defilement and immorality in thought, word, and deed. When David said he had committed to live a blameless life and not set any vile thing before his eyes (Psalm 101:2–3), and when Job said he had made a covenant with his eyes not to gaze lustfully at a woman (Job 31:1), this is what they were talking about. We are called to turn our attention to things that are pure and not let ourselves be corrupted with impurity.

Here is the question we need to ask about the things we see and hear and think about: *Will this cleanse my soul or dirty it?* This applies not only to sexual issues but to any kind of immoral thought or behavior. But many people do tend to think of sex first when they think of biblical purity, and there's a good reason for that. It's one of the areas in which our culture has become particularly impure.

Studies show that some sexual sin is as addictive as cocaine, and trying hard to quit—getting rid of a porn addiction, for example—is almost impossible to do on your own. It's a pseudo-intimacy that will eventually destroy your relationships. It multiplies fears and creates the need to cover things up. God wants you to see sex as holy and pure because that's how He made it. He loves it and wants the marriage bed to be holy, set apart for that special purpose. Anything outside of that purpose is impure, and if that's an issue you struggle with, I strongly encourage you to get help. I've counseled countless men over the years who privately lived with a secret porn addiction that was destroying their souls. Years of duplicity, shame, guilt, and fear of being found out strangled their intimacy with God and often their intimacy with their spouse. God wants so much better for us.

But pornography isn't the only sexual impurity our culture deals with. It's only the most obvious. Some are much more subtle, like movies that blur the lines between right and wrong and turn our sympathies in opposite directions. You've probably seen plots like these—a woman is married to a really self-centered, unappealing jerk of a husband and falls in love with a likable, selfless guy who seems just right for her. We find ourselves rooting against that marriage, don't we? Her affair doesn't bother us; we just want her to find true love. And all of a sudden, we've been sucked into one of the enemy's strategies for skewing our morals and making impurity look pure.

The battle for our lives is not out there in the world. It's in our hearts and minds.

The battle for our lives is not out there in the world. It's in our hearts and minds. The weapons of our warfare are not fleshly but powerful for pulling down spiritual strongholds. We need to take every thought captive and make it obedient to Christ (2 Corinthians 10:3–5). Have conversations with your children about what's going into their minds and, without any judgment, find out where you can help. Examine your own filters too. Ask yourself if the things you take in are cleansing or corrupting. Let your mind dwell on whatever is pure.

● *Whatever Is Lovely*

This word refers to things that are attractive, winsome, and beautiful. It's a wonderful word that calls for a response of love and warmth rather than bitterness, criticism, and vengeance. It urges us to smell the roses, look at rainbows, watch kids playing in the park, think about pleasant memories, read or watch something encouraging, and enjoy the pleasant things God has put into our world. It calls us to notice good things.

I found myself driving at about 6:30 one morning recently and noticed the red-and-pink sky behind the puffy clouds in front of me. It was beautiful—one of those moments that makes you think, *Oh, Lord, that's just amazing.* I had been listening to songs on my phone, shuffled so that they come up randomly. And the one that came on in that moment was written by a young man who was one of my son's best friends. He died of cancer at twenty-five, and his song, "Restore Me," brought back a flood of memories of what God had done and how He orchestrates our lives and walks with us through our joys and our pains. It softened my heart and made me appreciate the beauty all around me—the ocean and the redwoods, the clouds and the colors of the sun against the sky, things we don't always appreciate when our faces are glued to a screen.

By contrast, when I got home later that day and turned on the news, the stories of violence and murder were disturbing. I flipped to a PBS channel, which often plays encouraging documentaries, and the program airing then was disturbing too. Within ten minutes, I had gone from a glorious moment to sadness and anger about all the injustices in this messed-up world. Everything that was on my screen went into my heart and completely changed my thoughts and feelings.

So the question to ask about things that are lovely is, *Will this renew my heart or harden it?* We don't need to stick our heads in the sand and avoid every hint of bad news, but we do need balance, and news programs are not going to give it to us. They give us constantly flowing streams of everything that's wrong, and very occasionally something that is right. Meanwhile, hundreds of millions of acts of kindness are happening all around us. Children are being welcomed into the world, people are being generous and loving, people in need are being reached with food and fresh water, women are being rescued from the sex trade. Yes, there's a sex trade to begin with, and yes, people are hungry and thirsty. But many people focus only on those tragedies and completely miss all the wonderful things going on too. Choosing not to dwell on whatever isn't lovely is healthy. We're aware of those things, but we are not meant to fixate on them.

What you allow into your mind the first and last thirty to forty-five minutes of your day will shape your subconscious thoughts. You either starve your fear and feed your faith or do the opposite. Make sure you are choosing to think about things that are lovely.

● Whatever Is Admirable

Paul then adds the idea of thinking of things that are commendable, of good reputation, gracious. *Admirable* literally means fair spoken or well reported. It describes things that are fit for God to hear rather than false, ugly, impure words that do not line up with who He is. Paul follows this word, and really the whole list, with the clarifying words *excellent* and *praiseworthy*. We are to turn our minds toward whatever is virtuous, wholesome, and good.

Here's the question to ask with this instruction: *Can I recommend this to someone who looks up to me?* That's a sobering thought, but it's an important one. If you've ever been watching something and felt the need to change the channel before someone else walked in the room; if you've ever modified your behavior because you want to present the right face to someone else; if you've ever had to clean up your words or actions because impressionable people are watching, then you have a sense of what this instruction is about.

Imagine sitting on your couch watching something on your TV, phone, or laptop, and the resurrected Jesus walks in and sits down next to you. "May I join you?" He asks.

Obviously, you say yes.

Now, how comfortable are you with His presence, with Him seeing what you see, knowing what you think? And how comfortable would you be with Him looking on while you allow others in your household, even young children, to see what you're seeing? What would He say about what your habits are doing to your own heart and mind, and what would He say about how those habits are affecting others? If you are the representation of Jesus to other people around you—young children or people new in the faith—what impression are they getting? Can you recommend this movie, this scene, this conversation to them? Is it admirable?

If you're like me, you've had the sobering thought that if some people look up to you as the model Christian, that's not a good situation to be in for either of us. But people do. If you are a follower of Jesus, to many people you are a representative of Jesus. The song many of us have sung to our children, "Be Careful Little Eyes What You See," is good advice for us too. Not because God is looking down in judgment but, as the song says, because He is looking down in love. He wants the best for us.

Matt Maher and my son, Jason Ingram, wrote a song based on Zephaniah 3:17 that begins with the line, "I flirt with the world, it steals my love for you."³ It goes on to talk about how God delights in His children and sings over us. There is nothing condemning in that thought. It expresses the heart of a Father who wants to protect us from harm and help us find our satisfaction in Him.

When we put things in our minds that distance us from our Father's nature and character, we are driving a wedge in the relationship. He is not withdrawing His love from us—He never does that—but our fellowship with Him suffers. We stop sensing His presence and experiencing His love as we should. Guilt and shame keep us from drawing close to Him, even though drawing close is exactly what we need when we feel guilt and shame.

If you need help for a problem with pornography, violence, or other destructive and addictive thoughts, plenty of ministries and caring friends can help you plug into accountability groups, offer wise counsel, and encourage you with grace-filled conversations. You will never find yourself "too far gone," "too late," or "too" anything for God's help. But whatever you do, cultivate your connection with the Father. Saturate your mind with God-filled thoughts.

Saturate your mind with God-filled thoughts.

This is not just a call to a superspiritual mindset. Just read, listen to, watch, and think about healthy things. I recently finished listening to an audio book on the life of Winston Churchill, and the ways he responded with courage to things happening in the war, though not necessarily "spiritual," were certainly admirable, noble, and worthy of praise. I read a book on the life of Martin Luther and was inspired by many of his actions. Some of the things I read and listen to are about faith and Christian experiences, but others are about the beauty and truth God has woven into the world.

The statistics for depression and anxiety in our country and our world are alarming, especially among teens, and much of the problem is what people think about. If we're the product of our thought life, it only makes sense to fill our lives with good things. Paul's categories of thought cover a lot of territory—anything with moral excellence that will inspire us and motivate us to love God and others. Think about such things. New mental habits are life changing.

Put It into Practice

The point, Paul says, is not just to know about these things and agree that they are good. It's to put them into practice. That's what he says in verse 9, pointing to his own habits and practices as an example: "Whatever you have learned or received or heard from me, or seen in me." He is essentially telling them that their appetite for truth and their application of it (what they have learned and received) and the instruction and modeling they have seen in him are prompts for an ongoing lifestyle. His instruction to put these things into practice does not point to a onetime event. It's a lasting, habitual, ongoing life of thinking new things and living a new life.

Why is this important? Because *your thought life determines your future.* Whatever your hopes are, whatever dreams you've had, whatever calling you've sensed from God, all of it will be affected and even determined by the ways you think. Your passions and joys, your expectations for the kinds of friends and family you will have and the kind of work you will do, these

Your thought life determines your future.

forward-looking pictures are informed and shaped by your thought patterns today.

Paul addressed this dynamic in his letter to the Romans in pretty graphic terms, and I'm sharing it in the Amplified Version–Classic Edition (with implied meanings in brackets) because of how thoroughly it expresses his language:

> For those who are according to the flesh and are controlled by its unholy desires set their minds on and pursue those things which gratify the flesh, but those who are according to the Spirit and are controlled by the desires of the Spirit set their minds on and seek those things which gratify the [Holy] Spirit.
>
> Now the mind of the flesh [which is sense and reason without the Holy Spirit] is death [death that comprises all the miseries arising from sin, both here and hereafter]. But the mind of the [Holy] Spirit is life and [soul] peace [both now and forever].
>
> [That is] because the mind of the flesh [with its carnal thoughts and purposes] is hostile to God, for it does not submit itself to God's Law; indeed it cannot.
>
> So then those who are living the life of the flesh [catering to the appetites and impulses of their carnal nature] cannot please or satisfy God, or be acceptable to Him. (Romans 8:5–8 AMP-CE)

Did you notice how focused this passage is on our thought life? And that those who are catering to carnal appetites and impulses *cannot please* God? But that we are given an invitation here to let our minds be empowered and guided by the Holy Spirit, which leads to life and peace? We cannot keep putting unwholesome, untrue, impure things in our minds and also expect to walk out God's purposes for us. Transformation always begins with our thinking.

How do we accomplish this? Through the principle of a renewed mind:

> Do not be conformed to this world (this age), [fashioned after and adapted to its external, superficial customs], but be transformed (changed) by the [entire] renewal of your mind [by its new ideals and its new attitude], so that you may prove [for yourselves] what is the good and acceptable and perfect will of God, *even* the thing which is good and acceptable and perfect [in His sight for you]. (Romans 12:2 AMP-CE, italics added)

In other words, as we allow our minds to be renewed into new thought patterns and godly perspectives, the good and perfect will of God increasingly plays out in our lives.

Notice that this is not an overnight process. I've been a Christian for more than four decades and still have to be intentional about some of the most basic things I was learning in those early years after coming to Christ. But I've seen transformation in my life, in the lives of those I love, and in many I've spoken to over the years. I know this **Transformation always begins with our thinking.** works. I have witnessed God responding faithfully to every move toward Him and every effort to think in renewed ways.

I have a little card on top of my remote control. It asks the questions we've covered in this chapter. Before I watch, listen to, or spend time thinking about something, I remind myself to consider these questions: *Is this true? Does it honor God? Is it right or wrong? Will it cleanse or dirty my soul? Will it renew or harden my heart? Would I recommend it to someone who looks up to me?* And a final one that fits the overall passage: *Will it bring peace or fear into my life?*

What lies do you believe? What harmful attitudes or patterns have you adopted? What thoughts fall short of God's character? Whatever deceptions and distortions have become a part of your life, pray about and think through practical ways you can replace them with whatever is good and true. Don't condemn yourself, but do seek change—persistently. Fill your heart and mind with truth. One of the best things you can do for yourself and the people who care about you is to establish biblical filters for your thought life and literal filters on your devices to help you continually choose whatever is true, noble, right, pure, lovely, and admirable.

Filters for Your Thought Life

Is this true or false?

Is this right or wrong?

Will it cleanse my soul or dirty it?

Will this renew my heart or harden it?

Can I recommend this to someone who looks up to me?

Will it bring peace or fear into my life?

Years ago, I realized I had been believing a lie for most of my life. This lie was much of the driving force behind my type A personality, the reason I always felt compelled to fill holes in my life. The lie was that I am a prisoner of the opinions of the important, influential people in my life.

Some might call it being a "people pleaser," which came from being the son of an alcoholic father and learning how to keep the peace all the time. But whatever the source, I would agonize when my best judgment and even direction from the Lord was different from people I respected. I thought disagreeing with someone would irreparably harm our relationship, so I created an unhealthy lifestyle of trying to please everyone. It was frustrating and challenging, and simply trying hard to change didn't work. I had to address the lie.

So I made some cards I could carry around with me to remind me of truth. On one side is the lie I believed: *People only love me if I prove my worth, please them, and agree with them.* On the other side is the truth: *People love me and are for me, and they want me to live a life of joy, rhythm, rest, and fruitfulness in all areas of my life. I am accepted, loved, and valued for who I am.* Whenever the lie pops up, I pull out the card, read the lie to expose it, and say, "Stop." Then I read the truth on the other side. I'm setting my mind on the Spirit, not on the flesh. I'm choosing to think on the things that are true, noble, right, pure, lovely, and admirable.

I would strongly encourage you to do that. If you commit to shifting your thoughts toward truth, you just might be shocked at what God does as you renew your mind. If you think it's a good idea but never actually act on it, nothing will change. If you just try harder without addressing the lies, little will change. But if you saturate your mind in truth, the lies eventually cannot remain. Your mind is renewed.

The Promise of Peace

The promise Paul declares after his instructions on changing how we think is this: "The God of peace will be with you." Remember, peace is *shalom*, a rich, full expression of God's goodness in every area of your life. You receive not only His peace but His blessing, power, presence, and provision. He wants to fulfill the desires of your heart.

That strikes at the heart of the biggest lie most of us will ever believe: that God is not for us, that He will not come through for us unless we measure up. The truth is that God is outlandishly on your side. He wants to fill your life with His goodness. He is always ready to forgive. "Lord, you are so good, so ready to forgive, so full of unfailing love for all who ask for your help" (Psalm 86:5 NLT). That's a picture of David turning his thoughts toward what is good and true, and I think we all need that perspective. Many of us, me included, are predisposed to think of God with His arms crossed and His toe tapping, as though He is disappointed that we haven't been quite good enough and is waiting for us to do better. It's a lie. Scripture gives us a completely different picture.

The truth is that God is outlandishly on your side.

You can change the way you think about these things. You can overcome the lies that produce fears, anxieties, regrets, and other distorted perceptions. But it will require guarding your mind like never before, being diligent about what goes in and what is kept out. It may require some radical rearranging of the things that come into your house, onto your screens, into your own mind, and into the lives of your children or grandchildren. You will have to reorient your thought life and monitor the things that shape it.

If you need any advice on how to get started, here's a game plan I've found to be very useful:

Read: The Bible	10 minutes
Pray: Talk with God	7 minutes
Listen: Sit quietly and listen	3 minutes
Apply: A specific truth, e.g., serve someone	1 minute

I created a three-week video journey called "Daily Discipline with Chip" in which I show how to meet with God, hear His voice, and understand His Word. I never go more than ten minutes, and I ask you to invest another ten every day for those three weeks. It grew out of the "sheltering in place" situation when COVID-19 first hit. Of all the tools or teaching I've ever done, this had the greatest, most positive impact on people, as they learned not just to "have devotions" but to renew their mind and actually experience God's power and presence.

That's roughly twenty minutes a day of spending time with God, and if you follow this plan, I strongly believe God will show up in your life like never before. Your thoughts and emotions won't change overnight, but a process of change will begin. After a week, you'll probably notice a difference. In two or three weeks, that difference will be much more obvious. In a month, three months, maybe a year, you'll be astonished at how your thoughts have changed. Those insecurities, addictions, anger issues, coping mechanisms, or whatever your particular issues happen to be will shift into far healthier ways of thinking. You will begin to see a new you. And you'll be very aware that the God of *shalom*—of wholeness, fullness, completeness, goodness, and satisfaction—is with you.

QUESTIONS FOR DISCUSSION AND REFLECTION

1. How does our thought life affect our emotions?

2. How would you describe the quality of your thought life? What adjustments do you sense God would have you make in what you view, read, and think?

3. Why is habitual practice of the truth so vital if we are to experience God's peace? Why do inconsistencies and discrepancies in our integrity create stress and lack of peace in our lives?

4. What insight has God given you in this chapter to help you experience His peace in your life? How will you choose to cooperate with His process in your life? Who might be able to help you?

CHAPTER 4

Choose Peace in Difficult Circumstances

When COVID-19 first spread around the world in the spring of 2020 and whole nations were sent home to shelter in place, many people discovered that their gods—the props they depended on to give them peace—had failed. The isolation and loss of security removed many of the distractions and coping mechanisms we tend to use to avoid our fundamental spiritual issues. It revealed the cracks in the "society of escape" we talked about in chapter 2. When our society was forced to slow its pace, addictions, domestic conflict, and depression increased. We had no sporting events or daily interactions at work or school to distract us. Fear over losing jobs, savings, and social opportunities crept in.

The world's discontentment became much more apparent under the spotlight of the pandemic.

Contentment may seem like a simple state of mind, but all it takes is a crisis to demonstrate how elusive it can be. Nearly every human being longs for that place where striving, struggling, and endless treadmills of trying to get ahead are no longer needed. We want to get past that feeling of everything we reach for being just beyond our grasp. We simply want to be content. And for most people, that means living beyond the turmoil of difficult circumstances.

Contentment is not about living beyond difficulties. It's about having peace in the midst of them. We can't be truly content unless we're anchored in something much greater than the trials and turmoil around us. Once we are, it really does become a simple concept. But "simple" and "easy" are not the same thing. For many people, that simple concept is extremely difficult to put into practice.

In our fallen nature, we are not very content beings. Part of that is by design; God has wired us to long for advances in our own spiritual growth and in the growth of His kingdom. But a self-focus distorts that God-given ambition and turns it toward having a little (or a lot) more money or a higher status, being better looking or being a little taller or a little shorter, having a better house or living in a better neighborhood, piling up a few more accolades and getting more compliments, and on and on. And all those things we think will make us content end up satisfying us for a moment—until we're discontent again and start reaching for more.

One definition of *contentment* is being happy enough with what you have or who you are, not desiring something more or different. In other words, it's being satisfied—not complacent, but not unhappy with where you are either. You realize what you have and who you are is good—not perfect, but enough to be fulfilled.

How content are you? In quiet moments when you have nothing to distract you, how unsettled do you feel? In all honesty, what do you believe would make you content? The clearer you get with that, the more powerfully God will speak to you in the following pages. If you're able to identify those longings—the things that make you think, *When I have that, I'll be happy. When I become that, I'll feel satisfied*—you'll recognize which ones will really bring contentment and which ones won't.

The problem with contentment, in purely human terms—in our natural, self-focused ambitions—is that the horizon is always moving. You can probably remember a time when you really wanted something and actually ended up getting it. When you're just learning to drive, you think you'd be content with any kind of car, even an old, beat-up junker. But when you get it and it starts having problems, you begin to think of a better car that runs well. Then when you've got that one, you want one that runs well and looks nice. Then you want one that runs well, looks nice, and sends a certain message about where you are in life. It's human nature; we all tend to think that way with cars, houses, degrees, jobs, even relationships. The goal just keeps moving, perhaps to something better, or maybe even just to anything else, as long as it's different.

Two drastic extremes have emerged as people have tried to solve this problem of contentment throughout the ages. One response has been to get more—to keep acquiring, conquering, achieving, expanding, and never stopping until you run out of objectives. The Roman Empire is a good example of that thirst for conquest. There's always a little bit more to acquire, a few more territories to conquer, a lot more wealth and power to be gained.

That didn't work for the Empire—one of the biggest reasons for its downfall was the difficulty in governing such a vast territory—and we know from experience it doesn't work for us personally either. Sure, it's nice to have things, and there's something very satisfying about climbing the ladder or accumulating a bit more. But you've probably noticed how your desires keep changing—how last year's phone that made you so happy then doesn't have all the best features now, or those stylish clothes don't make you feel quite as trendy a few months later. There's no end to that process. J. Paul Getty was once asked what it takes to really be satisfied. His answer was, "Just a little bit more." He recognized the futility. Contentment and the peace we seek never quite come.

The other extreme approach to this problem of contentment is detachment. If you don't care about anything, then you're always content with what you have. This is a prominent theme in some Eastern religions, some streams of Western philosophy, and certain periods and branches of Christian thought. A Stoic philosopher recommended envisioning your clay pots breaking as practice for experiencing the death of your loved ones because both are inevitable; close attachments lead to greater discontentment when they are lost. Stoics believed virtue mattered above all else, and everything else was valuable only insofar as it aided the practice of virtue. This line of reasoning encourages releasing things, acquiring less, and even giving up what you have in order to have peace. It also quenches love because love involves too much emotion. As scholar and historian T. R. Glover suggested, the Stoics made the heart a desert and called it peace.[1]

In extreme forms, this approach to contentment is called "asceticism." It majors on self-denial, but it never quite succeeds in creating peace or contentment. Human beings were designed for more than the bare essentials, materially and relationally, and even though it's good to know how to get by in times of hardship—we'll see Paul's statement on that soon—deprivation and detachment don't lead to peace. In fact, they usually lead to even greater anxiety.

How Can Our Souls Be Satisfied?

If getting more and more doesn't give us contentment, and if desiring less and less doesn't bring it either, we have a bit of a problem. How can we experience the peace we long for?

Paul, inspired by the Holy Spirit, gives us an answer in Philippians 4. Empowered by God's Spirit, we can actually live our lives in such a way that whether we feel like we're on a mountaintop or in a deep valley, we can say, "It is well with my soul." As with virtually everything in the Christian life, this is a journey, not an instant fix. But it's profound and desperately needed in a world that is constantly on a search for happiness.

Remember, when Paul writes, he is in confinement and awaiting trial to determine if he will live or die. He has been through several difficult years, and really a difficult life since becoming a Christian. He has scars and probably some broken bones that have never fully healed and is living under house arrest or in a Roman prison cell. But he has a good relationship with the Philippian church, and apart from instructions about the relational conflict there, his letter is mostly filled with words of joy and celebration of God's goodness.

During his confinement, the believers at Philippi sent one of their own to Paul with a monetary gift—a very useful favor, since Roman prisoners usually had to support themselves without any means of employment. One of the reasons for Paul's letter is to thank them for their generosity.

> I rejoiced greatly in the Lord that at last you renewed your
> concern for me. Indeed, you were concerned, but you had
> no opportunity to show it. I am not saying this because
> I am in need, for I *have learned to be content whatever
> the circumstances*. I know what it is to be in need, and I
> know what it is to have plenty. *I have learned the secret
> of being content in any and every situation*, whether well
> fed or hungry, whether living in plenty or in want. I can do
> all this through him who gives me strength. (Philippians
> 4:10–13, italics added)

Here Paul is essentially saying, "I know we had some great times together and saw God do some amazing things in birthing this church, but we've lost track of each other over the years. I've always known you cared, and I rejoice that you've taken this opportunity to show it." He says they have "renewed" their concern for him—the same word for a dormant flower now beginning to bloom. It's a beautiful picture, and Paul is actually happy in the midst of these difficult circumstances.

In fact, that's how this section of the letter begins: "I rejoiced greatly." And in order to assure them that this joy is genuine, he goes on to say that he is not actually in need but is at peace with whatever he has, whether a lot or a little. "I have learned the secret of being content in any and every situation," he tells them, "whether well fed or hungry, whether living in plenty or in want."

Twice in this short passage Paul says, "I have learned." This isn't present tense. It comes from past experience, and it's a skill Paul already has in his repertoire. On one hand, he has a brilliant mind, a great education, an upper-crust pedigree from a respected family, Roman citizenship, and at least in his early adulthood, a sterling reputation. He has had well-off friends like Barnabas and has known what the finer life is like. On the other hand, he has been beaten within a lash of his life on multiple occasions (and once left for dead), shipwrecked, betrayed by close friends who left the faith, imprisoned, insulted, scandalized, and plotted against. He has worn the scars and felt the hunger pangs to prove it. He knows hardship as well as anybody and more than most. And in all the ups and downs, the thread that connects all these experiences is a supernatural relationship with Jesus.

Clearly this is not theory or just a philosophy for Paul. If someone were to put this in modern terms, it's like saying, "I've had tons of money in the bank, gone to the finest restaurants, driven the best cars, and felt like everything was going my way. And I've also been broke, had close friends walk out on me, lost my health, lived with pain, and felt like everything is going against me. And through my relationship with Christ, I can honestly say at any of those moments, 'I'm fine.'" The last line of this passage (v. 13) is the key: "I can do all this through him who gives me strength."

For Paul, then, peace is not a thing to be achieved but a secret to be discovered. There's a way to find it apart from all the strategies of conquest and detachment the world has come up with. It's possible to be truly at peace, not just faking it, in every situation in life, even when we aren't thrilled with what's going on. It isn't dependent on circumstances. You can actually be satisfied with who you are, where you are, what you have, and what you're doing as long as you're abiding in a deep relationship with Jesus.

Peace is not a thing to be achieved but a secret to be discovered.

This kind of contentment does not mean lying back on the couch and letting whatever is going to happen just happen. It isn't fatalism. You can still press ahead toward becoming everything you want to be in the process. Paul certainly did. It's a detachment from outward circumstances and anxieties, but not from inner purpose and personal relationships. Even in the midst of all the ups and downs of that turbulent journey, there's a supernatural peace in your heart.

But that raises an obvious question. How do ordinary people like you and me experience this kind of supernatural peace?

The Answer: Four Principles, Four Practices

Paul understood that contentment is a moving target. He knew from experience that gaining more and more would never be enough, and there were plenty of Stoics in his day to demonstrate that getting less and less—or becoming more and more detached—wasn't the answer either. So in this passage to the Philippians, where he calls contentment a "secret," he lays out four principles and practices we can follow to obtain it.

Keep in mind that these are doable principles and practices, not unreachable ideals. They are steps we can take to learn to be at peace 24/7, just as we learned to ride a bike or mastered a professional skill. We've touched on some of them, but we need to look at them in more depth. When we learn these, we are equipped for any situation we will ever encounter.

PRINCIPLE 1: Contentment is not dependent on our circumstances. Most of us have been taught unconsciously that there's a huge gap between our circumstances and our desires, and all we need to do is close that gap and we'll be happy. That's what the commercials tell us, right? We've been exposed to this message all our lives because it's the way the world thinks. I call it "the when-then syndrome": *When* you get married, get that job, have that house, drive that car, or whatever your particular desire is, *then* you'll be satisfied. Maybe you're waiting for your marriage to hit on all cylinders or your kids to grow up with good and healthy behaviors. It might be a certain career or a level of achievement within that career. It can be really big-ticket items or smaller steps along the way, like making a team or having enough money to remodel the kitchen. Large or small, the issue is always "when." And when "when" happens, "then" contentment and peace come.

> **The only way to get out of this never-ending cycle is to identify and break the lie.**

As we've seen, this is a lie. Lots of people have gotten from the "when" to the "then" and are still very unhappy. Like cats chasing their tails, they keep increasing the speed of the chase but still never catch up. The only way to get out of this never-ending cycle is to identify and break the lie. How?

PRACTICE 1: Be grateful. Develop the discipline of thanking God for what you have rather than focusing on what you don't have. Gratitude is a very effective antidote to the never-ending chase. Billions of dollars are spent every year on advertising that is designed to make people discontent and put the possibility of contentment in front of them through a certain product or lifestyle—food, drink, clothing, jobs, cars, diets, surgery, grooming products, and on and on. Any of these can be enjoyed and might be nice to have. None of them have the power to make us content in themselves.

Paul interrupts this human tendency of focusing on what we don't have to say, "I have learned to be content whatever the circumstances." The rest of the letter backs that up. He rejoices and gives thanks throughout for all the great things that are happening. He even turns all the negative circumstances in chapter 1—his imprisonment, rivalrous preachers, and the possibility of his death—into positive situations that he is grateful for. Moment by moment, he has learned by practice to give thanks for what he does have, even in the midst of hardship.

Gratitude is not just a nice suggestion.

Gratitude is not just a nice suggestion. In three short verses in a letter to the Thessalonians, he makes it a command: "Rejoice always, pray continually, give thanks in all circumstances; for this is God's will for you in Christ Jesus" (1 Thessalonians 5:16–18). We are called to be thankful.

I've learned the hard way how a lack of gratitude can subtly but tragically turn us into very discontent people. I married a wonderful woman named Theresa without any premarital counseling or experience in what married life was supposed to be like. We both loved God, I was going to seminary, and that was supposed to be enough. That saying about "opposites attracting" was true for us. And at first, that was awesome. Our differences drew us together like magnets.

But several months into our marriage, those opposites became sticking points. What I once saw as "faithful" became "rigid." Where she once had integrity, now she was just picky. And my list of complaints was growing. Overall, I think we had a pretty good marriage. But my focus was on the 10 percent that was really rubbing me the wrong way. I thought that if she could just improve on five or six things, we would have a great marriage. When . . . then.

I helped Theresa embark on a self-help program designed just for her so she could be the wife she needed to be. She became my project. If we could just focus on those areas she needed to develop and change, things would get better. I didn't say any of this, of course. I wasn't that naïve. But it didn't make sense to me that we would drive each other crazy if we both loved God, loved each other, and were headed into the ministry. It's embarrassing to look back and see how arrogant I was about marriage and my own less-than-desirable traits that were producing conflict.

In the process of getting some wise pastoral counseling, however, which God graciously provided for us, I began the practice of being grateful and thanking God for the beauty and gifts and joys He had put into my wife. I quit focusing on the 10 percent that seemed, to me, to be lacking and celebrated the good that was there. It was a discipline at first—minds trained in "fix it" mode don't turn their attention away from the problems very easily—but over time, that discipline gave me a much more accurate perspective. I came to appreciate Theresa more and more, and it changed my world and our marriage.

I try to apply that same practice to every area of life. I still do it for my marriage; we still go through emotional challenges, and sometimes it helps to go to a coffee shop and start writing down, "She's so faithful, she prays for me, she's an amazing mother and grandmother, she's godly, she's kind and beautiful," and all the other wonderful qualities she has.

But this is just as effective with kids, jobs, lifestyles, and every other area of life. Most of us already have plenty of practice staring at the glass half-empty—or even the glass 2 percent empty—and need to be retrained to see what's there. When we do, our emotions change. We become less depressed and more content. Eventually we overflow with joy.

That's what Paul seemed to do not only in Philippians but in most of his letters. It profoundly changes our emotions and strips our discontentment of its foundation. The first and best thing we can do to grow in our experience of peace in difficult circumstances is to habitually practice being thankful.

PRINCIPLE 2: Contentment is an attitude we learn, not a thing we achieve. This secret to contentment dispels a very powerful myth: that contentment is a future event. Many of us seem to think there is a big breakthrough event waiting out there for us, something like a life lottery that takes us from just getting by to overabundance. That "lotto" can revolve around a person, an event, or a state of being, but it's still anchored in when-then thinking. And whenever it comes, we'll be happy.

In Philippians 4:11–12, Paul stresses that he has learned. Already. Our search for peace is not out there, external to us and waiting for us to get there. It is based on God doing something within us. It's internal and already available.

PRACTICE 2: Be teachable. If you really want to learn this skill of contentment as a way of life, add to your gratitude the art of being teachable. In whatever circumstances you face, ask God what He wants to teach you instead of telling Him what you want Him to change.

What would happen if a little mental recorder could track all your thoughts and play them back? What would your prayers sound like? For many of us, prayer requests focus on things we want God to give us, problems we want Him to solve, people we want Him to change, and situations we want Him to create or get us out of. We present Him with an agenda, as if His role is to be the genie who makes us happy, satisfied, and fulfilled.

Ask God what He wants to teach you instead of telling Him what you want Him to change.

God does promise to provide for us, protect us, and answer our prayers. No question about that. But He isn't our genie, and His agenda is somewhat different from ours. He doesn't buy into the lie that if we only had this or that thing, person, or situation, we'd be content. Prayers focused almost exclusively on those things very often come from discontent people.

People who are at peace begin with, "Thank You, Lord." Even when things are difficult—and there's nothing wrong with telling Him we don't like certain situations—we choose to give thanks. And then content people add something to their gratitude: "Lord, teach me. What do You want me to learn in these circumstances? What are You trying to accomplish here, and how can I cooperate with that?" We learn to participate in His plans and leverage our situations rather than insist that something about them be changed.

I have a good friend who feels stuck. That's not an uncommon feeling. You have probably felt that way at some point in your life; that point may even be right now. Perhaps you've experienced the feeling of being stuck in your marriage, your job, your home life, or your school, and you know how frustrating it can be to keep trying to get unstuck without seeing breakthrough. That's where this friend is. He's tried everything, and he's really bummed out. He just can't make the right things happen.

We met one morning for coffee, and he pulled out a pen and started diagramming on a napkin. "God spoke to me," he said. "I realized all the things I couldn't change, even though I had done all I could to change them." So he wrote down his life categories: God, family, himself.

"I always say it's God first, then my family, then me," he said. "Then I did a little profit-and-loss evaluation, an inventory of where I am and how I'm stuck. I keep hitting things that don't move, so I started wondering if God wanted to teach me something. And I asked."

He went on to describe his thought processes in conversation with God, and what he thought God was teaching him about his relationship with God, his family, and himself. He looked at all his activities and where his energy was going, and even though he mentally placed God first, most of what he was doing was directed toward himself. He realized his words—his commitment to place God first and his family next, above himself—didn't really line up with his actions. So he reorganized his life, reprioritized, moved some things around, and said, "Okay, I want to learn."

That changed things. He realized what we all eventually discover for ourselves: that the goal of life is not self-actualization. It's not to be fulfilled and have everything go our way. God's primary agenda in your life is to make you like His Son, to use all the ups and downs in a fallen world to develop that vital relationship with Jesus by the power of His Spirit, rooted in His Word, in the context of authentic community, so that little by little you begin to think, talk, and serve like Jesus. It's for moms, dads, children, siblings, coworkers, and neighbors to embody the nature of God in Christ.

God's primary agenda in your life is to make you like His Son.

If you've struggled with that same discrepancy between your stated priorities and your actual investments of time, energy, emotions, and resources, this is where it's leading. When that vital relationship with Jesus becomes your priority, there will be people in your life who don't understand how you can go through the hard times or the injustice you're facing, who wonder how you keep such a level head in the midst of successes and abundance, who can't believe you aren't undone by the financial crisis or the pandemic that everyone is so worried about, who see the same version of you no matter what you're going through. You may still experience and express a range of emotions through those ups and downs, and you may need to work through some of them with God, but you begin to take on His nature and His peace. You manifest a supernatural calm and confidence regardless of your circumstances. You seem a lot more like Jesus than the disciples in that storm-tossed boat.

That's God's agenda for you, and when you become teachable in the midst of your circumstances, you learn what you can change and stop focusing on things you can't change. In any situation, you are able to thank God for what you do have and quit dwelling on what you don't have. And you begin to see every circumstance as an opportunity to demonstrate something of the nature of God and see it being formed in you.

PRINCIPLE 3: Prosperity does not have the power to give us peace and contentment, nor poverty the power to take it away. The secret of contentment challenges our modern assumption that more is better. This assumption is an American ideal and a common belief in today's global economy. But if inner peace is not based on circumstances and is an attitude we can learn, it can't be tied to our prosperity or lack.

Paul demonstrates the point himself in verse 12: "I know what it is to be in need, and I know what it is to have plenty." He's had a lot, and he's had nothing, and neither situation has defined his level of contentment. His word for "plenty" was also commonly used for fattened livestock. In other words, he is saying he has lived in the lap of luxury and knows it can't deliver happiness. But he has also experienced extreme hardship, including being hungry, thirsty, cold, and naked. (He provides a longer list of examples in 2 Corinthians 11:24–28.) None of those situations, whether positive or negative, have changed his level of peace and contentment.

You may have experienced extremes too. I know I have. In many respects, I've been very blessed and fortunate to live in a rich society with access to good medical care and many luxuries not available in some parts of the world. But I've also been in situations where I didn't know if I was going to come out alive. I've heard biopsy reports that confirmed cancer in loved ones. I've wondered how I was going to make it without this person in my life or how family and friends were going to get by without me if something happened to me. I have to agree with Paul: those kinds of situations can't take peace away from me, and the opposite situations will never be able to give it to me. It has to come from something beyond our circumstances.

PRACTICE 3: Be flexible. We begin by being grateful and then by being teachable. But what happens when God shows you something you didn't necessarily want to learn? Being flexible means you are open to change—in your own life and in the world around you. It's not just asking God what He wants you to learn; it's asking how He wants you to change in light of what you're learning.

When my friend sat down at the table and showed me his list of priorities, he put it all in context. "I've got a huge presentation to make for this big corporation, and there's a lot riding on it. I normally obsess over these things and over-prepare for them, working through every detail and trying to make sure nothing is left to chance. My career feels like a high-stakes project, and I've always chosen to prioritize it. But my wife wanted to get away and have some fun. And since God had just showed me where I was mixing up my priorities . . . well, I did it." And he described how he got up really early in the morning to put in about two hours of work on the presentation, and said, "Lord, I really need You to show up." Then he leaned in and said, "What's amazing is that the presentation went better than it would have if I had spent the whole day on it."

He was flexible. He took what God had told him and applied it to a real-life situation, even though it went against his grain and required a huge shift in thinking. When God says, "Here's how I want you to be more like My Son," what's the next step? It isn't the status quo. You have to break the lie that prosperity is going to get you where you need to go.

I'm one of those weird people who is going to bed about the time everyone else is getting revved up to have a great evening. Then while everyone else is sleeping, I'm usually up working. It's just how God made me. But it isn't easy finding a good place to work in the wee hours of the morning.

I found a little coffee shop that bakes donuts and bagels all night long and serves the kind of coffee I like. I'd go in there to spend some time with God and begin my workday, and I got to know people who seem to share the same weird schedule. One of the regulars was a young man I got to know pretty well. He came to California, began coming to our church, and eventually got pretty involved, and went to work at a Christian camp at minimum wage.

One morning as we shared coffee and a bagel, I asked him about his spiritual journey. I was captivated as his story unfolded and said, "That would make a great book."

"That's why I come in here so early," he said. "I'm revising the first edition for a publisher. Would you like to read it?"

He handed me a copy of *True Riches*, and I read the back cover.[2] At twenty-three, he had a degree in finance and plenty of credentials. He told the story of having three credit cards and borrowing as much cash as he could on each one, working his way onto the trading floor in Chicago, and going from dead broke to being a multimillionaire at twenty-five, with everything the world has to offer in his lap. Then at twenty-eight he was broke again, and again earned it all back the next year.

"God wanted to teach me something," he said. "I could get anything in the world I wanted. Do you know how scary it is to say you know Christ alone can deliver but unconsciously believe otherwise? I went into a deep depression. So I came here to serve people at minimum wage because I wanted to learn to be content. I want peace that doesn't ride the waves of circumstances I can't control."

How many people know Christ, believe the Holy Spirit lives in their hearts and lives, claim the Bible as truth, and behind the curtain of their soul still believe they have to get a good enough SAT score, make that team, climb the corporate ladder, land at the right firm, find that perfect spouse, or move into the right neighborhood to find peace? We unconsciously buy into that lie that prosperity can deliver, even when our words deny it. Paul's words sound like radical Christianity to many believers.

The flip side of that truth is that poverty has no power to take away our peace. Just as prosperity can't deliver it, lack can't destroy it. Paul said he was content even in those times when he had nothing.

I'll never forget a time in the Philippines when I was on a basketball team that traveled throughout the islands to play local teams and share Christ with the community. A young Filipino who traveled with us desperately wanted to show me his home. "You've got to come see it," he said.

"Sure," I said, and we got on his motorcycle to weave in and out of Manila traffic—no rules, as far as I could tell—to get to where he lived. We were weaving in and out of "lanes," dodging cars and trucks and all sorts of other vehicles. I was starting to wonder what I had gotten into. I was praying the whole way that I'd get to see Theresa and the kids again.

A missionary friend warned me that the young man lived in the slums, but I had no idea exactly what that meant until we got there. It was like nothing I had experienced. There was a hill with cardboard shacks against each other as far as the eye could see. In one area, there were a few wooden crates—that was the upper-middle class, I think—and then a few "elite" shacks with tin roofs to help for the rain. Thousands upon thousands of people, with no evidence of plumbing in sight.

Somehow this passionate young man had figured out how to extend a wire a long way from the one light pole and through his roof, so he attached a light bulb and opened up his home at night to read Scripture for anyone who wanted to hear. He was proud to be the only one in his area with a light.

We walked through a maze of people to get to his nine-by-six room. He had dug out a smaller area where he cooked. He introduced me to his wife and sons and said, "Chip, I'm so glad you would come to my home." You'd think he owned the Taj Majal.

"Where do you sleep?" I asked.

He looked at me like I was crazy. "Right here." He pointed to a small cot. "I curl my body this way, my wife curls that way, and we put our boys in the middle." Then he pointed to where he cooked, as if to emphasize that he had a two-level house. He had a light bulb, a dug-out level, a large enough bed for four, and was grateful for how good God had been to him. The most striking thing about him was the smile that radiated from his face and the joy in his heart.

Poverty doesn't have the power to rob our peace.

Poverty doesn't have the power to rob our peace. Paul says you can learn to be content in any situation. Sure, you will always be able to improve your golf swing, update your home, or get a better position. Go for it. But don't hang your contentment on those things. If you will practice being *grateful*, become *teachable*, and are *flexible* in every situation, you will be very close to having the heart and soul of someone who might as well have a million dollars in the bank and fulfilling relationships all in order, wondering how life could get better.

PRINCIPLE 4: Only Christ has the power to give us a peace that transcends all life's variables. Even believers buy into the lie that contentment can be found apart from God. But the testimony of those who get what they wanted and realize how much they need Him is that it can't. We can't blame unbelievers for thinking that the right situations, possessions, relationships, accomplishments, and status will do it for them because that's all they know to envision. In fact, that's how many of them become believers—they reach their goals and realize there's still something missing. But no one reaches contentment and experiences peace that transcends life's variables without connecting to the God above them.

Everyone seems to have a conscious or unconscious box full of treasures that they keep striving to reach. It's like a pot at the end of the rainbow. It keeps people walking, working, running on the treadmill that never ends. Sometimes they even reach their dreams and step into that little picture they drew for themselves. But instead of sitting around the table celebrating all the time, instead of being satisfied with what they've achieved, they're still restless. The picture doesn't look quite as good in the hand as it did on the horizon. That box turns out to be surprisingly empty.

In 2015, I had the privilege of leading chapel for the Seattle Seahawks when they came to San Francisco to play the 49ers. It was the year after they had beat the Broncos to win the Super Bowl. As the players in the room discussed what I shared from the Scriptures, a theme emerged. They all talked about the "letdown." Not that it wasn't wonderful to be world champions and accomplish such a challenging goal, but over and over I heard, "I thought it would feel different"—that reaching the top would be a lot "bigger" or more satisfying. The dream of every athlete is to be the world champion in their sport, but even when you arrive, it doesn't have the power to bring lasting peace.

The reason so many people come to Christ after they have given all the time, energy, and focus to a goal that turned out to be unfulfilling is that they have finally realized their need. It's the same reason people come to Christ out of extraordinary pain. Success and pain can both lead to hunger and thirst for a Savior because the world system can't give us what we need.

Believers arrive at that same realization when we think our peace comes from Jesus *plus* a great family, a good job, or a healthy body. The "plus" always gets us in trouble. We essentially tell God that when He delivers the "plus" and adds it to Jesus, we'll be happy and fulfilled. That's a spiritual version of the same journey unbelievers go on, but that's not the way life works. It's still a lie. We may not end up as empty as those without Christ, but it can feel that way if we've placed our hopes in Him plus something else.

Many Christians have lost their peace and wonder why.

The energy, skills, talents, time, money, and other resources God gives us to do something great with our lives for the sake of His kingdom can be subtly, destructively turned inward. We end up chasing something that doesn't exist, and we come up empty. That's why one of the fastest growing professions among believers in the last few decades has been Christian counseling. I'm grateful for counselors—I've benefited from them myself—but one of the reasons they are so needed is that believers have bought into the never-ending chase for contentment. Many Christians have lost their peace and wonder why.

PRACTICE 4: Be confident. If only Christ can give you the peace that transcends all circumstances—if that's the final secret of success added to being *grateful*, *teachable*, and *flexible*—then that's where we turn for strength. Maybe you've tried to change before and no longer think you can. If so, Philippians 4:13 is the key: "I can do all this through him who gives me strength."

Moment by moment, relationship by relationship, decision by decision, through every disappointment, you can have confidence that you can fulfill everything God wants you to do. It doesn't come by lying on the couch and thinking you might try that someday. The confidence comes by faith.

By faith, you begin by thanking God for whatever you do have. Then you commit to being teachable and learning how God wants to direct you. You become flexible enough to embrace change, reorienting your life around what matters, putting God and others first, even when there's a cost or it goes against your deeply ingrained ways.

Is it hard? Of course. Is it possible? Absolutely. But here's the key: When you receive the power of His Word, energized by His Spirit, in the context of genuine, loving community relationships, God will give you whatever you need to have a quiet heart that is completely at peace. Through the fellowship of His Son and the power of His Spirit, you can respond with all the courage and faith you need to be content and have peace in any situation in life. You can do all things through the One who strengthens you.

I recently received a letter from someone who wanted to thank me for some teachings that had been helpful to him.

But after that, seemingly out of the blue, he added some comments that get right to the heart of this issue of contentment. I'll paraphrase his story, but it went something like this:

> It seems like I keep running into people who think that if they can only perform at a high enough level, if they can only get enough applause or admiration, their life will have meaning. In the past year, I've spoken to so many in these situations, and I've seen it in my own life. But that doesn't do it.
>
> People put everything into being on the cheerleading squad, working their way to the top of the corporate ladder, making the dean's list, wearing a Super Bowl ring, or becoming a major political player. They spend every ounce of time and energy on these earthly goals, convinced that when they achieve them, they will finally have the self-esteem and confidence and peace they desperately want.
>
> But it seems to me, when they reach the pinnacle of what they thought would be successful, the sense of self-worth and contentment they long for is conspicuously absent. And the reason, I think, is that their goals were centered on what other people think rather than on what God thinks.
>
> I remember a sportswriter named Gary Smith once interviewed boxing legend Muhammad Ali at the fighter's farmhouse. Ali took Smith on a tour of his estate and led him into the barn, and the writer saw all of Ali's trophies, ribbons, and awards on the shelf, collecting dust, some of them even spattered with pigeon droppings—Golden Gloves, Olympic gold, World Champion. As they surveyed all the boxing memorabilia getting ruined, Muhammad

Ali said something very quietly to Smith. With his lips barely moving, he said, "I had the world, and it wasn't nothin'. Look now."[3]

What do you have now? What are you aiming for? What would it look like for you to be grateful, to be teachable, to be flexible, and to be confident God could give you whatever you need so that, as you grow in your contentment and experience His peace, circumstances would no longer have the power to touch you?

Here's the bottom line: Contentment is not a passive acceptance of the status quo. It's the positive assurance that God has supplied your needs and the release from unnecessary desires. Will you still have desires? Of course. You don't need to detach from everything in order to be content. And you certainly don't need to go to the other extreme and try to get all you can as if your contentment depended on it.

> **You are called to peace, and you already have everything you need to enter into it.**

No, you are called to peace, and you already have everything you need to enter into it. You have enough faith, courage, and supernatural empowerment to apply Paul's four keys and grow in peace daily. The *shalom* of God, which transcends every circumstance you will ever face, will guard your heart and mind, and God Himself will be with you.

QUESTIONS FOR DISCUSSION AND REFLECTION

1. Why is it so difficult to be genuinely content? What factors in our world make this so? What factors in our hearts make this so?

2. Why are both historical positions toward contentment doomed to failure?

3. How do each of the principles and practices relate to your present circumstances and attitudes about personal peace?

4. What action step will you take to reflect obedience to God's provision for your personal peace?

5. If you are going through this study in a group, take time to pray for one another. Ask God to help each member embrace His game plan for a life of personal peace. If you are going through this as personal study, spend some time praying the same for yourself.

CHAPTER 5

Choose Peace
in a Materialistic Culture

E ven if you've never heard of a "scouting report," you've
probably done one.

In sports, your team puts together a scouting report by watching game film of another team and its players to figure out
their strengths and weaknesses, where they can be exploited,
where your strengths match up against their vulnerabilities,
and what strategy to use when you play them.

In war, a small group of soldiers goes out in advance of a
battle to scout out the adversary's positions and capabilities.
One of my friends from years ago who had been a squad
leader in Vietnam told me how he would frequently take

about a dozen men out on a circular scouting mission, and sometimes after going through thick jungle they would find themselves at the edge of open areas of rice paddies, completely exposed. He'd send a couple scouts out from the natural cover, flat on their bellies, to check everything out and then motion to the rest if everything was okay. A good scouting report was a matter of life and death, and he saw people die in his arms because the report was wrong.

But we do a lighter version of this in everyday life, don't we? If a school friend wants your son or daughter to come over and spend the night, you make some phone calls, ask a few questions, check the internet for any sex offenders in the area, and make sure it's okay. It's not paranoid; you just have to be careful. Or when older students see a guy or girl they might be interested in, they ask so-and-so to ask so-and-so for some details to see if he or she might be worth pursuing. If you're interested in a job opening, you probably do a little research on the employer and check in with friends who might know others who work there to make sure it's actually a good opportunity. We conduct our own little scouting reports all the time.

In this chapter, we're going to look at contentment's greatest competitor and discover some ways to beat it. We'll continue in Philippians 4 to find out how to have peace in a materialistic culture. But first, let's look at another of Paul's passages that is essentially a scouting report about our battle. This report is even more serious than the scouting missions my friend had to do in Vietnam. People could lose their lives if the reports from him or his men were wrong, but people can lose their souls for eternity if they don't understand our enemy's tactics and their own vulnerabilities. Paul is dealing with an extremely serious issue.

A good scouting report does four basic things:

1. It identifies the foe.
2. It tells us how formidable the foe is.
3. It describes the foe's tactics.
4. It identifies where we are vulnerable.

So when false teachers were gaining influence in the first-century church, Paul wrote to Timothy to warn him about what was happening.

> They have an unhealthy interest in controversies and quarrels about words that result in . . . constant friction between people of corrupt mind, who have been robbed of the truth and who think that godliness is a means to financial gain.
>
> But godliness with contentment is great gain. For we brought nothing into the world, and we can take nothing out of it. But if we have food and clothing, we will be content with that. Those who want to get rich fall into temptation and a trap and into many foolish and harmful desires that plunge people into ruin and destruction. For the love of money is a root of all kinds of evil. Some people, eager for money, have wandered from the faith and pierced themselves with many griefs. (1 Timothy 6:4–10)

A teaching going around suggested that everything will turn out great for those who love God. Paul was pointing out the absurdity of the idea that walking with God and loving Jesus is a way to get rich. Sounds pretty familiar, doesn't it? That idea is still around. But people who believe such things, according to Scripture, "have been robbed of the truth."

People can lose their souls for eternity if they don't understand our enemy's tactics.

By contrast, Paul argues, "Godliness with contentment is great gain." What we get from walking with God, serving Him, and loving Him is a sense of supernatural sufficiency and peace in Christ. And then He follows this up with two facts that explain why this is true: (1) we brought nothing into the world and can take nothing out of it; and (2) if we have food and clothing, that's enough for us to be content.

In other words, Paul says, these teachers are making false promises, and people are wasting their lives on them. We come into the world as naked babies, and people may put nice clothes on us and give us a lot of wonderful things, but when we die, it doesn't matter if they put us in an expensive, gilded casket or a simple wooden box. A hundred percent of human beings come in with nothing and leave with nothing. And if, in the meantime, we have food and clothing—literally, a "covering"—to keep us nourished and protected from the elements, we really have all we need.

Then comes the scouting report: "Those who want to get rich fall into temptation and a trap and into many foolish and harmful desires that plunge people into ruin and destruction" (v. 9). Where does the ruin and destruction come from? "The love of money is a root of all kinds of evil. Some people, eager for money, have wandered from the faith and pierced themselves with many griefs" (v. 10). Paul is bothered that this is happening and wants to make sure Timothy stewards his leadership well and steers people away from the dangers of this temptation. Whether rich or poor, it is extremely risky for people to crave something that could cause them to drift away from their faith.

The Scouting Report's Four Questions

If a good scouting report addresses four key questions—who the foe is, how formidable the foe is, what the foe's tactics are, and where our vulnerabilities are—we should expect to find answers to each of these in Paul's words to Timothy.

Who is our foe? The technical name for the adversary Paul identifies is *philarguria*. It's the word translated as "love of money"—greed, or what we would today call *materialism*, that belief we examined in the last chapter that we just need more, more, and more to be happy. That's the foe Paul was dealing with and that we continue to deal with today.

How formidable is our foe? Paul is not reserved in his vocabulary when describing the dangers of avarice. Certain words serve as cues that we are dealing with a very formidable foe: *plunge, ruin, destruction, all kinds of evil, wandered, pierced, griefs*. The love of money is not primarily a financial problem. It's a heart issue. It skews our priorities and damages our relationships. About 60 percent of failed marriages can trace the failure back to disagreements about finances.

This is a powerful, deadly, ruthless enemy that can distort and destroy our spiritual, physical, emotional, and relational life. It can affect our eternal destiny.

The love of money is not primarily a financial problem. It's a heart issue.

What are the foe's tactics? Notice the words *temptation*, *trap*, *foolish*, and *harmful desires*, and a clear strategy begins to emerge. Temptation is almost always the prompt or urge to get something good in a bad way. It's missing the mark, a trap or a lure, that shiny thing a fish sees before it bites into a hook. Money is like that. It promises power, position, popularity, possessions, and a lifestyle that we think will make life easier and better. But when we start chasing it, the hook catches us and draws us in directions we didn't necessarily want to go.

The pursuit of money can destroy relationships and alienate us from God, both of which are far too high a price to pay for what we get in return. Jesus said the worries of the world and the deceitfulness of riches keep the Word of God from growing in us (Matthew 13:22). Little by little, our lives are strangled, and we end up with emptiness.

No one starts pursuing money with the intention of wandering from the faith. It isn't a willful decision. It just happens. We don't consciously think, *I love God, want Him to use my life for His purposes, and long for a good marriage and a fruitful career, but I think I'll just throw that all away and chase money instead.* It doesn't work that way. That's why Jesus called it the "deceitfulness of wealth" (Matthew 13:22). We don't realize what is happening while it is happening. So, as Paul puts it, we wander from the faith. We drift away like someone in a boat so engrossed in what's going on around him that the current takes him downstream, past the dock, and on to who knows where.

That's what this word *wander* means (1 Timothy 6:10). You wake up one day and you're far from Christ. Your priorities are out of order, your marriage is tense, you are consumed with your work, debt begins to grow, your kids are seeing the worst side of you, and everyone picks up on the fact that your life is oriented around having more. The result? You're pierced with grief. That's a powerful tactic.

Where are we vulnerable? Remember, this is a heart issue. And the heart can be deceitful above all else (Jeremiah 17:9). As believers, we've been given a new heart (Jeremiah 31:31–34), but we still have the potential to step outside that new creation and act in old ways. For most of us, the issue is not whether we are being deceived or are greedy. The question is how greedy we are. We are vulnerable in our hearts because we live in a culture that is constantly saturating us with messages of materialism and greed. We are bombarded with advertisements that are designed for the sole purpose of creating discontentment and then offering a false solution. Our old shoes, heels, hemlines, tapered cuts, cars, perfumes, jewelry, hairstyles, home furnishings, colors, patterns, and more are not good enough. We must need something new. To some degree or another, we have all been hooked.

To some degree or another, we have all been hooked.

What are you going to do about that? The answer isn't necessarily to run in the other direction and avoid buying anything ever again. But if the consequences of the love of money are ruin, destruction, and grief, it demands that we each check our own hearts—frequently.

Jesus talked about money a lot, usually in a warning. He didn't say money was bad, necessarily; His ministry received donations (Luke 8:1–3). But He knew the dangers of serving money instead of God (Luke 16:13)—of turning our worship away from God and toward "mammon" and letting greed and materialism drive our lives. He understood where we were vulnerable.

We know from the context of Scripture as a whole that having money is not bad in itself, but it is dangerous. As we will see, Paul will go on in his instructions to Timothy to say, "Command those who are rich in this present world not to be arrogant nor to put their hope in wealth, which is so uncertain, but to put their hope in God, who richly provides us with everything for our enjoyment" (1 Timothy 6:17). He doesn't tell those who are rich in this present world not to be rich. He tells them where to invest their hearts. The desire for money can be a road to destruction or a great kingdom asset. But vulnerable, tempted hearts so often turn it to the former rather than the latter. As Paul continues his letter to the Philippians, we will see how he views money as a vehicle of true worship rather than as a means of materialistic gain. He shows us how to overcome this formidable foe of materialism and experience true peace.

Breaking the Grip of Greed: Three Principles, Three Practices

By God's grace, through the power of His Spirit and His Word, we really can break the grip of greed. We saw in Paul's instructions to the Philippians in the last chapter how to learn contentment: through being grateful, teachable, flexible, and confident in the power of Christ at work in us (Philippians 4:10–13). That's a priceless lesson. In the next few verses, Paul and the Philippian church model what this antidote to greed looks like in real life. From their example, we can see three principles and three corresponding practices that will strip greed of its power in our hearts and minds.

PRINCIPLE 1: **Develop personal compassion.** Greed hardens your heart. It turns your focus to money, which often translates into things and experiences, which often take a higher place in our lives than God and people. The only way to reverse that trend is to have our hearts tenderized, to soften them toward God and people. In other words, we must intentionally develop compassion.

PRACTICE 1: **Put others' needs ahead of your wants.** Developing compassion is the "what." This is the "how." Identify some of your wants, find someone with a real need, and then decide to let go of your want to meet their need. This will require time, energy, or money that you would have spent on yourself to be redirected to someone else. That's an act of compassion, and as you learn to do it eagerly rather than grudgingly, it undoes the power of greed in your heart.

Paul identifies this kind of compassion in the Philippian believers. Immediately after he says he can do all things through Christ, who gives him strength, he highlights their generosity: "It was good of you to share in my troubles" (Philippians 4:14). As far as we can tell, piecing together the origins of the Philippian church in Acts 16 and comments Paul makes in his letters, this church began about ten years earlier. The church was birthed in turmoil; it's where Paul and Silas were beaten and imprisoned overnight for starting a riot, when all they had done was to cast an evil spirit out of a slave girl. They worshiped in jail, an earthquake broke their chains and opened the doors, they shared the gospel with the jailer, and the believers meeting in Lydia's home began to multiply. But Paul left town after those turbulent events and developed a close bond with this church in the following years.

Here he recalls those early years, when the Philippian believers were supporting his ministry. "It was good of you," he tells them—it was beautiful, winsome, an act of true fellowship when they shared with him. When? In his "troubles," a technical word used in the New Testament for the pain and suffering that comes from sharing Christ.

Then Paul continues reminiscing about the old days: "Moreover, as you Philippians know, in the early days of your acquaintance with the gospel, when I set out from Macedonia, not one church shared with me in the matter of giving and receiving, except you only" (Philippians 4:15). At first, this was the only church in the region to partner with him in a giving-and-receiving relationship. He is essentially reminding them how they had put his needs ahead of their wants and thanking them for doing the same thing again in this new situation of need.

This idea of giving and receiving is threaded throughout the New Testament. Those who receive spiritual food supply financial provision to those who give it so the ministry can go forward. Paul makes the point often in his letters, and it's a huge reason the church advanced in the first century. Early believers developed compassion in contrast to the greed of their culture.

As a pastor for more than three and a half decades, I've rarely met sincere followers of Jesus who don't want to be more compassionate and meet the needs of those less fortunate. Unfortunately, there's a very subtle lie, a mindset that prevents them from living that out. It goes something like this: *Someday, when I am earning a lot more money and have extra income, I'm going to really help others and invest in churches and ministries that accomplish these God-ordained purposes.* They honestly believe that they need to get more in order to give.

I've discovered that almost everybody sees him- or herself as middle class. Those who make less than average still see themselves as better off than many; those who make millions think of the billionaires, not themselves, as the rich ones who are better off. And in most cases, people sincerely think they need more in order to be more compassionate.

But that's not how compassion works. In one of his letters to the Corinthians, Paul wrote about the churches in Macedonia, which included Philippi, and how they gave generously, "even beyond their ability" (2 Corinthians 8:3) in a time of extreme poverty. In fact, they begged for the opportunity to contribute to people in need (2 Corinthians 8:1–5). That's a mark of compassion. It isn't dependent on supply. Compassionate people give regardless of their financial status.

When I first learned this principle, I was poor. Theresa and I were making less than a thousand dollars a month, we had three kids, I was going to seminary full time, and a representative from a well-known ministry came to chapel to speak to us about poverty relief and education in places where kids were starving.

There were about a thousand students in chapel that day, and the speaker showed us a video of poor kids in severely impoverished places. *I really wish I could help them,* I thought, *but I can barely pay my rent!* At the end of the video, the guy got up and said, "You're probably wondering why I would come to a seminary to show you this. A lot of you are trying to work two jobs while being a full-time student, and you're barely making it. So why would I come here?"

Yes, I thought. *I'm wondering the same thing. Why would you come here?*

"Before I answer that question, let me ask you another question. How many of you take your family out for a fast-food meal a couple times a month, just as a little treat?"

Almost every hand went up. That was a huge treat for our family. Two kids' meals were shared among three kids, Theresa and I would split a burger, everybody would drink water—

about fifteen dollars for all of us. That was a deal. We always looked forward to it.

Then the speaker put up a slide of one of those kids. "Going to McDonald's twice a month is a want. Would you be willing to give up that want once a month in order to meet this child's need? Can you sacrifice fifteen dollars a month to feed, educate, and share God's Word with a child who would otherwise not be able to eat or go to school?"

I'll never forget walking home that day with a picture of a child living in poverty whom I had committed to help. That was more than three decades ago, and it softened my heart and started a journey of compassion that continues to this day. I never would have started that journey if I had waited to give until I was well-off, because most of us don't ever see ourselves as well-off. It has to start where you are.

What does a heart of compassion look like in your life? Where can you take some of your wants and translate them into meeting others' needs? It's possible to give without loving someone, but it isn't possible to love without giving. And when you give, your heart grows more tender and you cultivate your compassion. That's the first step in breaking the power of greed and experiencing the peace of Christ.

> **It's possible to give without loving someone, but it isn't possible to love without giving.**

PRINCIPLE 2: Develop a generous spirit. Money can not only harden our hearts, it can make us protective of what we have. In amassing more, we pay a lot of attention to guarding what we already have so that we aren't losing anything while we are gaining. I get to see this when I preach about giving. Bodies and expressions stiffen. Walls go up. Some people unconsciously cross their arms as if to say, "I don't want anyone trying to tamper with my finances."

PRACTICE 2: Release the very thing that has the power to consume you. Compassion is like a muscle. We need not only to make our hearts tender toward God and others but also to get them flowing outward. We need to develop a generous spirit. And Paul's words in Philippians tell us that we can develop a generous spirit by releasing the very thing that has the power to consume us.

"Even when I was in Thessalonica, you sent me aid more than once when I was in need" (Philippians 4:16). What does Paul mean by "even when I was in Thessalonica"? Thessalonica was a lot better off financially than Philippi, and the Thessalonian believers should have easily been able to support his ministry. But they didn't necessarily have the spiritual maturity to do so. The Philippians did. Again and again, they sent him aid, even when they were in need themselves. They were systematic about it.

Paul explicitly recommended a systematic plan to the Corinthians. "Now about the collection for the Lord's people: Do what I told the Galatian churches to do. On the first day of every week, each one of you should set aside a sum of money in keeping with your income, saving it up, so that when I come no collections will have to be made" (1 Corinthians 16:1–2). He encouraged them to release a portion of their income every single week in order to develop their generosity to God and people in need.

This is not another "ought" or "should" to make us feel guilty. The practice addresses a heart issue and works toward our advantage in growing us up spiritually and supporting the ministry of God's kingdom on earth. Paul isn't placing just one more obligation on us. He is showing us a way to freedom and peace.

To put this in perspective, think about the way we tip servers in restaurants. When the service is good, we usually leave 15 percent as a minimum, sometimes a little more, because that's the dining culture we've created. Servers get paid from gifts of gratitude for their service.

Why is it that most of us would never think of leaving less than 10 or 15 percent on a check for a restaurant server, yet less than 3 percent of American Christians give 10 percent of their income to God on a regular basis?[1] What has happened sociologically to make one seem standard and the other seem like a burdensome obligation? It certainly isn't because servers deserve more; they do great work, but they don't create the food. They just bring it. Our lives were created by God, and He sustains us with every breath and heartbeat. He sacrificed His Son for us, raised Him from the dead, covered our sin, put His Spirit within us, sealed us forever in our relationship with Him, gave us spiritual gifts, provides for us every day, and told us to remember that it all belongs to Him. Scripture gives us a tithe as a starting point for giving back to Him, yet more than 97 percent of American believers don't even attempt the starting point. Why?

If you wondered whether materialism and greed have a grip on your life, this might be an indicator. Are you more faithful to your waiter or waitress than you are to the God who created your food and bought your salvation? If so, and if you see a lot of inconsistencies in your giving, now is the time to break the power of *philarguria* over your life. Jesus said our hearts will be where our treasure is (Matthew 6:21). We generally invest in our loves and desires, and our loves and desires grow in the areas we've invested in. The only way to address this heart issue is to proactively do the things that will soften our heart and cultivate generosity. It is a step of faith that becomes a lifestyle with practice.

I'm still growing in this area too. I was standing in line to get coffee at an airport recently, and the lady in front of me ordered a mocha. For whatever reason, it took the barista behind the counter an extraordinary amount of time to fix it. Another customer waiting behind me gave up and left. I was just standing there nurturing a critical spirit, thinking, *Come on, buddy, this is getting ridiculous. And it's not where I usually get my coffee, so I bet it's not going to be nearly as good. I can't believe I'm waiting this long for a substandard coffee.* My impatience was rapidly decreasing my generosity and peace.

I finally got my coffee, and then I went over to the sugar-and-cream stand. The lid on the creamer was loose, so my attempt to put in just a little turned into a cup of mostly milk. I was afraid to pour any out because I didn't know if the barista would refill it. But I went over to him and said, "Hey, do you think I could get a little grace?"

"What do you mean?"

"Listen, I put way too much cream in. If I dump some out, could you pour some more coffee in so it'll turn the right color?"

"Sure, I could do that." And he added some more coffee and made it just right.

As he handed it back to me, I thought, *This is a good moment for me to change my attitude.* I reached in my pocket and handed him a dollar. "Here's an extra buck. I just want to tell you, it's great to be around people with such a good attitude."

His tense, stoic demeanor gave way to an ear-to-ear grin. "Thanks, man!"

"No, thank you. I really appreciate it." It was obvious he was new on the job and I wasn't the first impatient and frustrated customer of the day.

One dollar's worth of generosity changed two guys' attitudes—his and mine. He relaxed and felt encouraged, and my critical spirit was transformed into a pretty good feeling about being able to bless him.

Do you see what issue is at stake here? Greed and generosity are not just about money. They aren't even about whether the church is getting what it needs to continue its ministry. They are mindsets, lifestyles, perspectives on the world that affect our moment-by-moment interactions and our future, and ultimately determine our peace. If you want to beat greed, you need to develop personal compassion for people and a generous spirit that blesses them. And don't be surprised if your joy level goes up and your peace of mind multiplies.

PRINCIPLE 3: Develop an eternal perspective. If we really believe there's life after death, a heaven and a hell, and that certain good things await people in heaven who follow God's ways, it changes the way we live. We begin to live for eternity rather than only for the here and now.

PRACTICE 3: Understand the inseparable relationship between your money and authentic worship. This is addressed in a variety of ways throughout Scripture, but the bottom line is that our worship and money are inseparably connected. Most people tend to put them in two distinct categories— what happens in our hearts and at church is worship, and what happens in our bank accounts is an entirely different matter. But every financial decision we make ends up being a worship decision of some kind.

> Every financial decision we make ends up being a worship decision of some kind.

Unfortunately, many pastors and churches talk about money only in the context of needing some. And because of that, many congregation members have gotten the impression that they are seen merely as potential donors, and they become resistant to the dreaded financial appeals. But that's a distortion that I and many other pastors ought to apologize for. Jesus talked about money more than he talked about heaven and hell combined. Money shouldn't be a bad word in the church. It's actually a fundamental indicator of our worship.

When spiritual leaders talk about money, it should almost always be in the larger context of using it well, being grateful, aligning our families with God's values, protecting our marriages, teaching our kids, and honoring God with our worship. Yes, churches and ministries have budgets and need income, but that's not the point. The fundamental point and priority in discussing money is the heart of the believer. When money has the right place in the heart—as a means rather than an end, as an opportunity to give rather than an opportunity to get—the budget issues are usually fine. Above all else, money is a spiritual issue.

Paul turned his words in Philippians in exactly that direction. After writing in financial and business terms to describe the church's gifts to him, he suddenly shifts to spiritual terms:

> Not that I desire your gifts; what I desire is that more be credited to your account. I have received full payment and have more than enough. I am amply supplied, now that I have received from Epaphroditus the gifts you sent. They are a fragrant offering, an acceptable sacrifice, pleasing to God. (Philippians 4:17–18)

Notice the progression. He has said he can do all things through Christ who strengthens him. He has thanked them for their gifts, not only in his captivity in Rome but also way back in the earliest days of the church and in his ministry in Thessalonica. And now he wants to make sure they understand his motives—that he is not focused on receiving gifts and having his needs met. Instead, he is focused on the good the Philippians' generosity brings to their account.

That phrase, "credited to your account," is as financially oriented as it sounds—an accounting term about debits and credits. Paul is essentially saying that the Philippians' heavenly profit-and-loss statement is in great shape because of their generosity. He has "received full payment," a picture of having the receipt in his hand. He is "amply supplied," having accepted the gift they sent with Epaphroditus. Paul's financial standing is not the issue now. He is focused on something much more important: the "fragrant offering" and "acceptable sacrifice" of the Philippians' worship through giving, which is "pleasing to God." They gave money, and the gift is of enormous value in their spiritual account.

A literal translation of that passage could look something like this: "When you did that, it was like a burnt offering, a fragrant, sweet smell that went up into the nostrils of God. He looked at it not as money but as a sacrifice of worship to Him, and it brought great pleasure and joy to His heart."

Clearly the issue is bigger than money here. The Philippians' gift reflects an eternal perspective, and Paul is making sure they recognize the relationship between their money and their worship. Every time we make a financial decision, every time we spend our money on something, we are choosing not to spend it on other things. We are providing a picture of what's important to us. God wants us to use money to meet our needs, and He is certainly not opposed to satisfying many of our wants. With deep gratitude, being satisfied in those desires can reflect our worship too. But what are we prioritizing? What does the hierarchy in our hearts look like?

Where is God in that hierarchy? Where are other people's needs in relation to our own wants?

Those are heart issues, and they are represented by something as mundane as money. Put simply, my money goes to the people, places, and things that matter most to me. It's like an MRI of my soul, my values, and my true worship.

King David was once told to build an altar on the threshing floor of a man named Araunah. When David tried to buy the threshing floor, Araunah offered it freely to his king. But David insisted on paying for it, and his reason was profound: "I will not sacrifice to the LORD my God burnt offerings that cost me nothing" (2 Samuel 24:24). Gifts from the heart are not minimal offerings of things we'll never miss. They cost something. They are sacrifices. They are reflections of what we love.

As you think about that last sentence, what would your money say about whom and what you love? My purpose in asking is not to send you on a guilt trip but to help you take any blinders off and see that peace is impossible if your heart is held captive. Giving begins to open up your heart and bring you into a place of freedom.

That's how we overcome greed with an eternal perspective. When we give our time, energy, talents, and financial gifts as acts of worship, a spiritual transaction occurs. A "credit" is added to our spiritual account. We acknowledge that impressing people and accumulating and enjoying everything we can now is not the end of the line—that there's more at stake than what we can get and spend in the present. We adopt the long view and live generously because of it. We take the things of this world and turn them into something of eternal value, and greed loses its power in our lives.

Scouting Recommendations

A good scouting report doesn't just give you information about the enemy's and your own strengths and weaknesses. It makes some recommendations based on that information. So let's go back to that letter Paul wrote to Timothy, the scouting report we looked at earlier in this chapter, and see what his recommendations are. He gives them in the form of four specific commands that will start us on a lifelong journey of peace by beating the monster of greed.

Before we do, there are a couple of things I think you should know. I'm well aware that you may be feeling overwhelmed as you read this. You may be juxtaposing the antidote to greed—having compassion, giving generously, and seeing with an eternal perspective—with massive debts and real frustration with where you are financially. No matter how many pictures of starving children you see, you've got no margin to give. The hook isn't just in your mouth; it's deep down inside. Are you forever out of God's will, then? Of course not. You can get out of this through a process that begins today. We'll dive deeper into that in the next chapter.

The other thing you should know is that I used to be a skeptic about this kind of message. I mentioned earlier that I didn't grow up in the church, and I've run into a lot of bad teaching after becoming a Christian too. I know what it's like to read teaching like this and think, *This is just leading up to an appeal to give to his ministry,* or *That's the church for you—always trying to sustain itself by milking all it can out of gullible people.* Please be assured that I'm not asking you to give to any particular ministry, and if giving to a church is a problem right now, give to some charity that serves people at their point of need. I do believe God wants us to give a regular percentage to whichever church we are involved in, but the more important point right now is just learning to be generous. It's not a matter of anybody's bottom line; it's a matter of the heart.

The four commands in Paul's scouting recommendations are very clear and concise:

> Command those who are rich in this present world not to be arrogant nor to put their hope in wealth, which is so uncertain, but to put their hope in God, who richly provides us with everything for our enjoyment. Command them to do good, to be rich in good deeds, and to be generous and willing to share. In this way they will lay up treasure for themselves as a firm foundation for the coming age, so that they may take hold of the life that is truly life. (1 Timothy 6:17–19)

1. Put your hope in God. Here God is identified as the one who provides for our enjoyment. Yes, it is important to be sacrificial in our giving, but it's equally important to enjoy what God has given us. The word used here clearly conveys the physical pleasures of this life. Giving generously is not a call to live in asceticism and poverty but to richly enjoy all God's good gifts and to be extravagantly generous as well.

You can't enjoy things if you're always worried about making the payments, so make sure your hope and contentment are rooted in God above all else. Don't strive for things that promise to make you content. Be content. But then enjoy what He has provided.

2. Be rich in good deeds. Like the Philippians, do things in a way that adds to your spiritual account. Recognize where true wealth is. This is a call to personal involvement, not just financial gifts.

3. Be generous. Focus more on giving than on getting. That heart of compassion you have developed will serve as a great motivator for a generous lifestyle.

4. Be willing to share. Being generous and rich in good deeds means giving away your time, energy, money, and possessions. Consider all your assets—time, money, materials, skills, talents, wisdom, and more—as community property. You steward them, of course, and that means knowing how to measure them in ways that don't lead to burnout and exhaustion. But it also means sharing your finances and yourself with a bigger purpose in mind.

The last line of this passage is a great reminder of that larger purpose: "In this way they will lay up treasure for themselves as a firm foundation for the coming age, so that they may take hold of the life that is truly life." We do this because the way we live now not only has an impact on other lives but also affects the quality of our experience in eternity. In other words, this scouting report guarantees that we will win the game.

That's what it means to "take hold of life that is truly life." In this life, relationships work better, creditors don't call, and instead of feeling guilty about what God has provided, you can simply be grateful for it, appreciating every opportunity to enjoy His gifts and share them generously with others.

This scouting report guarantees that we will win the game.

That kind of life is not hanging on the next big thing or waiting for some fulfillment "out there." It's a life in which, whether in plenty or in want, you know you can do all things through Christ who strengthens you.

If you long for that kind of life, ask God now to show you the extent to which greed has infiltrated your heart. Sit quietly and let Him speak to you. Be completely honest with Him and yourself. Then ask Him to show you the first step out of it. Don't look at every problem or the whole mountain of debt, if you have one. Don't examine every area of your life just yet. Start with something specific that God shows you, and then go from there. Then ask Him for the "next step" toward a heart of compassion, a generous spirit, and an eternal perspective, and do what He says. Ask Him who might help you on this journey—a counselor, pastor, or financial planner. You will have begun an adventure that is far more fulfilling than anything money can buy.

QUESTIONS FOR DISCUSSION AND REFLECTION

1. In Paul's "scouting report," what is contentment's greatest competitor? What makes this adversary such a formidable foe?

2. The theme of the book of Philippians is joy. How does the Philippian model (4:14–18) produce joy and personal peace?

3. How has greed crept into your heart and mind? In what ways have you experienced the futility and emptiness of its promises?

4. What practical steps are you going to take to follow the Philippian model toward personal peace?

CHAPTER 6

Choose Peace
in Tests of Faith

We began this journey looking for peace in the midst of conflicts, anxieties, circumstances, and challenges of this world. This chapter doesn't end the journey, of course. My hope is that it becomes a launching point into a new way of life, the beginning of a discovery process that will lead you into a quality of life many Christians never get to experience.

But that will only happen if you get to the end and make a conscious decision to activate your faith in this area. The title of this book and its chapters have not urged you just to have peace. They have prompted you to *choose* peace. There's a reason for that. Your peace and contentment only come through commitments you have made to embrace the truths God has given us in Scripture and live them out.

Before we continue, let's review some of those truths we have discovered in the last few chapters. After giving us instructions on having peace in our relationships and overcoming our anxieties through prayer, Paul turned his attention to the issue of contentment, and we explored his scouting report about the enemy of greed and Jesus's warnings about the place of money in our lives. We saw several truths:

1. Contentment is learned (Philippians 4:10–13). There is a secret to contentment, and we can learn it as a skill that will apply to any situation in our lives, regardless of whether our circumstances appear good or bad. We can choose peace in every situation!

2. Greed must die before contentment can live (Philippians 4:14–18). The way we get greed to die is by developing personal compassion, cultivating a generous spirit, and adopting an eternal perspective. We develop compassion by giving up our wants to meet other people's needs; we cultivate generosity by releasing the very thing (money) that consumes us; and we develop an eternal perspective by realizing that our money and our worship are not two separate categories of life but are inextricably connected.

3. Our treasure both reveals and directs the affections of our hearts (Matthew 6:21). Wherever your time, energy, talents, skills, and money go, your heart will be there. It is connected to your treasure. Your treasure has the ability not only to reflect your heart but to direct it as well. At different times in my life, this has been a very effective way to sort out my priorities or work on a relationship. When I've sensed my heart was not where God or I wanted it, I've started putting my treasure—my time, money, or energy—into whatever area I've needed to address. Sometimes it was my wife or one of my kids; at other times, I've realized my heart was hard or insensitive to another person or group. It's amazing how God has changed my heart in those times. As I gave more of my time, energy, or money where I knew God wanted them, my heart followed my investment.

These steps of faith and obedience will dramatically increase the peace and contentment in our lives, and they are part of an ongoing process that will last the rest of our lives. But they are also contested because virtually every advance in God's kingdom faces challenges. We will go through tests, and we need to know what to do when we encounter them.

Truth be told, we never know where our heart and values really lie until they are tested. The coronavirus global pandemic was a wake-up call for many sincere Christians when it first hit in early 2020. In the wake of death and economic fallout, more than a few shared with me that when money or people were removed from their lives, they realized they had made them idols without even knowing it. Tests have a way of revealing our real priorities—and what we are actually counting on for peace.

The Problem—and the Solution

Peace is a wonderful thing. Intellectually, we all want contentment. But we've seen that the way to get peace and contentment can be very counterintuitive. We receive by giving.

And for many people, that presents a problem. If you're deeply in debt, sweating over a stack of bills, and facing upcoming expenses like tuition for your kids or income for your retirement years, you might despair over the idea of becoming more compassionate and generous. Who's going to take care of *you*? That's a really big question a lot of people in difficult situations are wrestling with. At some point in the last few chapters, you might have started thinking, *What about me?*

Paul addresses that question in Philippians 4:19: "My God will meet all your needs according to the riches of his glory in Christ Jesus." This is a personal God who meets *all* the needs of those who have learned to live generously and compassionately—even in their most trying times.

This is a personal God who meets *all* the needs of those who have learned to live generously and compassionately—even in their most trying times.

The church at Philippi was a generous church. As a whole, it didn't have a lot of money, though some of its members like Lydia were probably doing okay. They loved Paul, heard what was happening with him, decided his needs were bigger than some of their wants, and gave financially out of their compassion. Paul tells them in this letter that they have modeled the path of love and contentment—the life that is really life. So he reassured them, as if to say, "Here's what I want you to know. When you're generous like that and your priorities are in order, you can know when you're afraid of the future that my God—not the universe, not the force, not invisible factors or principles, but this very personal God—will supply all your needs." What kind of needs? Paul doesn't say. *All* is a big word. It includes spiritual, emotional, relational, physical, and financial needs. And He will do it according to the glorious riches of Jesus.

That's the promise: God's provision. If we will trust Him and live out this radical compassion and generosity, Paul says, God will make sure we have what we need. He'll take care of us.

With every promise, there's a premise—a condition we have to fulfill in order to receive what God is offering. We can never earn His gracious gifts, or course, but He does require us to respond in certain ways to receive them.

That's why some people who have been believers a long time come to a verse like this and think, *Okay, maybe in principle. But I've tried this, and it doesn't work.* No Christian really says that out loud, but we think things like this, don't we? We've prayed, God hasn't provided the way we thought He would, and we're left with unpaid bills and confusion about what went wrong. If this is you, let me try to clear up the confusion.

First, I'd suggest that sometimes we get our needs and our wants confused. If you've got enough to eat, a roof over your head, and you're warm in the winter, that's really all you need. God is not necessarily promising that you'll own your own home, have a second car, wear fancy clothes, and rest securely in your retirement plan, though He often graciously provides those things anyway. After giving generously, we might find ourselves unable to pay for our accustomed lifestyle and wonder why God isn't living up to His promise.

I had that very experience in seminary. I was working fulltime selling life insurance while going to school full-time, and my job was based entirely on commissions. I'd make about $900 a month, which even in 1980 wasn't much money for a family of five. But there were times when a client would not pass a physical exam, so I didn't get my commission. We got into some pretty tight situations trying to figure out how to pay for rent and food. We'd dig quarters out of the back seat, pleading with God and claiming Philippians 4:19. I could tell story after story of God providing for our needs at the last minute. A check from an NFL quarterback I had met while he was in high school paid for rent and groceries one month. Once when we had no money in the bank, a letter and check from a missionary in India came the day our bills were due. These kinds of things happened so often and in such amazing ways that I began to quit worrying about finances, even though I never knew exactly how God would provide.

I still remember a really big lesson God taught us about His provision. The husband of the lady next door in our apartment complex walked out on her. She had a newborn and an older boy about the same age as our twin boys. She and Theresa had become good friends, and early one morning while I was reading my Bible, Theresa came to me with a great concern and an outrageous thought: "Chip, she's going to get kicked out of her apartment. We need to pay her rent."

"Honey, surely you jest," I said semi-sarcastically. But I quickly realized she wasn't smiling. "Theresa, we'd only have $10 left in the bank if we did that."

"Chip, I believe God wants us to pay her rent."

As I prayed about it, the still, small voice of the Holy Spirit confirmed Theresa's prompting to me, but I still didn't think it was a good idea. So I did what most people do in that situation. I tried to talk myself out of it. I told myself that still, small voice must have just been my imagination because the Holy Spirit was surely more aware of our financial situation than that. But I've learned that when you get thoughts about helping someone at great cost to yourself in ways that would bring glory to God, it's probably not from you.

I finally gave in after about three days. I was reluctant, but I agreed to do it. And my heart really did go out to her. Wanting to help was not the problem. Having the means to do it seemed like a big one. But we took everything but $10 out of the bank and paid her rent.

About nine days later, our own rent was due. "Okay, Lord," I prayed. "Philippians 4:19. You're going to supply all my needs, right? My rent's due!"

No money came. I'd seen miraculous things happen for the last two years, but this time there was no provision. Our rent contract gave us a three-day grace period. Still, no money came the next day. Or the next. On the third day, we had to pay.

"Lord, it's Your reputation on the line. What are You doing? Philippians 4:19—does it work or not?" I was pretty upset.

"How can I trust You in the future if You don't come through after we've sacrificially given to help our neighbor in crisis?"

As I was half praying and half complaining, I walked into our little living room and saw our TV. It wasn't worth much, but I thought, *Is that a need or a want?* Then I saw the stereo system I'd had for a few years. It was pretty nice. *Is that a need or a want?* I remembered the collection of silver dollars I'd saved when I was a paper boy and thought, *Hmm, maybe God has supplied all my needs, and I'm still asking Him for something extra.* So Theresa and I loaded up the TV, the stereo, my silver dollars, and some of her jewelry and went to a pawn shop. We got about $450 for all of it and were just able to pay for our food and rent that month.

I learned a very important lesson from that experience. God has often supplied our needs, but we expect Him to define His provision by a certain standard of living we've set for ourselves. We tell Him we can't afford to do what He's asking us to do because we have to make a payment on that late model car we stretched our budget to get or we can't make our house payment on the nice home we thought we deserved. Don't get me wrong—God isn't opposed to our having and enjoying some of these things over and above our basic needs. But He doesn't want us to define those luxuries as our needs and demand that He meet them. We have to keep needs and wants in perspective.

We have to keep needs and wants in perspective.

That distinction aside, Paul gives us three very specific conditions about the promise of verse 19. If you're serious about God's peace and contentment, you need to take His promises seriously and know who they're for and how to apply them.

Condition 1: This is not for unbelievers. Paul is not making a blanket promise to everyone out there that God will always meet all their needs. He is writing to a church, and the provision of God is given to those who are "in Christ Jesus." God loves everyone, but He does not commit Himself to meet the needs of those who resist Him and remain outside of Christ.

Condition 2: This is not for all believers. I don't think every Christian can claim this promise. I don't believe it applies to believers who are living in willful disobedience or who are not honoring God in their finances. Christians can be disobedient in major areas of our lives. We can be completely reckless and self-centered with our finances, and I don't believe God is assuring us that He will always meet our needs under those conditions. He is gracious, and we have all experienced wonderful provision at times when we were not necessarily walking closely with Him. His provision is not dependent on our being perfect. But is His provision guaranteed whether we are following Him obediently or not? I don't think so. Paul had already commended the Philippians for their faithful attitude and actions and sacrificially meeting his needs, and this promise is given in that context. This promise is true for those in Christ who are seeking first God's kingdom and His righteousness (Matthew 6:33) in the arena of their finances.

Condition 3: This is for believers who choose to walk by faith. And in the context of this passage of Philippians, the evidence of faith is sacrificial giving. This promise is for when God's children say, "Lord, I want to obey You. From my love for You and the compassion in my heart, I want to give of my time, talent, and money to honor You with the first portion of my income or meet this specific need. And if You don't catch me, I'm in a bind." This particular promise is God's way of saying, "I'll catch you. I'm there." He is reassuring those who live generously and sacrificially that they are not going to lose out in the process.

The way to unlock God's promises is by faith—trusting in Him even when everything's on the line. More than anything, God wants to deepen and develop our relationship with Him. Being a follower of Jesus is not fundamentally about outward moral behavior, engaging in the right activities, serving in the church, giving a certain amount of money, or anything else that could be translated into a formula. He is after sons and daughters who love Him and express their love by trusting Him enough to do what He says because they know He is good and always has their best in mind.

God longs for His children to take steps of faith so He can bless them.

Hebrews 11:6 says that it's impossible to please God without faith—that those who come to Him must (1) believe that He really, truly exists and (2) know that He rewards those who diligently seek Him. Don't miss the significance of that. While many people see Him as a punisher of those who don't seek Him, He is actually eager to reward those who do. God longs for His children to take steps of faith so He can bless them. In the context of faith, He promises to take care of us.

To bring this back to our financial needs and this specific promise in Philippians, debt and financial messes are often evidence that we have a need for immediate gratification and are looking for peace and contentment in things that money can buy. We've seen how that's a dead end. God's response is to say that if we learn to release our future to Him, trust Him, walk with Him, and align with His nature and character, He'll satisfy all our needs. He even goes above and beyond that and satisfies many of our wants too; He richly provides all things for us to enjoy (1 Timothy 6:17). But this promise guarantees that our basic needs of food, clothing, and shelter will always be covered.

The Law of the Harvest

There's a principle behind this promise, and it goes all the way back to the Old Testament. It's found throughout Scripture, from Genesis to Revelation, originating in the character of God and evident in the life of Jesus. It's foundational to the kingdom of God. It's called the Law of the Harvest.

There are other names for it: the law of sowing and reaping, or the law of reciprocity. But however you position it, it is the way the kingdom of God works. In a passage that was not specifically about finances but certainly applies to them, Jesus shared this kingdom principle with His followers: "Give, and it will be given to you. A good measure, pressed down, shaken together and running over, will be poured into your lap. For with the measure you use, it will be measured to you" (Luke 6:38). In other words, whether you use a fifty-five-gallon drum or a teaspoon, you'll find things coming back to you in the same measure you give them.

The world says to get, get, and get some more, to go out and acquire as much as you can so you can be comfortable, significant, strong, and secure. God says the opposite—to give, give, and give some more because you are already significant and secure in Christ, and your demonstration of trust in Him will be rewarded accordingly. Where the world tries to judge, protect, look out for self-interests, and accumulate things, you are free to love, forgive, have compassion, and give. When you live in that freedom, God blesses you with ample return on everything you've given. Whatever you pour out, He fills back up in abundance.

You'll find things coming back to you in the same measure you give them.

This is not just a spiritual secret. It's evident even in nature. "Unless a kernel of wheat falls to the ground and dies, it remains only a single seed. But if it dies, it produces many seeds" (John 12:24). Creation declares the glory of God. This is how He has made the world. You can take grains of wheat and put them in the ground, and whatever you planted will multiply. You could have ground up that grain to make more bread, but by taking a portion of your harvest and planting it again, you get a greater harvest.

But here's the tricky part, the primary reason so many people neglect this profound principle: You rarely reap in the same season you sow. Seed takes time to grow. Many people don't see the fruit of their investments right away and give up. They decide it's better to get what they can while they can get it. The Law of the Harvest delays gratification but brings in much more fruit in the end. "A good measure, pressed down, shaken together and running over, will be poured into your lap."

Jesus applied the Law of the Harvest to His own life. He became like that grain of wheat that died in the ground but produced a great harvest.

> Being found in appearance as a man,
>   he humbled himself
>   by becoming obedient to death—
>   even death on a cross!
>
> Therefore God exalted him to the highest place
>   and gave him the name that is above every name,
> that at the name of Jesus every knee should bow,
>   in heaven and on earth and under the earth,
> and every tongue acknowledge that Jesus Christ is
>   Lord,
>   to the glory of God the Father. (Philippians
>   2:8–10)

With His very life, Jesus demonstrated that the way to receive is to give. He proved the ultimate secret of contentment.

Jesus applied the same secret of life, peace, and contentment to us. "Whoever wants to save their life will lose it, but whoever loses their life for me will save it" (Luke 9:24). Many people look at a verse like that with dread because they recognize that, at least on the surface, denying yourself and taking up an instrument of death seems literally to be a dead end.

This is where cognitive dissonance begins to do its work in us, isn't it? What seems at first to be dreadful is actually the key to life. We see it in nature; farmers use it all the time. We see it in Jesus; it's the means of our salvation. We see it throughout Scripture; it shows up again and again in the lives of biblical characters and the teachings of prophets and apostles. And if it's true—if this is an axiomatic, foundational truth of the kingdom of God—we must begin thinking completely differently about the way we live.

Seeing life in a different way is, of course, only a first step. It's a crucial one—we live in new ways only when we see in new ways—but we actually have to walk this out. And it's an exciting but sometimes scary process. If you're tired of hearing those stories of supernatural, timely provision in other people's lives and think they happen only with missionaries, pastors, and famous people, you need to know that this is possible for anybody who chooses to walk by genuine faith.

Step out, live, give, and care for others. Put the needs of others ahead of your wants. Then be patient and persistent. You can experience miraculous stories too.

Be patient and persistent. You can experience miraculous stories too.

That's because God is a rewarder of those who trust Him. Steps of faith may be counterintuitive, like giving generously in a time of financial strain, but He loves that kind of faith. There have been times when I really wrestled with the question of whether I trusted Him to take care of me; sometimes my answer was "maybe." You don't always feel like taking steps of faith, so don't make the mistake of overspiritualizing this process. Just obey. And expect God to provide.

Be careful, though. Many prosperity teachers have taken this kingdom principle and perverted it. They have persuaded vulnerable Christians to give them money in order to get money from God. We never "give to get." We give in accordance with God's will to honor Him, express our love, and meet the spiritual, emotional, and physical needs of others.

Applying the Law of the Harvest in Real Life

Paul takes us through that process in his second letter to the church at Corinth. The context of chapters 8–9 is a collection Paul is taking up for fellow believers in need. He refers to the generosity of the Macedonian churches as an example and says he has also been boasting to the Macedonians about the Corinthians' generosity. Threaded throughout this passage is the Law of the Harvest, the principle of sowing and reaping that is so deeply embedded in Scripture. In his words to the Corinthians, Paul outlines several important steps in how this process of living by faith works for ordinary people like you and me.

● *The Principle Restated:*

When you have a need, plant a seed.

Jesus broadly applied this agricultural picture to love, grace, and forgiveness in Luke 6:38. Paul applies the same principle specifically to the use of our resources. "Remember this: Whoever sows sparingly will also reap sparingly, and whoever sows generously will also reap generously" (2 Corinthians 9:6). If a farmer plants a few grains of wheat, he'll grow a little bit of wheat. If he plants thousands of seeds, he'll grow a lot. That's what Paul is saying here. It's very simple. If you want a lot, plant a lot. If you have a need, plant a seed.

This absolutely applies to financial situations, but please understand that it's much bigger than that. You'll see this work in virtually every area of life. What do we tell people who complain about not having any friends? We tell them to "be a friend" to someone else. The world says to get friends, to build yourself up, and focus on your own fulfillment through relationships. What would happen if we turned that around and focused our energy on offering friendship to others? What if we made it a priority to meet other people's needs and longings in relationships? Do you think that would end up being less fulfilling for us? No, when we sow generously, we reap generously.

The same is true with time. I can't figure out how this works, but when I have an overwhelming to-do list and not enough time to fit it in, I'm usually reminded of my long-ago commitment to give God the first part of each day. So I set my alarm a half hour earlier and give Him more time. What happens? He multiplies the fruit of the other hours in the day.

It's amazing how this works. If you need more time, give some time away. If you need love and affection, give love and affection. If you need friends, be a friend. If you need more grace for your mistakes, be more gracious toward those around you. Warning: Don't walk away if nothing happens immediately. Remember, we hardly ever reap in the same season we sow. I am completely confident you'll see some dramatic changes over time. More importantly, that's what Scripture promises. This is how God works.

I came across a parable years ago that helps me picture and remember this amazing kingdom principle:

> Once there was a man lost in the desert, near death from thirst. He wandered almost aimlessly through the burning sand for many days, growing weaker by the moment. At long last, he saw an oasis in the distance, palm trees indicating that there was water. He stumbled forward feverishly, fell beneath the shade of the trees, that he finally might quench his tortured thirst.
>
> But then he noticed something strange about this oasis: Instead of a pool of water or a spring bubbling up from the ground, he found a pump. And beside the pump were two objects: a small jar of water and a parchment note. The note explained that the leather gasket within the pump must be saturated with water for the pump to work. Within the jar was just enough water for this purpose. The note also warned that the reader should not drink from the jar. Every single drop must be poured into the opening at the base of the pump to soak the heat-dried gasket. Then, as the leather softens and expands, an unlimited supply of sweet water would be available. The parchment's final instructions were to refill the jar for the next traveler.
>
> The man faced a dilemma. He was dying of thirst, and he had found water. Not much, of course, and likely not

enough even to save his life. But it seemed the height of folly to pour it away down the base of the pump. On the other hand, if the note was accurate, by pouring out the small quantity of water, he would then have all the water he wanted. What should he do?[1]

What would you do? It's a simple choice, really. If the note isn't true, you will probably die anyway. But if the note is true, you'd be a fool not to follow its instructions. It would be the smartest, wisest, most important thing you could do. Yet pouring out that water seems insane, doesn't it?

The majority of people in the world are consuming whatever is available to them. Those who trust God and understand the Law of the Harvest are wiser than that. By faith, we pour out what we have in order to get an unlimited supply of it— good measure, pressed down, shaken together, running over.

That's the promise of Philippians 4:19. It actually creates a dilemma for us because we have to decide if we are going to believe it and take steps of faith or ignore and reject it as unlikely or untrue. Deciding it's true may take you down a path you've never been on before, and that's always a little scary, but it leads to powerful experiences with God and those stories of supernatural provision that we all love to hear. I believe you'll find that the promise really does apply to you.

The Procedure Outlined:

Give with the right motive.

There's a temptation in this promise, isn't there? Many people will turn it around for self-centered purposes and think, *Ah, so if I want to get rich, all I need to do is plant some seeds.* And they are following the letter of the Law of the Harvest but not the spirit behind it.

Rest assured: I am not teaching a health-and-wealth gospel here. We don't give in order to get. But in God's economy, giving does have certain consequences. Receiving is a by-product of giving because God is generous and wants to bless those who trust Him. He is not telling us to work a system; He is asking us to trust and become like Him—a generous giver who gives from compassion and love. Someone following a "me-centered" health-and-wealth gospel misses that part of the equation. Scripture strongly warns those among us who teach this (1 Timothy 6:3–11).

God's promises do not give us any license to try to cut a deal with Him. The Law of the Harvest is not a mathematical formula. When you hear someone say that if you give God a hundred, He'll give you a thousand, that person is playing a game. That makes God like a vending machine, and it disqualifies us from the promise.

The Law of the Harvest is not a mathematical formula.

Paul says it's important to give with the right motive. If you're giving to get, it's not giving. "Each of you should give what you have decided in your heart to give, not reluctantly or under compulsion, for God loves a cheerful giver" (2 Corinthians 9:7). Notice the phrasing: "what you have decided"; "not reluctantly"; not "under compulsion"; "a cheerful giver." That is full of right motives. You don't give that way when someone else is twisting your arm and making false promises. You give that way when your heart overflows with the goodness of God.

Giving "what you have decided" means being thoughtful about it. Thoughtful giving comes from pure motives. It isn't manipulative. I remember going to church when I was young and, if I was in a good mood, giving five bucks or so. If I wasn't in a good mood, maybe a dollar. And if I was on top of the world, I might throw in a twenty and be amazed at how generous I was. I didn't know anything about the Bible. It was kind of like going to a movie and paying for a ticket only if the movie was good. My giving was emotionally rooted in the moment.

God says not to give that way. Your motives need to be thoughtful. As we saw in Paul's other letter to the Corinthians, he recommended bringing your offering on the first day of the week according to the ways God has blessed you that week (1 Corinthians 16:1–2). It requires taking mental inventory of His goodness toward you. That's a good motive.

You also need to give "not reluctantly" and "not under compulsion." That means giving enthusiastically, not merely as an obligation or out of peer pressure. It's voluntary. You aren't responding to someone who ranted and raved about how delinquent everyone is in their donations, or to someone who is manipulating emotions and twisting arms. Anytime I hear a manipulative message about giving, I take that as a sign from God not to give there. I don't want to give under compulsion. I do want to give, but not with the wrong motive. I need to find a place where I can do that and trust that those who are asking me to give are full of integrity and inviting me to follow God's directions and not their agenda.

That leads to the final phrase: "God loves a cheerful giver." The word used here for *cheerful* is the same word we get *hilarious* from. We give with that kind of lighthearted joy. We get the word *miserable* from *miser* because stingy people, the Scrooges of the world, are generally not very happy. That tight-fisted spirit is right in line with the world's agenda of acquiring and accumulating, but it never leads to peace or contentment. Have you ever known anybody whose credit cards are maxed out and whose debts are piled up to be at peace? Neither have I. The Law of the Harvest says to give, release, trust, love, and be generous with your grace, forgiveness, time, talents, energies, money, and resources, and to do it from your heart. Be tenderhearted and compassionate. Give "hilariously." Be happy about it. And God's goodness will come running over, back into your lap. This is not a health-and-wealth gospel. It's a give-and-enjoy gospel. There's a world of difference.

> **This is not a health-and-wealth gospel. It's a give-and-enjoy gospel.**

Still not convinced? Stay with me as God invites you to *know for certain* that when you exercise the Law of the Harvest, He's more than got you covered.

● *The Promise Expanded:*

God will give you everything you need in every area of your life.

Try a fun exercise. Count how many times the words *all* and *every* show up in these verses:

God is able to bless you abundantly, so that in *all* things at *all* times, having *all* that you need, you will abound in *every* good work. As it is written:

> "They have freely scattered their gifts to the poor;
> their righteousness endures forever."

Now he who supplies seed to the sower and bread for food will also supply and increase your store of seed and will enlarge the harvest of your righteousness. You will be enriched in *every* way so that you can be generous on *every* occasion, and through us your generosity will result in thanksgiving to God. (2 Corinthians 9:8–11, italics added)

God is able to bless you abundantly in all things at all times, and you will be enriched in every way. Why? Not so you can hoard it and break the cycle of giving and receiving, but so you can be generous on every occasion and perpetuate the cycle. That's a sweeping promise.

Can God really mean this? A lot of people read these words and think, *That hasn't been my experience.* But if they think it through, they have to admit that this kind of giving hasn't been their experience either. Might I tactfully suggest that those things are connected?

Most Christians don't give of their time, talents, and resources this way. In fact, only 5 percent of Americans who claim the name of Christ even give a tithe of 10 percent of their income, let alone practice radical generosity.[2] Why? Either because they have never been taught, or they don't believe, or perhaps because it's frightening. What if God doesn't come through? That's why Paul spells out the promise: God is able. And His blessing comes to us at *all* times in *every* way.

Does this apply to financial needs? Emotional needs? Relational issues? Career paths? Well, what does "all" mean to you? It's comprehensive. Again, this doesn't mean God will satisfy every want in all these areas. It does mean, however, that He is watching over your needs and concerns, abundantly willing and able—and, in fact, eager—to meet you there.

Just as the Law of the Harvest suggests, Paul is giving us an agricultural metaphor throughout this passage. But look what he does in verse 9: "Now he who supplies *seed* to the sower and *bread* for food will also supply and increase your *store of seed* and will *enlarge the harvest of your righteousness*" (emphasis added). Do you see that? He suddenly unveils it as a spiritual issue.

God gives us seed to begin with, our provision to invest. It's different for everybody, but for everybody it's something. He also gives us bread for food. That's today's sustenance—His provision for our immediate needs. But He also supplies and increases our store of seed—the portion a farmer uses to put back into the ground, the remainder we can use to invest. Why? To "enlarge the harvest of our righteousness" so that we "will be enriched in every way." The reason God gives us increase is so our harvest will increase spiritually, emotionally, relationally, financially, and "every" other way. And the reason He expands our harvest in all these ways is not so we can have more, do more, and be more, but *so we can be even more generous*, starting the cycle all over again—all for the ultimate purpose of helping, caring for, and loving others in a way that causes them to look up and give thanks to God.

I like the way Randy Alcorn puts it: "God prospers me not to raise my standard of living, but to raise my standard of giving."[3] But it doesn't just happen. We have to take a step of faith to participate in the process of giving, receiving, increase of seed, increase of harvest, greater generosity, thanksgiving to God.

We have to take a step of faith to participate in the process.

One of the things Theresa and I have done is to draw a financial income line for what we need to live on. As long as I live, however much God gives me over that line, that's what I'm going to give away. I think that's something everyone should consider doing. You may strategically raise or lower that line at different seasons of life, but it is helpful in keeping your finances oriented around sacrifice and generosity. Otherwise, compromise creeps in. As we receive increase, we tend to habitually increase our standard of living but not our percentage of giving. Sadly, many sincere Christians have given 10 percent of their income for twenty or thirty years while their income has doubled or tripled. They give almost the way they pay bills—and miss the joy and adventure of the supernatural movement of God's Spirit in their finances.

Paul was encouraging this church to give more, not because it was easy for them but because it was part of God's purpose in blessing others and blessing them through their own gift. Paul was going to take this collection to Jerusalem, where

Jewish believers were going through hard times from a famine. Those brothers and sisters would eat the food that was provided through that collection and give thanks to God, praising Him for His provision. But they would know He doesn't usually provide in a vacuum. He provides through His people.

That's our calling—to be vessels of provision. We see a need, God puts it on our heart to do something about it, and the people who are blessed by that provision thank Him for it. Then He provides for us because we let Him provide for others through us.

The world's mentality is to see resources as part of one big, limited pie. They're limited. You have to get your piece of the pie because if you don't, there won't be enough left for you. That's not how it works in the kingdom of God because King Jesus has unlimited resources. He's the pie maker. When He finds people who will give away not only their slice but whole pies, He'll provide a truckload. He loves faith, and He rewards those who diligently seek Him.

He gives us an abundance so we can be abundantly generous.

Over the years, I've met godly men and women who have taken God up on His promise to be radically generous. They all tell me the same thing: "You can't out-give God." As one elderly saint told me, some people are streams, and some people are reservoirs. The water runs through streams, but it stays in reservoirs. When God finds a man or woman who will be a stream, He keeps pouring out the blessing because He knows it doesn't get stuck. It passes on to those who need it. He gives us an abundance so we can be abundantly generous.

An Invitation to Test Him

I remember as a kid playing with some friends on a roof. I don't know if we were allowed up there, but there we were. And the roof of the neighboring house looked pretty close— close enough to make you want to run fast and see if you could jump from one to the other. We knew it was risky. That's what made it so tempting. But it was dangerous enough for us to know it was a bad idea.

That is, until someone said, "I dare you!" That one phrase turns something that looks like a bad idea into a test of your manhood. It's hard to resist when you're twelve years old. And when it's followed by "I *double* dare you," well . . . it was almost an obligation. I landed on the edge, right on my stomach, and slid down. The roof was fine. I was okay. My ego was bruised.

When God says, "I dare you," it's a different story. He isn't provoking our egos. He's testing our faith, and the only reason He would do that is with our good in mind. I know of only one place in Scripture where He does that, and it's related to this issue of having a generous spirit, taking steps of faith, and releasing what we have so the Law of the Harvest can have its result. He so wants us to experience the reality of His supernatural power and grace that He gives us a very tangible, specific way to put our faith on the line and depend on Him.

The prophet Malachi was speaking to exiles who had returned to Jerusalem and were reestablishing Judah's culture and worship. It had been a long process, and some of them had grown lax in their commitments. One of those commitments was God's instructions to tithe—to give Him 10 percent of their income or harvest. So God dared them to see what would happen if they were faithful in this area. "Bring the whole tithe into the storehouse, that there may be food in my house. Test me in this . . . and see if I will not throw open the floodgates of heaven and pour out so much blessing that there will not be room enough to store it" (Malachi 3:10). He put His own reputation on the line. He just wanted them to take a step of faith.

Old Testament instructions for giving amounted to about 23 percent of a family's income to support the worship, social needs, and government of Israel's theocracy. Here God emphasizes the basic 10-percent tithe. Jesus urged people to keep tithing but to realize that the main point of the Law was justice and compassion, not a monetary amount. The number really isn't the key issue, but it's a great starting point. And I've seen God do amazing things in the lives of people who commit to it.

I'll never forget teaching this passage and principle when I pastored in Santa Cruz, California. The church was almost all new believers, and I was prompted to challenge everyone to "test God" for ninety days to give Him the first 10 percent of their income, live on the remaining 90 percent, and see what happens. The church was doing fine financially, so it wasn't about any need. I even told them that if they were concerned about any hidden agenda to give it to a charity that feeds orphans and the poor rather than to a church.

I could tell story after story of how people tested God in this promise and found Him faithful. A Chinese girl who came to faith brought her first portion the week she became a Christian. She shared with me how she had twice as many customers the next week. A man who was pretty well off but decided to increase his giving from 10 to 20 percent became the top salesman in a major company. A family realized after the ninety-day challenge that they had never had such peace in their home in all the years they had been married. Another family was forced to develop a budget, and that discipline carried over into multiple areas of their family life. I have a thick file folder of stories from people writing to tell how they had "tested God" and He rewarded their faith. Again and again, God keeps His promises.

I'm not saying you will necessarily be financially blessed if you tithe. I do believe God will take care of your needs, but this is not a formula for success. The promise is that if you give, God will give back in areas your heart needs the most. If you take steps of faith in any area of life and put God's promises to the test, He will show Himself to be faithful. You will be blessed in the areas your heavenly Father knows will mean the most to you. Into your need, He will bring contentment. Into your emptiness, He will bring fulfillment. And into the trials and turbulence of your life, He will bring peace.

QUESTIONS FOR DISCUSSION AND REFLECTION

1. What is the relationship between experiencing personal peace and living by faith?

2. Why is giving such an integral part of activating the faith in our lives that leads to peace?

3. In what area of your life do you have a great need? What would planting a seed look like in this area?

4. What specific step of faith or obedience has God directed you to take?

CONCLUSION

We started out with peace. We ended with provision. Why? Because our uncertainty about the future, our concern for our own well-being, and our desire to be fully provided for and have all our needs met are very often at the root of our lack of peace. But, as you know, there are literally hundreds, even thousands of potential events, situations, relationships, trends, messages, and moods that can unsettle us. We each have certain triggers and temptations in our lives that will disrupt our peace if we let them. The dominant message of this book is this: Don't let them.

In order to understand how to live out that message, we've looked at a lot of truths from chapter 4 of Philippians and other passages in this book, all of them aimed at bringing us into God's *shalom*: the peace, wholeness, fullness, and completeness of His will for us. In that place of peace, we resolve conflicts with others, get free from our anxieties, find contentment in difficult circumstances, develop compassion and generosity, and overcome the temptations of greed. But none of that happens without intentional, specific steps of faith. Simply agreeing with God's principles isn't the key to experiencing their benefits. We have to apply them. We have to make moment-by-moment choices, in even the most trying and chaotic situations, to walk in the peace we have already been given. And that means making decisions that might feel risky. In many ways, a step of faith takes us on a journey into the unknown.

But even though we don't always know where faith will lead us, we do know the character of the Faithful One. The promises He gives us are not speculations or wishful thinking. They do come with certain conditions, but they are not lined with fine print that only the superspiritual can see. The principles of His Word are not relevant only for culturally different people in an ancient world. They are for us today, and they are life changing. I invite you to commit to them—to take God at His word, test Him in His promises, and experience how He brings His *shalom*—His supernatural peace and wholeness—into your heart and life.

Remember, you already have the peace Jesus gave you. It's the same peace that sustained Him through numerous conflicts and disputes about His work and His messages, much opposition, many trials and temptations, and the ultimate sacrifice on behalf of a fallen, chaotic world. The Prince of Peace laid down His life so we might be able to walk in the peace He brings. It's a priceless gift. Face every crisis, every difficulty, every challenge of life with a profound, life-changing statement that gratefully receives, embraces, and enjoys that gift: *I choose peace.*

I Choose Peace
Teaching Series Notes

Dear Fellow Pastors, Small Group Leaders, Sunday School Teachers, and Entrepreneurs,

I hope this book has been a help to you, and if it has, I know many of you will want to teach, revise, and communicate this message of peace to others.

The foundation for this book came from my *I Choose Peace* teaching series, which we've made available to help you share this truth.

What follows are message notes to accompany parts 1 through 4 of the series. I encourage you to listen to the series for additional insights. Go to **www.LivingontheEdge .org/I-Choose-Peace-Book** to find these messages, which you can play directly from the site or download as audio MP3 files. To round out the teaching, parts 5 and 6 of the series are also available online.

The discussion questions in these notes are the same as those found in the preceding chapters. I encourage you to use the notes as well as the discussion questions when you teach these messages to help your listeners or group members apply these truths to their daily lives, just as readers of this book have done.

Message notes to all my other teachings are available to download for free on the Chip Ingram App or at Livingon theEdge.org. My heart's desire is to help you communicate God's Word in a way that is biblical, practical, clear, and life changing. It's an honor to partner with you.

Partnering Together to Share God's Peace,

CEO and Teaching Pastor, Living on the Edge

PART 1:
IN RELATIONAL CONFLICT

Philippians 4:1–5

Introduction: Three Approaches to Peace

- Inward
- Outward
- Upward

The World's Peace

The absence of disturbance and hostility, free from internal and external strife.

God's Peace: *Shalom*

1. Complete soundness or wholeness of health
2. Harmony in relationships
3. Success and fulfillment of purpose
4. Victory over one's enemies

Peace I leave with you; my peace I give you. I do not give to you as the world gives. Do not let your hearts be troubled and do not be afraid.

Jesus of Nazareth, John 14:27

With what one person would you most like to be at peace?

Choosing Peace in Relational Conflict (Philippians 4:1-5)

The context

Therefore, my brothers and sisters, you whom I love and long for, my joy and crown, stand firm in the Lord in this way, dear friends! (v. 1)

The plea for unity

I plead with Euodia and I plead with Syntyche to be of the same mind in the Lord. (v. 2)

The request for competent counsel

Yes, and I ask you, my true yokefellow, to help these women who have [contended] with me for the gospel, along with Clement and the rest of my fellow workers, whose names are in the Book of Life. (v. 3 BSB)

The command concerning relational focus

Rejoice in the Lord always. I will say it again: Rejoice! (v. 4)

The command concerning personal responsibility

Let your gentleness be evident to all. The Lord is near. (v. 5)

5 Ways to Diffuse Relational Conflict

1. Resolve to stop PROCRASTINATING. (v. 1)
2. Reevaluate your EXPECTATIONS. (v. 2)
3. Get competent outside HELP. (v. 3)
4. Refuse to allow ONE relationship to ruin your life. (v. 4)
5. Remember a right RESPONSE is more important than being RIGHT. (v. 5)

Discussion Questions

1. On a scale of 1–10, rank the level of stress and concern you are currently experiencing from any problem relationship.

2. Why does relational conflict rob us of peace? What price are you paying to allow this to continue?

3. What specific steps does the apostle Paul give to help resolve relational conflict? List them and discuss each.

4. Is there a relationship in your life that calls for you to follow this pattern? When and how will you follow God's plan for peace (as far as it depends on you)?

5. Who could help you turn your good intention into action this week?

PART 2

IN ANXIOUS MOMENTS

Philippians 4:6-7

Introduction

Jesus's promise

These things I have spoken to you, so that in Me you may have peace. In the world you have tribulation, but take courage; I have overcome the world.

John 16:33 NASB

- What exactly is anxiety?
- What causes anxiety?
  - Fear of the future
  - Conflict in the present
  - Regrets over the past
- How does anxiety affect us?

How can we overcome anxiety?

Choosing God's Peace When Anxiety Strikes (Philippians 4:6-7)

Do not be anxious about anything, but in every situation, by prayer and petition, with thanksgiving, present your requests to God. And the peace of God, which transcends all understanding, will guard your hearts and your minds in Christ Jesus.

Philippians 4:6–7

<u>Nothing</u> be anxious about

But in everything

- by prayer
- by petition
- with thanksgiving
- the <u>requests</u> of you <u>let be made known</u> to God.

And the <u>peace</u> of God
     ↓
   (surpassing all <u>understanding</u>)
      will <u>guard</u> the <u>hearts</u> of you
      and
      the thoughts of you
        in Christ Jesus

The Commands = the What

1. Negatively =
2. Positively =

Four Key Words = the How

PRAYER = worship and adoration.

PETITION = focus on your needs.

THANKSGIVING = focus on what God has done.

REQUESTS = outline your specific requests.

The Promise = the Why

   1. Peace and anxiety cannot COEXIST.

   2. Anxiety and biblical prayer cannot COEXIST.

Summary

Biblical PRAYER is God's antidote to anxiety.

This week, every time you feel anxious, remember the following word picture . . .

When ANXIETY pounds at the door of your heart, let PRAYER answer it as you RUN into your Father's arms!

Discussion Questions

   1. When do you tend to be anxious?

   2. What are the issues in your life that are "strangling" and "stressing" you mentally and emotionally?

   3. How will you put this message into practice? Who will help/encourage you in your battle to overcome anxiety?

   4. Is there a relationship in your life that calls for you to follow this pattern? Who in your relationship network struggles with anxiety and needs your help?

PART 3:
IN A BROKEN WORLD

Philippians 4:8-9

Introduction: Are You Feeding or Starving Your Fear?

University of Tennessee - 12-year study

Psychologically: "We are what we eat"

| Negative Thinking | → | Fearful Emotions | → | Ungodly Behavior | → | Devastating Consequences |

OR

| Positive Thinking | → | Peaceful Emotions | → | Godly Behavior | → | Fruitful Consequences |

Summary

Science and Scripture agree:

1. We are a product of our THOUGHT life. (Proverbs 23:7)
2. Our EMOTIONS flow from our thought life. (Romans 8:6)
3. What we allow to enter our mind is the most important DECISION we make each and every day. (Romans 12:2)

The Question: How can we choose peace in a broken world?

The Answer:

Finally, brethren, whatever is true, whatever is honorable, whatever is right, whatever is pure, whatever is lovely, whatever is of good repute, if there is any excellence and if anything worthy of praise, dwell on these things. The things you have learned and received and heard and seen in me, practice these things, and the God of peace will be with you.

Philippians 4:8–9 NASB 1995

Command #1: DWELL on these things . . .   Philippians 4:8

True: Objectively true, that which conforms to reality vs. things that are deceptive, illusions that promise peace and happiness.

Pre-view question: Is this TRUE or FALSE?

Honorable: "Sober," "serious," "worthy of respect," "inspires awe"—it refers to those things which reflect the weighty purposes of a believer's life.

Pre-view question: Does this HONOR or DISHONOR?

Right: "Righteous"; used in New Testament to refer to the Father, Jesus, God's actions, God's character. It pictures doing what is right when tempted.

Pre-view question: Is this morally RIGHT or WRONG?

Pure: From the same root word as "holy." It means free from defilement; sexual and moral purity in thought, word, and deed.

Pre-view question: Will this CLEANSE or DIRTY my soul?

Lovely: "Attractive," "winsome," "beautiful"; it pictures those things that call forth a response of love and warmth within us vs. bitterness, criticism, and vengeance.

Pre-view question: Will this RENEW or HARDEN my heart?

Good Repute: That which is "commendable," "gracious," "admirable"; it literally means "fair speaking." It describes the things which are fit for God to hear vs. ugly words, false words, and impure words.

Pre-view question: Could I RECOMMEND this to someone who looks up to me?

Summary

Virtue and/or Praise: A summary of sorts to "think on" anything that has moral excellence and will inspire and motivate us to love God and others.

Command #2: Habitually PRACTICE these things ... **Philippians 4:9a**

- Learned . . . Received: Appetite and application
- Heard . . . Saw: Instruction and modeling

Why? Your thought life determines your FUTURE. (Romans 8:5–8)

How? The principle of mind RENEWAL. (Romans 12:2)

Promise: The God of peace (*shalom*) will be WITH YOU. (Philippians 4:9b)

21 Minutes That Will Change Your Life

1. **Read:** The Bible	10 minutes
2. **Pray:** Talk with God	7 minutes
3. **Listen:** Sit quietly and listen	3 minutes
4. **Apply:** One specific truth, e.g., serve someone	1 minute

Discussion Questions

1. How does our thought life affect our emotions?

2. How would you describe the <u>quality</u> of your thought life? What adjustments do you sense God would have you make in what you **view, read,** and **think**?

3. Why is **habitual practice** of the truth so vital if we are to experience <u>God's peace</u>? Why does "duplicity" create <u>stress</u> and lack of peace in our lives?

4. What <u>insight</u> has God given you today to help you experience His **peace** in your life? How will you choose to cooperate with God's process in your life? Who will help you?

Resources

Reclaiming the Lost Art of Biblical Meditation by Robert Morgan

Good to Great in God's Eyes by Chip Ingram (Chapter 1: "Think Great Thoughts")

Topical Memory System by The Navigators Press

PART 4

IN DIFFICULT CIRCUMSTANCES

Philippians 4:10-13

Introduction: What Would It Take for You to Be Content?

Definition

content happy enough with what one has or is; not desiring something more or different; satisfied.

Webster's Dictionary

The Problem: The horizon is always moving.

Two Historical Solutions

1. Conquer, achieve, and acquire until satisfied.
2. Desire less and less until it doesn't matter.

The Question: How can we be satisfied ... today?

The Answer (Philippians 4:10-13)

The Occasion: A "Thank You" Note

I rejoiced greatly in the Lord that at last you have renewed your concern for me. Indeed, you have been concerned, but you had no opportunity to show it. (v. 10)

I am not saying this because I am in need, for I have learned to be content whatever the circumstances. (v. 11) I know what it is to be in need, and I know what it is to have plenty. I have learned the secret of being content in any and every situation, whether well fed or hungry, whether living in plenty or in want. (v. 12) I can do all this through him who gives me strength. (v. 13)

Conclusion

Contentment is not a thing to be achieved, but a secret to be discovered.

Four Principles – Four Practices

- **Principle #1:** Our contentment is not dependent on our <u>circumstances</u>.
  - Practice = BE THANKFUL / GRATEFUL (v. 10)

- **Principle #2:** Contentment is an attitude we <u>learn</u> not a thing we achieve.
  - Practice = BE TEACHABLE (v. 11)

- **Principle #3:** Prosperity does not have the power to give us contentment; nor <u>poverty</u> the power to take it away.
  - Practice = BE FLEXIBLE / CHANGEABLE (v. 12)

- **Principle #4:** Only Christ has the power to give us a contentment that transcends all life's variables.
  - Practice = BE CONFIDENT / TRUSTING (v. 13)

Summary

Contentment is not passive acceptance of the status quo, but the positive assurance that God has supplied one's needs, and the consequent release from unnecessary desires.

Discussion Questions

1. Why is it so difficult to be genuinely content? What factors in our world make this so? What factors in our hearts make this so?

2. Why are both historical positions toward contentment doomed to failure?

3. Walk through each of the principles and practices and discuss how they relate to your present circumstances and attitudes about personal peace.

4. What action step will you take to reflect obedience to God's provision for your personal peace?

5. Take time to pray for one another in your group. Ask God to help each one to embrace His game plan for a life of personal peace.

NOTES

Chapter 1 Choose Peace in Relational Conflict

1. Matthew Arnold, *Literature and Dogma* (Boston: James R. Osgood, 1875), xv, 94, 207, 217, 231.

2. Kerry Patterson, Joseph Grenny, Ron McMillan, and Al Switzler, *Crucial Conversations: Tools for Talking When Stakes Are High* (New York: McGraw Hill, 2012).

Chapter 2 Choose Peace in Anxious Moments

1. Paul D. Meier, Frank B. Minirth, and Frank Wichern, *Introduction to Psychology and Counseling* (Grand Rapids: Baker, 1982).

Chapter 3 Choose Peace in a Broken World

1. Jack Haskins, "The Trouble with Bad News," Department of Communications, University of Tennessee, 1981.

2. Tommy Newberry, *The 4:8 Principle* (Carol Stream, IL: Tyndale, 2007).

3. Matt Maher, "Sing over Your Children," ThankYou Music, 2009.

Chapter 4 Choose Peace in Difficult Circumstances

1. T. R. Glover, *The Conflict of Religions in the Early Roman Empire* (London: Methuen, 1909), 67.

2. Todd A. Sinelli, *True Riches* (Santa Cruz, CA: Lit Torch Publishing, 2001).

3. Gary Smith, "Ali and His Entourage: Life after the End of the Greatest Show on Earth," *Sports Illustrated*, October 10, 2014, accessed March 2020, https://www.si.com/boxing/2014/10/10/muhammad-ali-entourage.

Chapter 5 Choose Peace in a Materialistic Culture

1. American Donor Trends, Barna Research Report, June 3, 2013.

Chapter 6 Choose Peace in Tests of Faith

1. Jim Carpenter, "The Parable of the Pump," *Discipleship*, no. 35, 1986, 15.

2. American Donor Trends.

3. Randy Alcorn, *The Treasure Principle* (Portland: Multnomah, 2001), 73.

REFERENCES

Barclay, William. *The Letters to the Philippians, Colossians, and Thessalonians.* The Daily Study Bible Series. Rev. ed. Philadelphia: Westminster, 1975.

———. *More New Testament Words.* New York: Harper & Row, 1958.

Gaebelein, Frank E. *Ephesians to Philemon.* The Expositor's Bible Commentary Series, vol. 11. Grand Rapids: Zondervan, 1980.

Hendriksen, William. *Philippians, Colossians and Philemon.* New Testament Commentary Series. Grand Rapids: Baker, 1979.

Martin, Ralph P. *Philippians.* Tyndale New Testament Commentaries. Grand Rapids: Eerdmans, 1989.

Meier, Paul D., Frank B. Minirth, and Frank Wichern. *Introduction to Psychology and Counseling.* Grand Rapids: Baker, 1982.

Meyer, F. B. *Devotional Commentary on Philippians.* Grand Rapids: Kregel, 1979.

Robertson, Archibald T. *The Epistles of Paul.* Word Pictures in the New Testament, vol. 4. Nashville: Broadman, 1931.

Sunukjian, Donald R. *Invitation to Philippians: Building a Great Church through Humility.* Wooster, OH: Weaver Book Company, 2014.

Turner, Nigel. *Christian Words: Concise Word Studies to Help Anyone Understand the Unique Vocabulary of the Greek New Testament.* Nashville: Thomas Nelson, 1982.

Wiersbe, Warren W. *The Bible Exposition Commentary: An Exposition of the New Testament Comprising the Entire "BE" Series.* Wheaton: Victor Books, 1989.

Wuest, Kenneth S., ed. *Philippians–Hebrews; The Pastoral Epistles–First Peter in the Last Days.* Wuest's Word Studies in the Greek New Testament, vol. 2. Grand Rapids: Eerdmans, 1986.

Chip Ingram is the founder and CEO of Living on the Edge, an international teaching and discipleship ministry. A pastor for over thirty-five years, Chip is the author of many books, including *Discover Your True Self*, *Marriage That Works*, *Culture Shock*, *The Real Heaven*, *The Real God*, *The Invisible War*, and *Love, Sex, and Lasting Relationships*. Chip and his wife, Theresa, have four grown children and twelve grandchildren and live in California.

See Yourself the Way
GOD SEES YOU

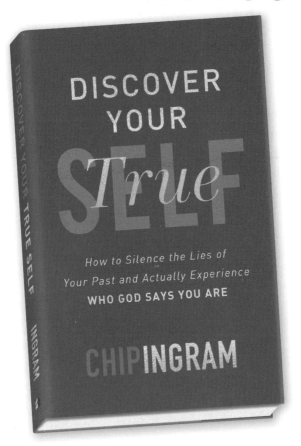

Chip Ingram wants to open your eyes to your true self, the "new you" that God sees; the person who is immeasurably valuable and beautiful. In this Scripture-soaked book, he shows you how getting God's perspective

- satisfies your search for significance
- undoes your shame
- makes you secure

- frees you from comparing yourself with others
- helps you discover your calling
- and more

More from
CHIP INGRAM

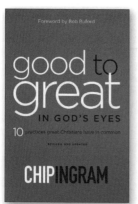

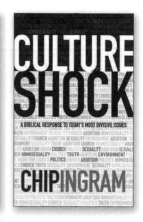

LIVING ON THE EDGE™

Head to **LivingontheEdge.org** for Chip's
daily broadcast, free online courses,
digital downloads, group studies, and more!

DOWNLOAD THE CHIP INGRAM APP

The Chip Ingram App provides you with daily radio programs,
message notes, discipleship videos, Chip's blog, and more.
Download it now and listen when it's most convenient for you.

Find it on iTunes, Apple Play and CarPlay, or the Amazon Appstore

Connect with
BakerBooks
Relevant. Intelligent. Engaging.

Sign up for announcements about
new and upcoming titles at

BakerBooks.com/SignUp

@ReadBakerBooks

Careers
in Focus

MECHANICS

THIRD EDITION

Ferguson

An imprint of Infobase Publishing

Careers in Focus: Mechanics, Third Edition

Copyright © 2008 by Infobase Publishing

Ferguson
An imprint of Infobase Publishing
132 West 31st Street
New York NY 10001

Library of Congress Cataloging-in-Publication Data

Careers in focus. Mechanics. — 3rd ed.
    p. cm.
    Includes bibliographical references and index.
    ISBN-13: 978-0-8160-7275-0
    ISBN-10: 0-8160-7275-2
    1. Machinery—Maintenance and repair—Vocational guidance. 2. Mechanics (Persons)—Vocational guidance. I. J.G. Ferguson Publishing Company. II. Title: Mechanics.
    TJ157.C37 2008
    621.8'16023—dc22
                                    2007038313

Ferguson books are available at special discounts when purchased in bulk quantities for businesses, associations, institutions, or sales promotions. Please call our Special Sales Department in New York at (212) 967-8800 or (800) 322-8755.

You can find Ferguson on the World Wide Web at http://www.fergpubco.com

Text design by David Strelecky
Cover design by Salvatore Luongo

Printed in the United States of America

MP MSRF 10 9 8 7 6 5 4 3 2 1

This book is printed on acid-free paper.

Table of Contents

Introduction

Mechanics maintain and repair machines and mechanical systems. It would be difficult to name an area of your life that is not affected by the work of mechanics. From the moment that we get out of bed, mechanics of all types help us accomplish our daily tasks. *Automobile service technicians* keep your car running smoothly so that you can get to school or work. *Aircraft mechanics* and *diesel mechanics* keep you safe when you travel by plane or train to far-away places. *General maintenance mechanics* keep your school, house, or workplace cool in the summer and warm in the winter. Did you ride an elevator today? If so, you can thank *elevator installers and repairers* for your safe and quick trip. Been to the doctor lately? We bet that you've never stopped to think about the *biomedical equipment technicians* who maintain and repair the medical equipment used to diagnose and treat you. And what about the food you eat every day? *Agricultural equipment technicians* and *farm equipment mechanics* maintain the equipment farmers use to plant and harvest the crops that eventually end up on your dinner table. There are even mechanics who repair the telephones and computers you use to communicate (*communications equipment technicians*); fix the musical instrument you play (*musical instrument repairers and tuners*) in band or just for fun; or fix the mountain bike you ride after school or work (*bicycle mechanics*). In short, through mechanics, our lives have been thoroughly changed for the better.

The work of mechanics has been revolutionized by technological development. Workers in the industry are now often trained in electrical operations and computer technology to work on the more high-tech engines, parts, and systems that comprise products such as automobiles, appliances, and aircraft.

Each of the careers in this industry offers its own opportunities for advancement. Workers with the best potential, however, are those who become skilled at what they do, seek further training or education, and are always aware that changing technology and a global economy will affect jobs and opportunities in their industry. Trade associations and unions, in an effort to improve the skill level of workers and keep them in the industry, often offer different levels of training and certification. Some are short-term programs, but many last several years because of the knowledge required in specific jobs.

In order to advance in their careers, some mechanics choose to travel the road from apprentice to journey worker. Others choose to move from programming to designing, while still others become trainers and supervisors or move into technical sales and customer support. Those who dream of owning their own business should remember that most of the small businesses in this industry are owned by people who came up through the ranks.

Employment for mechanics is closely tied to the economic conditions within their specific industry. Although economic conditions have improved during the last decade, employment opportunities have not increased proportionately. Many companies have laid off mechanics and are hiring fewer workers than in the past. In addition, automation is affecting employment opportunities for many workers. The manufacturing industry has been revolutionized by highly productive, computer-controlled machining and turning centers that change their own tools; transfer machines that completely machine, assemble, and test mass-produced products; and innovative metal removal and forming systems. Robots and robotic equipment are becoming more common and are being used in many areas where the work is tedious, repetitive, or dangerous. Automated inspection equipment, such as electronic sensors, cameras, X rays, and lasers, is increasingly being used to test and inspect parts during production.

All these factors have affected the career outlook for mechanics. However, there will always be opportunities for mechanics who have advanced training and knowledge of the latest electronic and computer technology.

Each article in this book discusses in detail a particular mechanical-related occupation. The articles in *Careers in Focus: Mechanics* appear in Ferguson's *Encyclopedia of Careers and Vocational Guidance* but have been updated and revised with the latest information from the U.S. Department of Labor, professional organizations, and other sources. The following paragraphs detail the sections and features that appear in the book.

The **Quick Facts** section provides a brief summary of the career, including recommended school subjects, personal skills, work environment, minimum educational requirements, salary ranges, certification or licensing requirements, and employment outlook. This section also provides acronyms and identification numbers for the following government classification indexes: the *Dictionary of Occupational Titles* (DOT), the *Guide to Occupational Exploration* (GOE), the National Occupational Classification (NOC) Index, and the Occupational Information Network (O*NET)-Standard

Occupational Classification System (SOC) index. The DOT, GOE, and O*NET-SOC indexes have been created by the U.S. government; the NOC index is Canada's career classification system. Readers can use the identification numbers listed in the Quick Facts section to access further information about a career. Print editions of the DOT (*Dictionary of Occupational Titles*. Indianapolis, Ind.: JIST Works, 1991) and GOE (*Guide for Occupational Exploration*. Indianapolis, Ind.: JIST Works, 2001) are available at libraries. Electronic versions of the NOC (http://www23.hrdc-drhc.gc.ca) and O*NET-SOC (http://online.onetcenter.org) are available on the Internet. When no DOT, GOE, NOC, or O*NET-SOC numbers are present, this means that the U.S. Department of Labor or Human Resources Development Canada have not created a numerical designation for this career. In this instance, you will see the acronym "N/A," or not available.

The **Overview** section is a brief introductory description of the duties and responsibilities involved in this career. Oftentimes, a career may have a variety of job titles. When this is the case, alternative career titles are presented. Employment statistics are also provided, when available. The **History** section describes the history of the particular job as it relates to the overall development of its industry or field. **The Job** describes the primary and secondary duties of the job. **Requirements** discusses high school and postsecondary education and training requirements, any necessary certification or licensing, and other personal requirements for success in the job. **Exploring** offers suggestions on how to gain experience in or knowledge of the particular job before making a firm educational and financial commitment. The focus is on what can be done while still in high school (or in the early years of college) to gain a better understanding of the job. The **Employers** section gives an overview of typical places of employment for the job. **Starting Out** discusses the best ways to land that first job, be it through the college career services office, newspaper ads, Internet employment sites, or personal contact. The **Advancement** section describes what kind of career path to expect from the job and how to get there. **Earnings** lists salary ranges and describes the typical fringe benefits. The **Work Environment** section describes the typical surroundings and conditions of employment—whether indoors or outdoors, noisy or quiet, social or independent. Also discussed are typical hours worked, any seasonal fluctuations, and the stresses and strains of the job. The **Outlook** section summarizes the job in terms of the general economy and industry projections. For the most part, Outlook information is obtained from the U.S. Bureau of Labor Statistics and is supplemented by information gathered from professional associations. Job growth terms follow those used in the *Occupational Outlook Handbook*. Growth described as "much faster than the average" means an increase of 27 percent or more. Growth described as "faster than the average" means an increase of 18 to 26 percent. Growth described as "about as fast as the average" means an increase of 9 to 17 percent. Growth described as "more slowly than the average" means an increase of 0 to 8 percent. "Decline" means a decrease by any amount. Each article ends with **For More Information,** which lists organizations that provide information on training, education, internships, scholarships, and job placement.

Careers in Focus: Mechanics also includes photographs, informative sidebars, and interviews with professionals in the field.

Aeronautical and Aerospace Technicians

OVERVIEW

Aeronautical and aerospace technicians design, construct, test, operate, and maintain the basic structures of aircraft and spacecraft, as well as propulsion and control systems. They work with scientists and engineers. Many aeronautical and aerospace technicians assist engineers in preparing equipment drawings, diagrams, blueprints, and scale models. They collect information, make computations, and perform laboratory tests. Their duties may include working on various projects involving aerodynamics, structural design, flight-test evaluation, or propulsion problems. Other technicians estimate the cost of materials and labor required to manufacture the product, serve as manufacturers' field service technicians, and write technical materials.

HISTORY

Both aeronautical engineering and the aerospace industry had their births in the early 20th century. The very earliest machine-powered and heavier-than-air aircraft, such as the first one flown by Wilbur and Orville Wright in 1903, were crudely constructed and often the result of costly and dangerous trial-and-error experimentation.

As government and industry took an interest in the possible applications of this new invention, however, our knowledge of aircraft and the entire industry became more sophisticated. By 1908, for instance, the Wright brothers had received their first government military contract, and by 1909, the industry had expanded to include additional airplane producers, such as Glenn Curtiss in the United States and several others in France.

Aeronautical engineering and the aerospace industry have been radically transformed since those early days, mostly because of the demands of two world wars and the tremendous increases in scientific knowledge that have taken place during this century. Aviation and aerospace developments continued after the end of World War II. The factories and workers that built planes to support the war were in place and the industry took off, with the jet engine, rocket propulsion, supersonic flight, and manned voyages outside the earth's atmosphere among the major developments. As the industry evolved, aeronautical and aerospace engineers found themselves taking on increasingly larger projects and were more in need of trained and knowledgeable assistants to help them. Throughout the years, these assistants have been known as engineering aides, as engineering associates, and, most recently, as aerospace technicians and technologists. Their main task today is to take on assignments that require technical skills but do not necessarily require the scientist's or engineer's special training and education.

THE JOB

There are no clear-cut definitions of aeronautical technology and aerospace technology; in fact, many employers use the terms interchangeably. This lack of a clear distinction also occurs in education, where many schools and institutes offer similar courses under a variety of titles: aeronautical, aviation, or aerospace technology. In general, however, the aerospace industry includes manufacturers of all kinds of flying vehicles: from piston- and jet-powered aircraft that fly inside the earth's atmosphere, to rockets, missiles, satellites, probes, and all kinds of manned and unmanned spacecraft that operate outside the earth's atmosphere. The term *aeronautics* is often used within the aerospace industry to refer specifically to mechanical flight inside the earth's atmosphere, especially to the design and manufacture of commercial passenger and freight aircraft, private planes, and helicopters.

The difference between technicians and technologists generally refers to their level of education. Technicians generally hold associate's degrees, while technologists hold bachelor's degrees in aeronautical technology.

Whether they work for a private company working on commercial aircraft or for the federal government, aerospace technicians work side by side with engineers and scientists in all major phases of the design, production, and operation of aircraft and spacecraft technology. The aerospace technician position includes collecting and recording data; operating test equipment such as wind tunnels and flight simulators; devising tests to ensure quality control; modifying mathematical procedures to fit specific problems; laying out experimental circuits to test scientific theories; and evaluating experimental data for practical applications.

The following paragraphs describe jobs held by aerospace technicians; some may be used in other industries as well. Fuller descriptions of the work of some of these titles are provided in the following paragraphs.

Aerospace physiological technicians operate devices used to train pilots and astronauts. These devices include pressure suits, pressure chambers, and ejection seats that simulate flying conditions. These technicians also operate other kinds of flight-training equipment such as tow reels, radio equipment, and meteorological devices. They interview trainees about their medical histories, which helps detect evidence of conditions that would disqualify pilots or astronauts from further training.

Aircraft launch and recovery technicians work on aircraft carriers to operate, adjust, and repair launching and recovery equipment such as catapults, barricades, and arresting nets. They disassemble the launch and recovery equipment, replace defective parts, and keep track of all maintenance activities.

Avionics technicians repair, test, install, and maintain radar and radio equipment aboard aircraft and spacecraft.

Computer technicians assist mathematicians and subject specialists in checking and refining computations and systems, such as those required for predicting and determining orbits of spacecraft.

Drafting and design technicians convert the aeronautical engineer's specifications and rough sketches of aeronautical and aerospace equipment, such as electrical and mechanical devices, into accurate drawings that are used by skilled craft workers to make parts for aircraft and spacecraft.

Electronics technicians assist engineers in the design, development, and modification of electronic and electromechanical systems. They assist in the calibration and operation of radar and photographic equipment and also operate, install, troubleshoot, and repair electronic testing equipment.

Engineering technicians assist with review and analysis of post-flight data, structural failure, and other factors that cause failure in flight vehicles.

Industrial engineering technicians assist engineers in preparing layouts of machinery and equipment, workflow plans, time-and-motion

Modern Aviation Timeline

1903: Orville and Wilbur Wright fly the first powered, heavier-than-air aircraft at Kitty Hawk, N.C.

1907: Paul Cornu, a French inventor, flies the first helicopter.

1908: The U.S. War Department purchases its first "flying machine" from the Wright Brothers.

1912: The air speed-meter is invented.

1913: The gyroscopic compass and gyroscopic stabilizer are invented.

1914-1918 (World War I): Airplanes are used by both sides to gather intelligence, direct artillery fire, and, later in the war, conduct raids on enemy troops, supply bases, and cities.

1919: The first sustained commercial flights begin between Paris and Brussels.

1924: The first round-the-world flight is completed.

1927: Air-cooled engines, which reduce the weight of planes and allow larger and faster planes to be produced, replace water-cooled engines.

1927: Charles Lindbergh makes the first nonstop solo flight across the Atlantic Ocean.

1929: The first electro-mechanical flight simulator is invented.

1929: The first rocket-powered plane is flown.

1931: The first jet engine is designed and patented.

1932: Amelia Earhart becomes the first aviatrix to fly solo across the Atlantic Ocean.

1939-1945 (World War II): Aviation plays a key role for both the Allied and Axis powers.

1947: Military test pilot Charles Yeager flies his rocket powered Bell X-1 aircraft faster than the speed of sound.

1952: The world's first turboprop light plane, the Cessna XL-19B, is flown in Wichita, Kans.

1958: The number of passengers flying across the Atlantic Ocean surpasses the number of those traveling the Atlantic via steamship for the first time.

1969: The Concorde, the first supersonic passenger jet, is flown for the first time.

1980: The first solar-powered aircraft is flown.

1989: The U.S. Air Force's B-2 "Spirit" bomber is launched. It combines composite materials with stealth technology.

1994: The Boeing 777, the first aircraft to be designed entirely using a computer, is test-flown.

2002: The hypersonic scramjet engine, which uses hydrogen fuel, is tested successfully in Australia. This technology could substantially reduce flight time for trans-Atlantic flights.

2003: The Concorde makes its last flight.

2005: The Airbus A380, the largest commercial aircraft in the world, debuts.

Source: American Institute of Aeronautics and Astronautics

studies, and statistical studies and analyses of production costs to produce the most efficient use of personnel, materials, and machines.

Instrumentation technicians test, install, and maintain electronic, hydraulic, pneumatic, and optical instruments. These are used in aircraft systems and components in manufacturing as well as research and development. One important responsibility is to maintain their assigned research instruments. As a part of this maintenance, they test the instruments, take readings and calibration curves, and calculate correction factors for the instruments.

Liaison technicians check on the production of aircraft and spacecraft as they are being built for conformance to specifications, keeping engineers informed as the manufacturing progresses, and they investigate any engineering production problems that arise.

Mathematical technicians assist mathematicians, engineers, and scientists by performing computations involving the use of advanced mathematics.

Mechanical technicians use metalworking machines to assist in the manufacture of one-of-a-kind parts. They also assist in rocket-fin alignment, payload mating, weight and center-of-gravity measurements, and launch-tower erection.

Target aircraft technicians repair and maintain pilotless target aircraft. They assemble, repair, or replace aircraft parts such as cowlings, wings, and propeller assemblies and test aircraft engine operation.

REQUIREMENTS

High School

A strong science and mathematics background is essential for entry into this field. High school courses that will be useful in preparing you for college-level study include algebra, trigonometry, physics, and chemistry. In addition to math and science, courses in social studies, economics, history, blueprint reading, drafting, and industrial and machine shop practice will provide a valuable background for a career in aerospace technology. Computer experience is also important. English, speech, and courses in the preparation of test reports and technical writing are extremely helpful to develop communication ability.

Postsecondary Training

There are a variety of training possibilities for potential aerospace technicians: two-, three-, or four-year programs at colleges or universities, junior or community colleges, technical institutes, or vocational-technical schools; industry on-the-job training; or work-study programs in the military. Graduates from a two- or three-year program usually earn an associate's degree in engineering or science. Graduates from a four-year program earn a bachelor's degree in engineering or science; in addition, several colleges offer four-year degree programs in aeronautical technology. There are also many technical training schools, particularly in areas where the aerospace industry is most active, that offer training in aeronautical technology. Aircraft mechanics, for instance, usually attend one of the country's roughly 200 training schools. However, many employers require graduates of such programs to complete a period of on-the-job training before they are granted full technician status. When selecting a school to attend, check the listings of such agencies as the Accreditation Board for Engineering and Technology and the regional accrediting associations for engineering colleges. Most employers prefer graduates of an accredited school.

In general, postsecondary programs strengthen the student's background in science and mathematics, including pretechnical training. Beyond that, an interdisciplinary curriculum is more helpful than one that specializes in a narrow field. Other courses, which are basic to the work of the aeronautical scientist and engineer, should be part of a balanced program. These include basic physics, nuclear theory, chemistry, mechanics, and computers, including data-processing equipment and procedures.

Certification or Licensing

Only a few aerospace technician positions require licensing or certification; however, certificates issued by professional organizations do enhance the status of qualified engineering technicians. Certification is usually required of those working with nuclear-powered engines or testing radioactive sources, for those working on aircraft in some test programs, and in some safety-related positions. Technicians and technologists working in areas related to national defense, and especially those employed by government agencies, are usually required to carry security clearances.

Other Requirements

Aeronautical and aerospace technicians must be able to learn basic engineering skills. They should enjoy and be proficient in mathematics and the physical sciences, able to visualize size, form, and function. The Aerospace Industries Association of America advises that today's aerospace production worker must be strong in the basics of manufacturing, have a knowledge of statistics, and have the ability to work with computers.

EXPLORING

Visiting an aerospace research or manufacturing facility is one of the best ways to learn more about this field. Because there are so many such facilities connected with the aerospace industry throughout the United States, there is sure to be one in nearly every area. The reference department of a local library can help students locate the nearest facility.

Finding part-time or summer employment at such a facility is, of course, one of the best ways to gain experience or learn more about the field. Such jobs aren't available for all students interested in the field, but you can still find part-time work that will give you practical experience, such as in a local machine shop or factory.

Students should not overlook the educational benefits of visiting local museums of science and technology or aircraft museums or displays. The National Air and Space Museum at the Smithsonian Institution in Washington, D.C., is one of the most comprehensive museums dedicated to aerospace. Some Air Force bases or naval air stations also offer tours to groups of interested students. The tours may be arranged by teachers or career guidance counselors.

The Junior Engineering Technical Society (JETS) provides students a chance to explore career opportunities in engineering and

technology, enter academic competitions, and design model structures. JETS administers a competition that allows students to use
their technology skills. The Tests of Engineering, Aptitude, Mathematics, and Science is an open-book, open-discussion engineering
problem competition. If your school doesn't have a JETS chapter,
check with other schools in your area; sometimes smaller schools
can form cooperatives to offer such programs.

EMPLOYERS

Aeronautical and aerospace technicians and technologists are prin-
cipally employed by government agencies, commercial airlines,
educational institutions, and aerospace manufacturing companies.
Most technicians employed by manufacturing companies engage in
research, development, and design; the remainder work in production, sales, engineering, installation and maintenance, and other
related fields. Those employed by government and educational institutions are normally assigned to do research and specific problem-
solving tasks. Airlines employ technicians to supervise maintenance
operations and the development of procedures for new equipment;
there are roughly 142,000 aircraft and avionics equipment mechanics and service technicians.

STARTING OUT

The best way for students to obtain an aeronautical or aerospace
technician's job is through their college or university's career services office. Many manufacturers maintain recruiting relationships
with schools in their area. Jobs may also be obtained through state
employment offices, newspaper advertisements, applications for government employment, and industry work-study programs offered by
many aircraft companies.

ADVANCEMENT

Aeronautical and aerospace technicians continue to learn on the job.
As they gain experience in the specialized areas, employers turn to
them as experts who can solve problems, create new techniques,
devise new designs, or develop practice from theory.

Most advancement involves taking on additional responsibilities.
For example, with experience, a technician may take on supervisory
responsibilities, overseeing several trainees, assistant technicians, or
others. Such a technician may also be assigned independent responsi-

bility especially on some tasks usually assigned to an engineer. Technicians with a good working knowledge of the company's equipment and who have good personalities may become company sales or technical representatives. Technicians seeking further advancement are advised to continue their education. With additional formal education, a technician may become an aeronautical or aerospace engineer.

EARNINGS

Aerospace technology is a broad field, so earnings vary depending on a technician's specialty, educational preparation, and work experience. In 2006, the median annual earnings for aerospace technicians were $53,300. Salaries ranged from less than $34,570 to more than $74,860 per year. Avionics technicians earned salaries that ranged from $32,540 to $63,090 or more in 2006. Benefits depend on employers but usually include paid vacations and holidays, sick pay, health insurance, and a retirement plan. Salary increases will likely be held to a minimum over the next few years as the industry struggles to achieve a new balance after years of cutbacks and difficult markets. Nearly all companies offer some form of tuition reimbursement for further education. Some offer cooperative programs with local schools, combining classroom training with practical paid experience.

WORK ENVIRONMENT

The aerospace industry, with its strong emphasis on quality and safety, is a very safe place to work. Special procedures and equipment make otherwise hazardous jobs extremely safe. The range of work covered means that the technicians can work in small teams in specialized research laboratories or in test areas that are large and hospital-clean.

Aerospace technicians are at the launch pad, involved in fueling and checkout procedures, and back in the blockhouse sitting at an electronic console. They work in large test facilities or in specialized shops, designing and fabricating equipment. They travel to test sites or tracking stations to construct facilities or troubleshoot systems. Working conditions vary with the assignment, but the work climate is always challenging, and coworkers are well-trained, competent people.

Aeronautical technicians may perform inside activities involving confined detail work, they may work outside, or they may combine both situations. Aeronautical and aerospace technicians work in many situations: alone, in small teams, or in large groups. Commonly, technicians participate in team projects, which are coordinated efforts of scientists, engineers, and technicians working on specific assignments. They concentrate on the practical aspects of the project and must get along well with and interact cooperatively with the scientists responsible for the theoretical aspects of the project.

Aerospace technicians must be able to perform under deadline pressure, meet strict requirements and rigid specifications, and deal with potentially hazardous situations. They must be willing and flexible enough to acquire new knowledge and techniques to adjust to the rapidly changing technology. In addition, technicians need persistence and tenacity, especially when engaged in experimental and research tasks. They must be responsible, reliable, and willing to accept greater responsibility.

Aerospace technology is never far from the public's attention, and aeronautical technicians have the additional satisfaction of knowing that they are viewed as being engaged in vital and fascinating work.

OUTLOOK

The U.S. Department of Labor predicts that employment of aircraft and avionics mechanics and service technicians will grow about as fast as the average for all occupations. Although the aerospace industry is predicted to grow more slowly than the average for all industries through 2014, an increase in air traffic and the improving finances of national airlines in the years since the terrorist attacks on the United States in 2001 will translate to modest employment growth. Increased military spending on defense aircraft and aerospace equipment represents additional growth. Job openings will occur as technicians retire or seek employment in other industries. The Aerospace Industries Association (AIA) predicts aerospace companies will be looking for qualified technicians in fields such as laser optics, mission operations, hazardous materials procedures, production planning, materials testing, computer-aided design, and robotic operations and programming.

FOR MORE INFORMATION

For a list of accredited technology programs, contact
Accreditation Board for Engineering and Technology Inc.
111 Market Place, Suite 1050
Baltimore, MD 21202-4012

Tel: 410-347-7700
http://www.abet.org

Contact the AIA for publications with information on aerospace technologies, careers, and space.
Aerospace Industries Association (AIA)
1000 Wilson Boulevard, Suite 1700
Arlington, VA 22209-3928
Tel: 703-358-1000
http://www.aia-aerospace.org

For career information and information on student branches of this organization, contact the AIAA.
American Institute of Aeronautics and Astronautics (AIAA)
1801 Alexander Bell Drive, Suite 500
Reston, VA 20191-4344
Tel: 800-639-2422
http://www.aiaa.org

For career and scholarship information, contact
General Aviation Manufacturers Association
1400 K Street, NW, Suite 801
Washington, DC 20005-2402
Tel: 202-393-1500
http://www.gama.aero

JETS has career information and offers high school students the opportunity to "try on" engineering through a number of programs and competitions. For more information, contact
Junior Engineering Technical Society
1420 King Street, Suite 405
Alexandria, VA 22314-2750
Tel: 703-548-5387
Email: info@jets.orghttp://www.jets.org

SEDS is an international organization of high school and college students dedicated to promoting interest in space. The United States national headquarters are located at the Massachusetts Institute of Technology. Contact
Students for the Exploration and Development of Space (SEDS)
MIT Room W20-401
77 Massachusetts Avenue

Cambridge, MA 02139-4307
Email: mitseds-officers@mit
http://www.mit.edu/~mitseds

For more information on career choices and schools in Canada, contact
Aerospace Industries Association of Canada
60 Queen Street, Suite 1200
Ottawa, ON K1P 5Y7 Canada
Tel: 613-232-4297
Email: info@aiac.ca
http://www.aiac.ca

Agricultural Equipment Technicians

OVERVIEW

Agricultural equipment technicians work with modern farm machinery. They assemble, adjust, operate, maintain, modify, test, and even help design it. This machinery includes automatic animal feeding systems; milking machine systems; and tilling, planting, harvesting, irrigating, drying, and handling equipment. Agricultural equipment technicians work on farms or for agricultural machinery manufacturers or dealerships. They often supervise skilled mechanics and other workers who keep machines and systems operating at maximum efficiency. Approximately 33,000 agricultural equipment technicians are employed in the United States.

HISTORY

The history of farming equipment stretches back to prehistoric times, when the first agricultural workers developed the sickle. In the Middle Ages, the horse-drawn plow greatly increased farm production, and in the early 1700s, Jethro Tull designed and built the first mechanical seed planter, further increasing production. The industrial revolution brought advances in the design and use of specialized machinery for strenuous and repetitive work. It had a great impact on the agricultural industry, beginning in 1831 with Cyrus McCormick's invention of the reaper.

In the first half of the 20th century, governmental experiment stations developed high-yield, standardized varieties of farm crops. This, combined with the establishment of agricultural equipment-producing companies, caused a boom in the production of farm machinery. In the late 1930s, the abundance of inexpensive petroleum spurred the development of gasoline- and diesel-run farm machinery. During the early 1940s, the resulting explosion in complex and powerful farm machinery multiplied production and replaced most of the horses and mules used on farms in the United States.

Modern farming is heavily dependent on very complex and expensive machinery. Highly trained and skilled technicians and farm mechanics are therefore required to install, operate, maintain, and modify this machinery, thereby ensuring the nation's farm productivity. Recent developments in agricultural mechanization and automation make the career of agricultural equipment technicians both challenging and rewarding. Sophisticated machines are being used to plant, cultivate, harvest, and process food; to contour, drain, and renovate land; and to clear land and harvest forest products in the process. Qualified agricultural equipment technicians are needed not only to service and sell this equipment, but also to manage it on the farm.

Farming has increasingly become a highly competitive, big business. A successful farmer may have hundreds of thousands or even millions of dollars invested in land and machinery. For this investment to pay off, it is vital to keep the machinery in excellent operating condition. Prompt and reliable service from the farm equipment manufacturer and dealer is necessary for the success of both farmer and dealer. Interruptions or delays because of poor service are costly for everyone involved. To provide good service, manufacturers and dealers need technicians and specialists who possess agricultural and engineering knowledge in addition to technical skills.

THE JOB

Agricultural equipment technicians work in a wide variety of jobs both on and off the farm. In general, most agricultural equipment technicians find employment in one of three areas: equipment manufacturing, equipment sales and service, and on-farm equipment management.

Equipment manufacturing technicians are involved primarily with the design and testing of agricultural equipment such as farm machinery; irrigation, power, and electrification systems; soil and water conservation equipment; and agricultural harvesting and processing equipment. There are two kinds of technicians working in this field: agricultural engineering technicians and agricultural equipment test technicians.

Agricultural engineering technicians work under the supervision of design engineers. They prepare original layouts and complete detailed drawings of agricultural equipment. They also review plans, diagrams, and blueprints to ensure that new products comply with company standards and design specifications. In order to do this they must use their knowledge of biological, engineering, and design principles. They also must keep current on all of the new equipment and materials being developed for the industry to make sure the machines run at their highest capacity.

Agricultural equipment test technicians test and evaluate the performance of agricultural machinery and equipment. In particular, they make sure the equipment conforms with operating requirements, such as horsepower, resistance to vibration, and strength and hardness of parts. They test equipment under actual field conditions on company-operated research farms and under more controlled conditions. They work with test equipment and recording instruments such as bend-fatigue machines, dynamometers, strength testers, hardness meters, analytical balances, and electronic recorders.

Test technicians are also trained in methods of recording the data gathered during these tests. They compute values such as horsepower and tensile strength using algebraic formulas and report their findings using graphs, tables, and sketches.

After the design and testing phases are complete, other agricultural equipment technicians work with engineers to perform any necessary adjustments in the equipment design. By performing these functions under the general supervision of the design engineer, technicians do the engineers' "detective work" so the engineers can devote more time to research and development.

Large agricultural machinery companies may employ agricultural equipment technicians to supervise production, assembly, and plant operations.

Most manufacturers market their products through regional sales organizations to individual dealers. Technicians may serve as *sales representatives* of regional sales offices, where they are assigned a number of dealers in a given territory and sell agricultural equipment directly to them. They may also conduct sales-training programs for the dealers to help them become more effective salespeople.

These technicians are also qualified to work in sales positions within dealerships, either as *equipment sales workers* or *parts clerks*. They are required to perform equipment demonstrations for customers. They also appraise the value of used equipment for trade-in allowances. Technicians in these positions may advance to sales or parts manager positions.

Some technicians involved in sales become *systems specialists*, who work for equipment dealerships, assisting farmers in the planning and installation of various kinds of mechanized systems, such as irrigation or materials-handling systems, grain bins, or drying systems.

In the service area, technicians may work as *field service representatives*, forming a liaison between the companies they represent and the dealers. They assist the dealers in product warranty work, diagnose service problems, and give seminars or workshops on new service information and techniques. These types of service technicians may begin their careers as specialists in certain kinds of repairs. *Hydraulic specialists*, for instance, maintain and repair the component parts of hydraulic systems in tractors and other agricultural machines. *Diesel specialists* rebuild, calibrate, and test diesel pumps, injectors, and other diesel engine components.

Many service technicians work as service managers or parts department managers. *Service managers* assign duties to the repair workers, diagnose machinery problems, estimate repair costs for customers, and manage the repair shop.

Parts department managers in equipment dealerships maintain inventories of all the parts that may be requested either by customers or by the service departments of the dealership. They deal directly with customers, parts suppliers, and dealership managers and must have good sales and purchasing skills. They also must be effective business managers.

Technicians working on the farm have various responsibilities, the most important of which is keeping machinery in top working condition during the growing season. During off-season periods, they may overhaul or modify equipment or simply keep the machinery in good working order for the next season.

Some technicians find employment as *on-farm machinery managers*, usually working on large farms servicing or supervising the servicing of all automated equipment. They also monitor the field operation of all machines and keep complete records of costs, utilization, and repair procedures relating to the maintenance of each piece of mechanical equipment.

REQUIREMENTS

High School

You should take as many mathematics, technical/shop, and mechanical drawing classes as you can. Take science classes, including courses in earth science, to gain some insight into agriculture, soil conservation, and the environment. Look into adult education programs available to high school students; in such a program, you may be able to enroll in pre-engineering courses.

Postsecondary Training

A high school diploma is necessary, and some college and specialized experience is also important. A four-year education, along with some continuing education courses, can be very helpful in pursuing work, particularly if you're seeking jobs with the government.

Postsecondary education for the agricultural equipment technician should include courses in general agriculture, agricultural power and equipment, practical engineering, hydraulics, agricultural-equipment business methods, electrical equipment, engineering, social science, economics, and sales techniques. On-the-job experience during the summer is invaluable and frequently is included as part of the regular curriculum in these programs. Students are placed on farms, functioning as technicians-in-training. They also may work in farm equipment dealerships where their time is divided among the sales, parts, and service departments. Occupational experience, one of the most important phases of the postsecondary training program, gives students an opportunity to discover which field best suits them and which phase of the business they prefer. Upon completion of this program, most technical and community colleges award an associate's degree.

Other Requirements

The work of the agricultural equipment technician is similar to that of an engineer. You must have knowledge of physical science and engineering principles and enough mathematical background to work with these principles. You must have a working knowledge of farm crops, machinery, and all agricultural-related products. You should be detail-oriented. You should also have people skills, as you'll be working closely with professionals, other technicians, and farmers.

EXPLORING

If you live in a farming community, you've probably already had some experience with farming equipment. Vocational agriculture education programs in high schools can be found in most rural settings, many suburban settings, and even in some urban schools. The teaching staff and counselors in these schools can provide considerable information about this career.

Light industrial machinery is now used in almost every industry. It is always helpful to watch machinery being used and to talk with people who own, operate, and repair it.

Summer and part-time work on a farm, in an agricultural equipment manufacturing plant, or in an equipment sales and service business offers opportunities to work on or near agricultural and light industrial machinery. Such a job may provide you with a clearer idea about the various activities, challenges, rewards, and possible limitations of this career.

EMPLOYERS

Approximately 33,000 agricultural equipment technicians are employed in the United States. Depending on their area of specialization, technicians work for engineers, manufacturers, scientists, sales and services companies, and farmers. They can also find work with government agencies, such as the U.S. Department of Agriculture.

STARTING OUT

It is still possible to enter this career by starting as an inexperienced worker in a machinery manufacturer's plant or on a farm and learning machine technician skills on the job. However, this approach is becoming increasingly difficult due to the complexity of modern machinery. Because of this, some formal classroom training is usually necessary, and many people find it difficult to complete even part-time study of the field's theory and science while also working a full-time job.

Operators and managers of large, well-equipped farms and farm equipment companies in need of employees keep in touch with colleges offering agricultural equipment programs. Students who do well during their occupational experience period usually have an excellent chance of going to work for the same employer after graduation. Many colleges have an interview day on which personnel representatives of manufacturers, distributors, farm owners or managers, and dealers are invited to recruit students completing technician programs. In general, any student who does well in a training program can expect employment immediately upon graduation.

ADVANCEMENT

Opportunities for advancement and self-employment are excellent for those with the initiative to keep abreast of continuing developments in the farm equipment field. Technicians often attend company schools in sales and service or take advanced evening courses in colleges.

EARNINGS

Agricultural technicians working for the government may be able to enter a position at GS-5 (government wage scale), which was $25,623 in 2007. The U.S. Department of Labor reports that median annual earnings for agricultural equipment mechanics were $29,460 in 2006. Hourly wages ranged from less than $9.30 ($19,340 a year) to more than $20.77 ($43,210 a year). Those working on farms often receive room and board as a supplement to their annual salary. The salary that technicians eventually receive depends—as do most salaries—on individual ability, initiative, and the supply of skilled technicians in the field of work or locality. There is opportunity to work overtime during planting and harvesting seasons.

In addition to their salaries, most technicians receive fringe benefits such as health and retirement packages, paid vacations, and other benefits similar to those received by engineering technicians. Technicians employed in sales are usually paid a commission in addition to their base salary.

WORK ENVIRONMENT

Working conditions vary according to the type of field chosen. Technicians who are employed by large farming operations will work indoors or outdoors depending on the season and the tasks that need to be done. Planning machine overhauls and the directing of such work usually are done in enclosed spaces equipped for it. As implied by its name, field servicing and repairs are done in the field.

Some agricultural equipment sales representatives work in their own or nearby communities, while others must travel extensively.

Technicians in agricultural equipment research, development, and production usually work under typical factory conditions: some work in an office or laboratory; others work in a manufacturing plant; or, in some cases, field testing and demonstration are performed where the machinery will be used.

For technicians who assemble, adjust, modify, or test equipment and for those who provide customer service, application studies, and maintenance services, the surroundings may be similar to large automobile service centers.

In all cases, safety precautions must be a constant concern. Appropriate clothing, an acute awareness of one's environment, and careful lifting or hoisting of heavy machinery must be standard. While safety practices have improved greatly over the years, certain risks do exist. Heavy lifting may cause injury, and burns and cuts are always possible. The surroundings may be noisy and grimy. Some work is performed in cramped or awkward physical positions. Gasoline fumes and odors from oil products are a constant factor. Most technicians ordinarily work a 40-hour week, but emergency repairs may require overtime.

OUTLOOK

The *Occupational Outlook Handbook* reports that employment of agricultural equipment technicians is expected to grow more slowly than the average for all occupations through 2014. However, agricultural equipment businesses now demand more expertise than ever before. A variety of complex specialized machines and mechanical devices are steadily being produced and modified to help farmers improve the quality and productivity of their labor. These machines require trained technicians to design, produce, test, sell, and service them. Trained workers also are needed to instruct the final owners in their proper repair, operation, and maintenance.

In addition, the agricultural industry is adopting advanced computer and electronic technology. Computer skills are becoming more and more useful in this field. Precision farming will also require specialized training as more agricultural equipment becomes hooked up to satellite systems.

As agriculture becomes more technical, the agricultural equipment technician will assume an increasingly vital role in helping farmers solve problems that interfere with efficient production. These opportunities exist not only in the United States, but also worldwide. As agricultural economies everywhere become mechanized, inventive technicians with training in modern business principles will find expanding employment opportunities abroad.

FOR MORE INFORMATION

To read equipment sales statistics, agricultural reports, and other news of interest to agricultural equipment technicians, visit
Association of Equipment Manufacturers
6737 West Washington Street, Suite 2400
Milwaukee, WI 53214-5647
Tel: 414-272-0943
Email: info@aem.org
http://www.aem.org

Visit the following Web site to learn about publications and read industry news:

Farm Equipment Manufacturers Association
1000 Executive Parkway, Suite 100
St. Louis, MO 63141-6369
Tel: 314-878-2304
Email: info@farmequip.org
http://www.farmequip.org

For information on student chapters and the many activities available, contact

National FFA Organization
6060 FFA Drive
PO Box 68960
Indianapolis, IN 46268-0960
Tel: 317-802-6060
Email: membership@ffa.org
http://www.ffa.org

Aircraft Mechanics

QUICK FACTS

School Subjects
Computer science
Technical/shop

Personal Skills
Mechanical/manipulative
Technical/scientific

Work Environment
Indoors and outdoors
One location with some
travel

Minimum Education Level
Some postsecondary training

Salary Range
$31,080 to $47,740 to
$71,780+

Certification or Licensing
Recommended

Outlook
About as fast as the average

DOT
621

GOE
05.03.01

NOC
2244, 7315

O*NET-SOC
49-3011.00, 49-3011.01,
49-3011.02, 49-3011.03

OVERVIEW

Aircraft mechanics examine, service, repair, and overhaul aircraft and aircraft engines. They also repair, replace, and assemble parts of the airframe (the structural parts of the plane other than the power plant or engine). There are about 142,000 aircraft mechanics working in the United States.

HISTORY

On December 17, 1903, Wilbur and Orville Wright made history's first successful powered flight. The Wright brothers—who originally built and repaired bicycles—designed, built, and repaired their airplane, including the engine, making them the first airplane mechanics as well. In the early years of aviation, most airplane designers filled a similar scope of functions, although many had people to assist them. As the aviation industry grew, the various tasks required to design, build, operate, and repair aircraft became more specialized. However, because of the instability of early planes and the uncertainty of the weather and other conditions, it was often necessary for pilots to have a strong working knowledge of how to repair and maintain their aircraft. In later years, one important route to becoming a pilot was to start as an aircraft mechanic.

As aircraft became capable of flying faster, for longer distances, and at higher altitudes, and especially after aircraft began to carry passengers, the role of the aircraft mechanic became vital to the safety of the aircraft and the growth of the aviation industry. New technologies have continually been introduced into the design of aircraft, and mechanics needed to be familiar with all the systems, from the airframe to the engine to the control systems. The complexity of airplane design increased to the point where the mechanics themselves began to specialize. Some mechanics had the skills to work on the entire aircraft. Others were able to work on the airframe, on the engines, or on the power plant. Some mechanics functioned as repairers, who completed minor repairs to the plane. Mechanics were assisted by technicians, who were often training to become fully qualified mechanics. With the introduction of electronics into aircraft, some mechanics specialized as avionics technicians.

The Air Commerce Act of 1926 imposed regulations on the commercial airlines and their fleets. The Federal Aviation Agency, later called the Federal Aviation Administration (FAA), also established training and licensing requirements for the mechanics servicing the airplanes. Mechanics were also an important part of the armed forces, especially as the world entered World War II, in which air power became a vital part of successful military operations.

The growth of the general aviation industry, which includes all flights operated outside of the airlines, provided still more demand for trained mechanics. The introduction of ultralight aircraft in the 1970s brought air flight back to its origins: these craft were often sold as kits that the purchasers had to build and repair themselves.

THE JOB

The work of aircraft mechanics employed by the commercial airlines may be classified into two categories, that of line maintenance mechanics and overhaul mechanics.

Line maintenance mechanics are all-around craft workers who make repairs on all parts of the plane. Working at the airport, they make emergency and other necessary repairs in the time between when aircraft land and when they take off again. They may be told by the pilot, flight engineer, or head mechanic what repairs need to be made, or they may thoroughly inspect the plane themselves for oil leaks, cuts or dents in the surface and tires, or any malfunction in the radio, radar, and light equipment. In addition, their duties include changing oil, cleaning spark plugs, and replenishing the hydraulic and oxygen systems. They work as fast as safety permits so the aircraft can be put back into service quickly.

Overhaul mechanics keep the aircraft in top operating condition by performing scheduled maintenance, making repairs, and conducting inspections required by the FAA. Scheduled maintenance programs are based on the number of hours flown, calendar days, or a combination of these factors. Overhaul mechanics work at the airline's main overhaul base on either or both of the two major parts of the aircraft: the airframe, which includes wings, fuselage, tail assembly, landing gear, control cables, propeller assembly, and fuel and oil tanks; or the power plant, which may be a radial (internal combustion), turbojet, turboprop, or rocket engine.

Airframe mechanics work on parts of the aircraft other than the engine, inspecting the various components of the airframe for worn or defective parts. They check the sheet-metal surfaces, measure the tension of control cables, and check for rust, distortion, and cracks in the fuselage and wings. They consult manufacturers' manuals and the airline's maintenance manual for specifications and to determine whether repair or replacement is needed to correct defects or malfunctions. They also use specialized computer software to assist them in determining the need, extent, and nature of repairs. Airframe mechanics repair, replace, and assemble parts using a variety of tools, including power shears, sheet-metal breakers, arc and acetylene welding equipment, rivet guns, and air or electric drills.

Aircraft powerplant mechanics inspect, service, repair, and overhaul the engine of the aircraft. Looking through specially designed openings while working from ladders or scaffolds, they examine an engine's external appearance for such problems as cracked cylinders, oil leaks, or cracks or breaks in the turbine blades. They also listen to the engine in operation to detect sounds indicating malfunctioning components, such as sticking or burned valves. The test equipment used to check the engine's operation includes ignition analyzers, compression checkers, distributor timers, and ammeters. If necessary, the mechanics remove the engine from the aircraft, using a hoist or a forklift truck, and take the engine apart. They use sensitive instruments to measure parts for wear and use X-ray and magnetic inspection equipment to check for invisible cracks. Worn or damaged parts are replaced or repaired; then the mechanics reassemble and reinstall the engine.

Aircraft mechanics adjust and repair electrical wiring systems and aircraft accessories and instruments; inspect, service, and repair pneumatic and hydraulic systems; and handle various servicing tasks, such as flushing crankcases, cleaning screens, greasing moving parts, and checking brakes.

Mechanics may work on only one type of aircraft or on many different types, such as jets, propeller-driven planes, and helicopters. For greater efficiency, some specialize in one section, such as the electrical system, of a particular type of aircraft. Among the specialists, there are airplane electricians; pneumatic testers and pressure sealer-and-testers; aircraft body repairers and bonded struc-

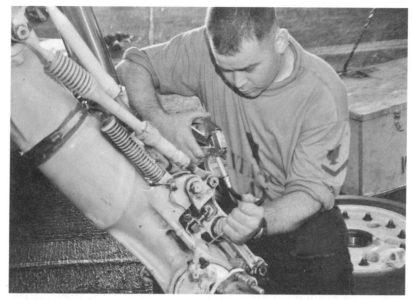

Aircraft mechanics must be able to work with precision and have better-than-average strength and physical dexterity. *(U.S. Department of Defense)*

tures repairers, such as burnishers and bumpers; and air conditioning mechanics, aircraft rigging and controls mechanics, plumbing and hydraulics mechanics, and experimental-aircraft testing mechanics. *Avionics technicians* are mechanics who specialize in the aircraft's electronic systems.

Mechanics who work for businesses that own their own aircraft usually handle all necessary repair and maintenance work. The planes, however, generally are small and the work is less complex than in repair shops.

In small, independent repair shops, mechanics must inspect and repair many different types of aircraft. The airplanes may include small commuter planes run by an aviation company, private company planes and jets, private individually owned aircraft, and planes used for flying instruction.

REQUIREMENTS

High School

The first requirement for prospective aircraft mechanics is a high school diploma. Courses in mathematics, physics, chemistry, and mechanical drawing are particularly helpful because they teach the principles involved in the operation of an aircraft, and this knowledge is often necessary to making the repairs. Machine shop, auto mechanics, or electrical shop are important courses for gaining many skills needed by aircraft mechanics.

Postsecondary Training

At one time, mechanics were able to acquire their skills through on-the-job training. This is rare today. Now most mechanics learn the job either in the armed forces or in trade schools approved by the FAA. The trade schools provide training with the necessary tools and equipment in programs that range in length from two years to 30 months. In considering applicants for certification, the FAA sometimes accepts successful completion of such schooling in place of work experience, but the schools do not guarantee an FAA certificate. There are about 170 such schools in the United States.

The experience acquired by aircraft mechanics in the armed forces sometimes satisfies the work requirements for FAA certification, and veterans may be able to pass the exam with a limited amount of additional study. But jobs in the military service are usually too specialized to satisfy the FAA requirement for broad work experience. In that case, veterans applying for FAA approval will have to complete a training program at a trade school. Schools occasionally give some credit for material learned in the service. However, on the plus side, airlines are especially eager to hire aircraft mechanics with both military experience and a trade school education.

Certification or Licensing

FAA certification is necessary for certain types of aircraft mechanics and is usually required to advance beyond entry-level positions. Most mechanics who work on civilian aircraft have FAA authorization as airframe mechanics, power plant mechanics, or avionics repair specialists. Airframe mechanics are qualified to work on the fuselage, wings, landing gear, and other structural parts of the aircraft; power plant mechanics are qualified for work on the engine. Mechanics may qualify for both airframe and power plant licensing, allowing them to work on any part of the plane. Combination airframe and power plant mechanics with an inspector's certificate are permitted to certify inspection work done by other mechanics. Mechanics without certification must be supervised by certified mechanics.

FAA certification is granted only to aircraft mechanics with previous work experience: a minimum of 18 months for an airframe or power plant certificate and at least 30 months working with both engines and airframes for a combination certificate. To qualify for an inspector's certificate, mechanics must have held a combined airframe and power plant certificate for at least three years. In addition, all applicants for certification must pass written and oral tests and demonstrate their ability to do the work authorized by the certificate.

Other Requirements

Aircraft mechanics must be able to work with precision and meet rigid standards. Their physical condition is also important. They need more than average strength for lifting heavy parts and tools, as well as agility for reaching and climbing. And they should not be afraid of heights, since they may work on top of the wings and fuselages of large jet planes.

In addition to education and certification, union membership may be a requirement for some jobs, particularly for mechanics employed by major airlines. The principal unions organizing aircraft mechanics are the International Association of Machinists and Aerospace Workers and the Transport Workers Union of America. In addition, some mechanics are represented by the International Brotherhood of Teamsters.

EXPLORING

Working with electronic kits, tinkering with automobile engines, and assembling model airplanes are good ways of gauging your ability to do the kinds of work performed by aircraft mechanics. A guided tour of an airfield can give you a brief overall view of this industry. Even better would be a part-time or summer job with an airline in an area such as the baggage department. Small airports may also offer job opportunities for part-time, summer, or replacement workers. You may also earn a student pilot certificate at the age of 16 and may gain more insight into the basic workings of an airplane that way. Kits for building ultralight craft are also available and may provide even more insight into the importance of proper maintenance and repair.

More exotic types of engines also exist, such as rocket engines and scramjets, which can boost an aircraft to more than seven times the speed of sound. However, these types of engines are rarely seen outside of rare, highly experimental aircraft.

EMPLOYERS

Of the roughly 142,000 aircraft mechanics currently employed in the United States, more than half work for air transportation companies, according to the U.S. Department of Labor. Each airline usually has one main overhaul base, where most of its mechanics are employed. These bases are found along the main airline routes or near large cities, including New York, Chicago, Los Angeles, Atlanta, San Francisco, and Miami.

About 18 percent of aircraft mechanics work for the federal government. Many of these mechanics are civilians employed at military aviation installations, while others work for the FAA, mainly in Oklahoma City, Atlantic City, Wichita, and Washington, D.C. About 14 percent of mechanics works for aircraft assembly firms. Most of the rest are general aviation mechanics employed by independent repair shops at airports around the country, by businesses that use their own planes for transporting employees or cargo, by certified supplemental airlines, or by crop-dusting and air-taxi firms.

STARTING OUT

High school graduates who wish to become aircraft mechanics may enter this field by enrolling in an FAA-approved trade school. (Note that there are schools offering this training that do not have FAA approval.) These schools generally have placement services available for their graduates.

Another method is to make direct application to the employment offices of companies providing air transportation and services or the local offices of the state employment service, although airlines prefer to employ people who have already completed training. Many airports are managed by private fixed-base operators, which also operate the airport's repair and maintenance facilities. The field may also be entered through enlistment in the armed forces.

ADVANCEMENT

Promotions depend in part on the size of the organization for which an aircraft mechanic works. The first promotion after beginning employment is usually based on merit and comes in the form of a salary increase. To advance further, many companies require the mechanic to have a combined airframe and power plant certificate, or perhaps an aircraft inspector's certificate.

Advancement could take the following route: journeyworker mechanic, head mechanic or crew chief, inspector, head inspector, and shop supervisor. With additional training, a mechanic may advance to engineering, administrative, or executive positions. In larger airlines, mechanics may advance to become flight engineers, then copilots and pilots. With business training, some mechanics open their own repair shops.

EARNINGS

Although some aircraft mechanics, especially at the entry level and at small businesses, earn little more than the minimum wage, the

Earnings by Specialty, 2006

Industry	Mean Annual Earnings
Oil and gas extraction	$59,840
Scheduled air transportation	$58,080
Nonscheduled air transportation	$49,620
Federal executive branch	$48,760
Aerospace product and parts manufacturing	$45,800
Support activities for air transportation	$40,730

Source: U.S. Department of Labor

median annual income for aircraft mechanics was about $47,740 in 2006, according to the U.S. Department of Labor. The top 10 percent earned more than $71,780, while the bottom 10 percent earned $31,080 or less. Mechanics with airframe and powerplant certification earn more than those without it. Overtime, night shift, and holiday pay differentials are usually available and can greatly increase a mechanic's annual earnings.

Most major airlines are covered by union agreements. Their mechanics generally earn more than those working for other employers. Contracts usually include health insurance and often life insurance and retirement plans as well. An attractive fringe benefit for airline mechanics and their immediate families is free or reduced fares on their own and many other airlines. Mechanics working for the federal government also benefit from the greater job security of civil service and government jobs.

WORK ENVIRONMENT

Most aircraft mechanics work a five-day, 40-hour week. Their working hours, however, may be irregular and often include nights, weekends, and holidays, as airlines operate 24 hours a day, and extra work is required during holiday seasons.

When doing overhauling and major inspection work, aircraft mechanics generally work in hangars with adequate heat, ventilation, and lights. If the hangars are full, however, or if repairs must be made quickly, they may work outdoors, sometimes in unpleasant weather. Outdoor work is frequent for line maintenance mechanics, who work at airports, because they must make minor repairs and preflight checks at the terminal to save time. To maintain flight schedules, or to keep from inconveniencing customers in general aviation, the mechanics often have to work under time pressure.

The work is physically strenuous and demanding. Mechanics often have to lift or pull as much as 70 pounds of weight. They may stand, lie, or kneel in awkward positions, sometimes in precarious places such as on a scaffold or ladder.

Noise and vibration are common when testing engines. Regardless of the stresses and strains, aircraft mechanics are expected to work quickly and with great precision.

Although the power tools and test equipment are provided by the employer, mechanics may be expected to furnish their own hand tools.

OUTLOOK

Despite recent fluctuations in air travel, the outlook for aircraft mechanics should remain steady over the course of the next decade. Employment opportunities will open up due to fewer young workers entering the labor force, fewer entrants from the military, and more retirees leaving positions. But the job prospects will vary according to the type of employer. Less competition for jobs is likely to be found at smaller commuter and regional airlines, FAA repair stations, and in general aviation. These employers pay lower wages and fewer applicants compete for their positions, while higher paying airline positions, which also include travel benefits, are more in demand among qualified applicants. Mechanics who keep up with technological advancements in electronics, composite materials, and other areas will be in greatest demand.

Employment of aircraft mechanics is likely to increase about as fast as the average for all occupations through 2014, according to the U.S. Department of Labor. The demand for air travel and the numbers of aircraft created are expected to increase due to population growth and rising incomes. However, employment growth will be affected by the use of automated systems that make the aircraft mechanic's job more efficient.

FOR MORE INFORMATION

For career information, contact
   Federal Aviation Administration
   800 Independence Avenue, SW, Room 810
   Washington, DC 20591-0001
   Tel: 866-835-5322
   http://www.faa.gov/careers

For information on aviation maintenance and scholarships, contact
Professional Aviation Maintenance Association
400 Commonwealth Drive
Warrendale, PA 15096-0001
Tel: 866-865-7262
Email: hq@pama.org
http://www.pama.org

Appliance Service Technicians

OVERVIEW

Appliance service technicians install and service many kinds of electrical and gas appliances, such as washing machines, dryers, refrigerators, ranges, and vacuum cleaners. Some repairers specialize in one type of appliance, such as air conditioners, while others work with a variety of appliances, both large and small, used in homes and business establishments. There are approximately 50,000 appliance service technicians employed in the United States.

HISTORY

Although some small home appliances, including irons and coffee makers, were patented before the 20th century began, only a few types were in general use before the end of World War I. Around that time, however, more efficient and inexpensive electric motors were developed, which made appliances more affordable to the public. In addition, electric and gas utility companies began extending their services into all parts of the nation. As a result, many new laborsaving appliances began to appear on the market. Eventually, consumers began to rely increasingly on a wide variety of machines to make everyday tasks easier and more pleasant, both at home and at work. Soon, many kinds of equipment, such as washing machines and kitchen ranges, were considered an essential part of middle-class life.

Since the end of World War II, there has been a tremendous growth in the use and production of home appliances. The increasing use of appliances has created the need for qualified people to install, repair, and service them. Today's service technicians need a different mix of knowledge and skills than was needed by the appliance repairers of years ago, however, because today's appliances often involve complex electronic parts. The use of electronic components is advantageous to consumers because the electronic appliances are more reliable. However, the fact that modern appliances need fewer repairs means that the demand for appliance technicians is no longer growing as fast as the use of new appliances.

THE JOB

Appliance technicians use a variety of methods and test equipment to figure out what repairs are needed. They inspect machines for frayed electrical cords, cracked hoses, and broken connections; listen for loud vibrations or grinding noises; sniff for fumes or overheated materials; look for fluid leaks; and watch and feel other moving parts to determine if they are jammed or too tight. They may find the cause of trouble by using special test equipment made for particular appliances or standard testing devices such as voltmeters and ammeters. They must be able to combine all their observations into a diagnosis of the problem before they can repair the appliance.

Technicians often need to disassemble the appliance and examine its inner components. To do this, they often use ordinary hand tools like screwdrivers, wrenches, and pliers. They may need to follow instructions in service manuals and troubleshooting guides. To understand electrical circuitry, they may consult wiring diagrams or schematics.

After the problem has been determined, the technician must correct it. This may involve replacing or repairing defective parts, such as belts, switches, motors, circuit boards, or gears. The technician also cleans, lubricates, and adjusts the parts so that they function as well and as smoothly as possible.

Those who service gas appliances may replace pipes, valves, thermostats, and indicator devices. In installing gas appliances, they may need to measure, cut, and connect the pipes to gas feeder lines and to do simple carpentry work such as cutting holes in floors to allow pipes to pass through.

Technicians who make service calls to homes and businesses must often answer customers' questions and deal with their complaints.

They may explain to customers how to use the appliance and advise them about proper care. These technicians are often responsible for ordering parts from catalogs and recording the time spent, the parts used, and whether a warranty applies to the repair job. They may need to estimate the cost of repairs, collect payment for their work, and sell new or used appliances. Many technicians who make service calls drive light trucks or automobiles equipped with two-way radios or cellular phones so that as soon as they finish one job, they can be dispatched to another.

Many appliance service technicians repair all different kinds of appliances; there are also those who specialize in one particular kind or one brand of appliances. *Window air-conditioning unit install-ers and technicians,* for example, work only with portable window units, while *domestic air-conditioning technicians* work with both window and central systems in homes.

Household appliance installers specialize in installing major household appliances, such as refrigerators, freezers, washing machines, clothes dryers, kitchen ranges, and ovens; *household appliance technicians* maintain and repair these units.

Small electrical appliance technicians repair portable household electrical appliances such as toasters, coffee makers, lamps, hair dryers, fans, food processors, dehumidifiers, and irons. Customers usually bring these types of appliances to service centers to have them repaired.

Gas appliance technicians install, repair, and clean gas appliances such as ranges or stoves, heaters, and gas furnaces. They also advise customers on the safe, efficient, and economical use of gas.

REQUIREMENTS

High School

Appliance technicians usually must be high school graduates with some knowledge of electricity (especially wiring diagrams) and, if possible, electronics. If you are interested in this field, you should take as many shop classes as possible to gain a familiarity with machines and tools. Electrical shop is particularly helpful because of the increasing use of electronic components in appliances. Mathematics and physics are good choices to build knowledge of mechanical principles. Computer classes will also be useful.

Postsecondary Training

Prospective technicians are sometimes hired as helpers and acquire most of their skills through on-the-job experience. Some employers assign such helpers to accompany experienced technicians when they are sent to do repairs in customers' homes and businesses. The trainees observe and assist in diagnosing and correcting problems with appliances. Other employers assign helpers to work in the company's service center where they learn how to rebuild used appliances and make simple repairs. At the end of six to 12 months, they usually know enough to make most repairs on their own, and they may be sent on unsupervised service calls.

An additional one to two years of experience is often required for trainees to become fully qualified. Trainees may attend service schools sponsored by appliance manufacturers and study service manuals to familiarize themselves with appliances, particularly new models. Reading manuals and attending courses is a continuing part of any technician's job.

Many technicians train at public or private technical and vocational schools that provide formal classroom training and laboratory experience in the service and repair of appliances. The length of these programs varies, although most last between one and two years. Correspondence courses that teach basic appliance repair are also available. Although formal training in the skills needed for appliance repair can be a great advantage for job applicants, newly graduated technicians should expect additional on-the-job training to acquaint them with the particular work done in their new employer's service center.

Certification or Licensing

In some states, appliance technicians may need to be licensed or registered. Licenses are granted to applicants who meet certain standards of education, training, and experience and who pass an examination. Since 1994, the Environmental Protection Agency (EPA) has required certification for all technicians who work with appliances containing refrigerants known as chlorofluorocarbons. Since these refrigerants can be harmful to the environment, technicians must be educated and tested on their handling in order to achieve certification to work with them.

The National Appliance Service Technician Certification Program (NASTeC) offers certification on four levels: refrigeration and air conditioning; cooking; laundry and dishwashing; and universal technician (all three specialties). To earn NASTeC certification, candidates must pass a basic skills exam and at least one of the three specialty exams. Technicians who pass all four exams are certified as NASTeC universal technicians.

The Professional Service Association (PSA) also offers certification to appliance repairers. The PSA offers the following certifications to technicians who pass an examination: certified master technician, certified technician, certified service manager, and certified consumer specialist. Certification is valid for four years, at which time technicians must apply for recertification and pass another examination. Certified technicians who complete at least 15 credit hours of continuing education annually during the four years do not need to retake the examination to gain recertification. Additionally, the certified graduate technician designation is available to vocational school graduates who have completed their training. After working for two years as an appliance service technician, holders of this designation can seek to upgrade to the master technician designation.

The North American Retail Dealers Association offers a certification program for those who recover refrigerant from appliances categorized as "Type I" by the EPA. These include refrigerators and freezers designed for home use, room air conditioners including window models, packaged terminal air conditioners, packaged terminal heat pumps, dehumidifiers, under-the-counter icemakers, vending machines, and drinking water coolers. Contact the association for more information on certification requirements.

Other Requirements

Technicians must possess not only the skills and mechanical aptitude necessary to repair appliances but also skills in consumer relations. They must be able to deal courteously with all types of people and be able to convince their customers that the products they repair will continue to give satisfactory service for some time to come. Technicians must work effectively with little supervision, since they often spend their days alone, going from job to job. It is necessary that they be accurate and careful in their repair work, as their customers rely on them to correct problems properly.

EXPLORING

You can explore the field by talking to employees of local appliance service centers and dealerships. These employees may know about part-time or summer jobs that will enable you to observe and assist with repair work. You can also judge interest and aptitude for this work by taking shop courses, especially electrical shop, and assembling electronic equipment from kits.

EMPLOYERS

Currently, about 50,000 appliance service technicians are employed throughout the United States in service centers, appliance manufacturers, retail dealerships, and utility companies. They may also be self-employed in independent repair shops or work at companies that service specific types of appliances, such as coin-operated laundry equipment and dry-cleaning machines.

STARTING OUT

One way of entering this occupation is to become a helper in a service center where the employer provides on-the-job training to qualified workers. To find a helper's job, prospective technicians should apply directly to local service centers or appliance dealerships. They also can watch area newspaper classified ads for entry-level jobs in appliance service and repair.

For those who have graduated from a technical or vocational program, their schools' career services offices may also prove helpful.

ADVANCEMENT

Advancement possibilities for appliance service technicians depend primarily on their place of employment. In a small service center of three to five people, advancement to a supervisory position will likely be slow, because the owner usually performs most of the supervisory and administrative tasks. However, pay incentives do exist in smaller service centers that encourage technicians to assume a greater share of the management load. Technicians working for large retailers, factory service centers, or gas or electric utility companies may be able to progress to supervisor, assistant service manager, or service manager.

Another advancement route leads to teaching at a factory service training school. A technician who knows the factory's product, works with proficiency, and speaks effectively to groups can conduct classes to train other technicians. Technical and vocational schools that offer courses in appliance repair work may also hire experienced repairers to teach classes.

Some service technicians aspire to opening an independent repair business or service center. This step usually requires knowledge of business management and marketing and a significant investment in tools, parts, vehicles, and other equipment.

Some technicians who work for appliance manufacturers move into positions where they write service manuals, sell appliances, or act as manufacturers' service representatives to independent service centers.

EARNINGS

The earnings of appliance technicians vary widely according to geographic location, type of equipment serviced, workers' skills and experience, and other factors. In 2006, the median annual salary for home appliance technicians was about $33,860, according to the U.S. Department of Labor. At the low end of the salary scale, some technicians earned less than $19,490. Technicians at the high end of the pay scale earned $53,750 or more per year. Trainees are usually paid less than technicians who have completed their training period. Employees of gas utility companies and other large companies generally command higher hourly wages than those who work for service centers. Some service centers, however, offer incentives for technicians to increase their productivity. Some of these incentive plans are very lucrative and can allow a proficient worker to add considerably to his or her salary.

Opportunities for overtime pay are most favorable for repairers of major appliances, such as refrigerators, stoves, and washing machines. In addition to regular pay, many workers receive paid vacations and sick leave, health insurance, and other benefits such as employer contributions to retirement pension plans.

WORK ENVIRONMENT

Appliance technicians generally work a standard 40-hour week, although some work evenings and weekends. Repairers who work on cooling equipment, such as refrigerators and air conditioners, may need to put in extra hours during hot weather. In general, there is little seasonal fluctuation of employment in this occupation, since repairs on appliances are needed at all times of the year and the work is done indoors.

Technicians encounter a variety of working conditions depending on the kinds of appliances they install or repair. Those who fix small appliances work indoors at a bench and seldom have to handle heavy objects. Their workplaces are generally well lighted, properly ventilated, and equipped with the necessary tools.

Repairers who work on major appliances must deal with a variety of situations. They normally do their work on site, so they may spend several hours each day driving from one job to the next. To do repairs, they may have to work in small or dirty spaces or in other uncomfortable conditions. They may have to crawl, bend, stoop, crouch, or lie down to carry out some repairs, and they may have to move heavy items. Because they work in a variety of environments, they may encounter unpleasant situations, such as dirt, odors, or pest infestation.

In any appliance repair work, technicians must follow good safety procedures, especially when handling potentially dangerous tools, gas, and electric currents.

OUTLOOK

The U.S. Department of Labor reports that through 2014 the total number of repairers is expected to grow more slowly than the average for all occupations. Although Americans will certainly continue buying and using more appliances, today's machines are often made with electronic components that require fewer repairs than their nonelectronic counterparts. Thus, the dependability of the technology built into these new appliances will restrain growth in the repair field. Most openings that arise will be due to workers leaving their jobs who must be replaced. However, the employment outlook will remain good, with job openings outnumbering job seekers, since relatively few people wish to enter this industry. Opportunities are expected to be better for wage and salary workers than self-employed technicians who service appliances in peoples' homes.

FOR MORE INFORMATION

For information on the National Appliance Service Technician Certification Program, contact
> International Society of Certified Electronics Technicians
> 3608 Pershing Avenue
> Fort Worth, TX 76107-4527
> Tel: 800-946-0201
> Email: info@iscet.org
> http://www.iscet.org

For industry information, contact
> National Appliance Service Association
> PO Box 2514
> Kokomo, IN 46904-2514
> Tel: 765-453-1820
> Email: nasahq@sbcglobal.net
> http://www.nasa1.org

For information on the Refrigerant Recovery Certification Test Program, contact
> North American Retail Dealers Association
> 4700 West Lake Avenue
> Glenview, IL 60025-1468
> Tel: 800-621-0298
> Email: nardasvc@narda.com
> http://www.narda.com

For information on a career as an appliance service technician and certification, contact

Professional Service Association
71 Columbia Street
Cohoes, NY 12047-2939
Tel: 888-777-8851
Email: psa@psaworld.com
http://www.psaworld.com

Automobile Collision Repairers

OVERVIEW

Automobile collision repairers repair, replace, and repaint damaged body parts of automobiles, buses, and light trucks. They use hand tools and power tools to straighten bent frames and body sections, replace badly damaged parts, smooth out minor dents and creases, remove rust, fill small holes or dents, and repaint surfaces damaged by accident or wear. Some repairers also give repair estimates. There are approximately 223,000 automobile collision repairers working in the United States, with approximately 10 percent specializing in automotive glass installation and repair.

HISTORY

The proliferation of the automobile in American society in the 1920s meant new opportunities for many who had not traveled far beyond their hometown. It also created something else by the thousands—jobs. One profession necessitated by America's new love for automobiles was that of the collision repairer. With ill-prepared roads suddenly overrun by inexperienced drivers, accidents and breakdowns became a common problem.

Automobiles were significantly simpler in the early years. Body repairs often could be performed by the owner or someone with general mechanical aptitude. Minor body dents, if they did not affect driving, were usually left alone. As cars became more complex and as society grew ever more fond of their automobiles, the need for qualified collision repairers grew.

Automobiles suddenly became major status symbols, and people were no longer indifferent to minor dents and fender-benders. To many, dents were intolerable. New body styles and materials made body repairs a difficult job. To meet this new demand, some automobile mechanics shifted their focus from repairs under the hood to repairs to the body of automobiles.

By the 1950s, automobile body repair garages were common in cities throughout the United States. More drivers carried vehicle insurance to protect against loss due to an accident. The insurance industry began to work more closely with automobile collision repairers. Since traffic control methods and driving rules and regulations were not very well established, frequent car accidents kept these repair garages busy year-round. Most collision repairers learned the trade through hands-on experience as an apprentice or on their own through trial and error. When automakers began packing their cars with new technology, involving complex electrical circuitry, computer controlled mechanisms, and new materials, as well as basic design changes, collision repairers found themselves in need of comprehensive training.

THE JOB

Automobile collision repairers repair the damage vehicles sustain in traffic accidents and through normal wear. Repairers straighten bent bodies, remove dents, and replace parts that are beyond repair. Just as a variety of skills are needed to build an automobile, so a range of skills is needed to repair body damage to vehicles. Some body repairers specialize in certain areas, such as painting, welding, glass replacement, or air bag replacement. All collision repairers should know how to perform common repairs, such as realigning vehicle frames, smoothing dents, and removing and replacing panels.

Vehicle bodies are made from a wide array of materials, including steel, aluminum, metal alloys, fiberglass, and plastic, with each material requiring a different repair technique. Most repairers can work with all of these materials, but as car manufacturers produce vehicles with an increasing proportion of lightweight fiberglass, aluminum, and plastic parts, more repairers specialize in repairing these specific materials.

Collision repairers frequently must remove car seats, accessories, electrical components, hydraulic windows, dashboards, and trim to get to the parts that need repair. If the frame or a body section of the vehicle has been bent or twisted, frame repairers and straighteners can sometimes restore it to its original alignment and shape. This is done by chaining or clamping it to an alignment machine, which uses hydraulic pressure to pull the damaged metal into position. Repairers use specialty measuring equipment to set all components, such as engine parts, wheels, headlights, and body parts, at manufacturer's specifications.

After the frame is straightened, the repairer can begin to work on the car body. Newer composite car bodies often have "panels" that can be individually replaced. Dents in a metal car body can be corrected in several different ways, depending on how deep they are. If any part is too badly damaged to repair, the collision repairers remove it with hand tools, a pneumatic metal-cutting gun, or acetylene torch, and then weld on a replacement. Some dents can be pushed out with hydraulic jacks, pneumatic hammers, prying bars, and other hand tools. To smooth small dents and creases, collision repairers may position small anvils, called dolly blocks, against one side of the dented metal. They then hit the opposite side of the metal with various specially designed hammers. Tiny pits and dimples are removed with pick hammers and punches. Dents that cannot be corrected with this treatment may be filled with solder or a puttylike material that becomes hard like metal after it cures. When the filler has hardened, the collision repairers file, grind, and sand the surface smooth in the correct contour and prepare it for painting. In many shops the final sanding and painting are done by other specialists, who may be called *automotive painters.*

Since more than the body is usually damaged in a major automobile accident, repairers have other components to repair. Advanced vehicle systems on new cars such as anti-lock brakes, air bags, and other "passive restraint systems" require special training to repair. Steering and suspension, electrical components, and glass are often damaged and require repair, removal, or replacement.

Automotive painting is a highly skilled, labor-intensive job that requires a fine eye and attention to detail for the result to match the pre-accident condition. Some paint jobs require that less than the whole vehicle be painted. In this case, the painter must mix pigments to match the original color. This can be difficult if the original paint is faded, but computer technology is making paint matching easier.

A major part of the automobile collision repairer's job is assessing the damage and providing an estimate on the cost to repair it. Sometimes, the damage to a vehicle may cost more to repair than the vehicle is worth. When this happens, the vehicle is said to be "totaled," a term used by collision repairers as well as insurance companies. Many body repair shops offer towing services and will coordinate the transfer of a vehicle from the accident scene as well as the transfer of a totaled vehicle to a scrap dealer who will salvage the useable parts.

An automobile collision repairer prepares a truck to be repainted after it was damaged by a collision with a deer. (*Journal Courier/ Steve Warmowski, The Image Works*)

The shop supervisor or repair service estimator prepares the estimate. They inspect the extent of the damage to determine if the vehicle can be repaired or must be replaced. They note the year, model, and make of the car to determine type and availability of parts. Based on experience with similar types of repair and general industry guidelines, estimates are calculated for parts and labor and then submitted to the customer's insurance company. One "walk around" a car will tell the collision repairer what needs to be investigated. Since a collision often involves "hidden" damage, supervisors write up repair orders with specific instructions so no work is missed or, in some cases, done unnecessarily. Repair orders often indicate only specific parts are to be repaired or replaced. Collision repairers generally work on a project by themselves with minimal supervision. In large, busy shops, repairers may be assisted by helpers or apprentices.

REQUIREMENTS

High School
Technology demands more from the collision repairer than it did 10 years ago. In addition to automotive and shop classes, high school students should take mathematics, English, and computer classes. Adjustments and repairs to many car components require numer-

ous computations, for which good mathematics skills are essential. Reading comprehension skills will help a collision repairer understand complex repair manuals and trade journals that detail new technology. Oral communication skills are also important to help customers understand their options. In addition, computers are common in most collision repair shops. They keep track of customer histories and parts and often detail repair procedures. Use of computers in repair shops will only increase in the future, so students will benefit from a basic knowledge of them.

Postsecondary Training

A wide variety of training programs are offered at community colleges, vocational schools, independent organizations, and manufacturers. As automotive technology changes, the materials and methods involved in repair work change. With new high-strength steels, aluminum, and plastics becoming ever more common in newer vehicles and posing new challenges in vehicle repair, repairers will need special training to detect the many hidden problems that occur beyond the impact spot. Postsecondary training programs provide students with the necessary skills needed for repairing today's vehicles.

Certification or Licensing

Collision repairers may be certified by the National Institute for Automotive Service Excellence. Although certification is voluntary, it is a widely recognized standard of achievement for automobile collision repairers and the way many advance. Collision repairers who are certified are more valuable to their employers than those who are not and therefore stand a greater chance of advancement.

Other Requirements

Automobile collision repairers are responsible for providing their own hand tools at an investment of approximately $6,000 to $20,000 or more, depending on the technician's specialty. It is the employer's responsibility to provide the larger power tools and other test equipment. Skill in handling both hand and power tools is essential for any repairer. Since each collision repair job is unique and presents a different challenge, repairers often must be resourceful in their method of repair.

While union membership is not a requirement for collision repairers, many belong to the International Association of Machinists and Aerospace Workers; the International Union, United Automobile, Aerospace and Agricultural Implement Workers of America; the Sheet Metal Workers International Association; or the International Brotherhood of

Teamsters. Most collision repairers who are union members work for large automobile dealers, trucking companies, and bus lines.

EXPLORING

Many community colleges and park districts offer general auto maintenance, mechanics, and body repair workshops where students can get additional practice working on real cars and learn from experienced instructors. Trade magazines such as *Automotive Body Repair News* (http://www.abrn.com) are an excellent source for learning what's new in the industry. Such publications may be available at larger public libraries or vocational schools. Many journals also post current and archived articles on the Internet.

Working on cars as a hobby provides invaluable firsthand experience in repair work. A part-time job in a repair shop or dealership allows a feel for the general atmosphere and the kind of problems repairers face on the job as well as provide a chance to learn from those already in the business.

Some high school students may gain exposure to automotive repairs through participation in organizations, such as SkillsUSA. SkillsUSA coordinates competitions in several vocational areas, including collision repair. The collision repair competition tests students' aptitudes in metal work, MIG welding, painting, alignment of body and frame, painting, estimation of damage to automobiles, and plastic identification and repair. SkillsUSA is represented in all 50 states. If your school does not have a SkillsUSA chapter, ask your guidance counselor about starting one or participating in a co-op arrangement with another school.

EMPLOYERS

Approximately 223,000 automobile collision repairers are employed in the United States. Most work for body shops specializing in body repairs and painting, including private shops and shops operated by automobile dealers. Others work for organizations that maintain their own vehicle fleets, such as trucking companies and automobile rental companies. About one of every five automobile collision repairers is self-employed, operating small shops in cities large and small.

STARTING OUT

The best way to start out in the field of automobile collision repair is, first, to attend one of the many postsecondary training programs available throughout the country and, second, to obtain certification. Trade and technical schools usually provide job placement assistance for their graduates. Schools often have contacts with local employers who seek highly skilled entry-level employees. Often, employers post job openings at nearby trade schools with accredited programs.

Although postsecondary training programs are considered the best way to enter the field, some repairers learn the trade on the job as apprentices. Their training consists of working for several years under the guidance of experienced repairers. Fewer employers today are willing to hire apprentices because of the time and cost it takes to train them, but since there currently is a shortage of high quality entry-level collision repair technicians, many employers will continue to hire apprentices who can demonstrate good mechanical aptitude and a willingness to learn. Those who do learn their skills on the job will inevitably require some formal training if they wish to advance and stay in step with the changing industry.

Internship programs sponsored by car manufacturers or independent organizations provide students with excellent opportunities to work with prospective employers. Internships can also provide students with valuable contacts who will be able to refer the student to future employers and provide a recommendation to potential employers once they have completed their training. Many students may even be hired by the company at which they interned.

ADVANCEMENT

With today's complex automobile components and new materials requiring hundreds of hours of study and practice to master, employers encourage their employees to advance in responsibility by learning new systems and repair procedures. A repair shop's reputation will only go as far as its employees are skilled. Those with good communications and planning skills may advance to shop supervisor or service manager at larger repair shops or dealerships. Those who have mastered collision repair may go on to teaching at postsecondary schools or work for certification agencies.

EARNINGS

Salary ranges of collision repairers vary depending on level of experience, type of shop, and geographic location. The median annual salary for automotive body and related repairers was $35,180 in 2006, according to the U.S. Department of Labor. At the lower end of the pay scale, repairers with less experience and repairers employed by smaller shops tended to earn less; experienced repairers with management positions earned more. The lowest paid 10 percent earned $21,000 or less, and the top 10 percent $59,720 or more. In many repair shops and dealerships, collision repairers can make more by working on commission, typically earning 40 to 50 percent of the labor costs charged to customers. Employers often guarantee a minimum level of pay in addition to commissions.

Benefits packages vary from business to business. Most repair technicians can expect health insurance and a paid vacation from employers. Other benefits may include dental and eye care, life and disability insurance, and a pension plan. Employers usually cover a technician's work clothes and may pay a percentage of the cost of hand tools they purchase. An increasing number of employers pay all or most of an employee's certification training, dependent on the employee passing the test. A technician's salary can increase through yearly bonuses or profit sharing if the business does well.

WORK ENVIRONMENT

Collision repair work is generally noisy, dusty, and dirty. In some cases, the noise and dirt levels have decreased as new technology such as computers and electrostatic paint guns are introduced. Automobile repair shops are usually well ventilated to reduce dust and dangerous fumes. Because repairers weld and handle hot or jagged pieces of metal and broken glass, they wear safety glasses, masks, and protective gloves. Minor hand and back injuries are the most common problems of technicians. When reaching in hard-to-get-at places or loosening tight bolts, collision repairers often bruise, cut, or burn their hands. With caution and experience, most learn to avoid hand injuries. Working for long periods in cramped or bent positions often results in a stiff back or neck. Collision repairers also lift many heavy objects that can cause injury if not handled carefully; however, this is less of a problem with new cars as automakers design smaller and lighter parts for better fuel economy. Automotive painters wear respirators and other protective gear, and they work in specially ventilated rooms to keep from being exposed to paint fumes and other hazardous chemicals. Painters may need to stand for hours at a time as they work.

By following safety procedures and learning how to avoid typical problems, repairers can minimize the risks involved in this job. Likewise, shops must comply with strict safety procedures to help employees avoid accident or injury. Collision repairers are often under pressure to complete the job quickly. Most repairers work a standard 40-hour week but may be required to work longer hours when the shop is busy or in emergencies.

OUTLOOK

Like many service industries, the collision repair industry is facing a labor shortage of skilled, entry-level workers in many areas of the country. Demand for collision repair services is expected to remain consistent, at the least, as the number of cars in the nation grows, and employment opportunities are expected to increase about as fast as the average for all occupations through 2014. This demand, paired with technology that will require new skills, translates into a healthy job market for those willing to undergo the training needed. According to *Automotive Body Repair News,* as the need for skilled labor is rising, the number of people pursuing collision repair careers is declining. In many cases, vocational schools and employers are teaming up to recruit new workers.

Changing technology also plays a role in the industry's outlook. New automobile designs have body parts made of steel alloys, aluminum, and plastics—materials that are more time consuming to work with. In many cases, such materials are more prone to damage, increasing the need for body repairs.

The automobile collision repair business is not greatly affected by changes in economic conditions. Major body damage must be repaired to keep a vehicle in safe operating condition. During an economic downturn, however, people tend to postpone minor repairs until their budgets can accommodate the expense. Nevertheless, body repairers are seldom laid off. Instead, when business is bad, employers hire fewer new workers. During a recession, inexperienced workers face strong competition for entry-level jobs. People with formal training in repair work and automobile mechanics are likely to have the best job prospects in such times.

FOR MORE INFORMATION

For information on scholarships, contact
Automotive Aftermarket Industry Association
7101 Wisconsin Avenue, NW, Suite 1300
Bethesda, MD 20814-3415
Tel: 301-654-6664
Email: aaia@aftermarket.org
http://www.aftermarket.org

For information on training opportunities, contact
Inter-Industry Conference on Auto Collision Repair
5125 Trillium Boulevard
Hoffman Estates, IL 60192-3600
Tel: 800-422-7872
http://www.i-car.com

For information on accredited training programs, contact
National Automotive Technicians Education Foundation
101 Blue Seal Drive, Suite 101
Leesburg, VA 20175-5646
Tel: 703-669-6650
http://www.natef.org

For information on certification, contact
National Institute for Automotive Service Excellence
101 Blue Seal Drive, SE, Suite 101
Leesburg, VA 20175-5646
Tel: 877-273-8324
http://www.asecert.org

Automobile Service Technicians

OVERVIEW

Automobile service technicians maintain and repair cars, vans, small trucks, and other vehicles. Using both hand tools and specialized diagnostic test equipment, they pinpoint problems and make the necessary repairs or adjustments. In addition to performing complex and difficult repairs, technicians perform a number of routine maintenance procedures, such as oil changes, tire rotation, and battery replacement. Technicians interact frequently with customers to explain repair procedures and discuss maintenance needs. Approximately 803,000 automotive service technicians work in the United States.

HISTORY

By the mid-1920s, the automobile industry began to change America. As automobiles changed through the years, mechanics—or automobile service technicians, as they are now called—have kept them running. The "Big Three" automobile makers—Ford, General Motors, and Chrysler—produced millions of cars for a public eager for the freedom and mobility the automobile promised. With the ill-prepared roads suddenly overrun by inexperienced drivers, accidents and breakdowns became common. People not only were unskilled in driving but also were ignorant of the basic maintenance and service the automobile required. It suddenly became apparent that a new profession was in the making.

In 1899, the American Motor Company opened a garage in New York and advertised "competent mechanics always on hand to make repairs when necessary." Gradually, other repair "garages" opened in larger cities, but they were few and far between. Automobiles were much simpler in the early years. Basic maintenance and minor repairs often could be performed by the owner or someone with general mechanical aptitude.

As cars became more complex, the need for qualified technicians grew. Dealerships began to hire mechanics to handle increasing customer concerns and complaints. Gas stations also began to offer repair and maintenance services. The profession of automobile mechanic was suddenly in big demand.

By the 1950s, automobile service and repair garages were common throughout the United States, in urban and rural areas alike. Most mechanics learned the trade through hands-on experience as an apprentice or on their own through trial and error. When automakers began packing their cars with new technology, involving complex electrical circuitry, and computer-controlled mechanisms as well as basic design changes, it became apparent that mechanics would need comprehensive training to learn new service and repair procedures. Until the 1970s, there was no standard by which automobile service technicians were trained. In 1972, the National Institute for Automotive Service Excellence (ASE) was established. It set national training standards for new technicians and provided continuing education and certification for existing technicians when new technology became widespread in the field.

Today, the demand for trained, highly skilled professionals in the service industry is more important than ever. To keep up with the technology that is continually incorporated in new vehicles, service technicians require more intensive training than in the past. Today, mechanics who have completed a high level of formal training are generally called automobile service technicians. They have studied the complexities of the latest automotive technology, from computerized mechanisms in the engine to specialized diagnostic testing equipment.

THE JOB

Many automobile service technicians feel that the most exciting part of their work is troubleshooting—locating the source of a problem and successfully fixing it. Diagnosing mechanical, electrical, and computer-related troubles requires a broad knowledge of how cars work, the ability to make accurate observations, and the patience to determine what went wrong. Technicians agree that it frequently is more difficult to find the problem than it is to fix it. With experience, knowing where to look for problems becomes second nature.

Generally, there are two types of automobile service technicians: *generalists* and *specialists*. Generalists work under a broad umbrella of repair and service duties. They have proficiency in several kinds of light repairs and maintenance of many different types of automobiles. Their work, for the most part, is routine and basic. Specialists concentrate in one or two areas and learn to master them for many different car makes and models. Today, in light of the sophisticated technology common in new cars, there is an increasing demand for specialists. Automotive systems are not as easy or as standard as they used to be, and they now require many hours of experience to master. To gain a broad knowledge in auto maintenance and repair, specialists usually begin as generalists.

When a car does not operate properly, the owner brings it to a service technician and describes the problem. At a dealership or larger shop, the customer may talk with a *repair service estimator,* who writes down the customer's description of the problem and relays it to the service technician. The technician may test-drive the car or use diagnostic equipment, such as motor analyzers, spark plug testers, or compression gauges, to determine the problem. If a customer explains that the car's automatic transmission does not shift gears at the right times, the technician must know how the functioning of the transmission depends on the engine vacuum, the throttle pressure, and—more common in newer cars—the onboard computer. Each factor must be thoroughly checked. With each test, clues help the technician pinpoint the cause of the malfunction. After successfully diagnosing the problem, the technician makes the necessary adjustments or repairs. If a part is too badly damaged or worn to be repaired, he or she replaces it after first consulting the car owner, explaining the problem, and estimating the cost.

Normal use of an automobile inevitably causes wear and deterioration of parts. Generalist automobile technicians handle many of the routine maintenance tasks to help keep a car in optimal operating condition. They change oil, lubricate parts, and adjust or replace components of any of the car's systems that might cause a malfunction, including belts, hoses, spark plugs, brakes, filters, and transmission and coolant fluids.

Technicians who specialize in the service of specific parts usually work in large shops with multiple departments, car diagnostic centers, franchised auto service shops, or small independent shops that concentrate on a particular type of repair work.

Tune-up technicians evaluate and correct engine performance and fuel economy. They use diagnostic equipment and other computerized devices to locate malfunctions in fuel, ignition, and emissions-control systems. They adjust ignition timing and valves and may replace spark plugs, points, triggering assemblies in electronic ignitions, and other components to ensure maximum engine efficiency.

Electrical-systems technicians have been in healthy demand in recent years. They service and repair the complex electrical and computer circuitry common in today's automobile. They use both sophisticated diagnostic equipment and simpler devices such as ammeters, ohmmeters, and voltmeters to locate system malfunctions. As well as possessing excellent electrical skills, electrical-systems technicians require basic mechanical aptitude to get at electrical and computer circuitry located throughout the automobile.

Front-end technicians are concerned with suspension and steering systems. They inspect, repair, and replace front-end parts such as springs, shock absorbers, and linkage parts such as tie rods and ball joints. They also align and balance wheels.

Brake repairers work on drum and disk braking systems, parking brakes, and their hydraulic systems. They inspect, adjust, remove, repair, and reinstall such items as brake shoes, disk pads, drums, rotors, wheel and master cylinders, and hydraulic fluid lines. Some specialize in both brake and front-end work.

Transmission technicians adjust, repair, and maintain gear trains, couplings, hydraulic pumps, valve bodies, clutch assemblies, and other parts of automatic transmission systems. Transmissions have become complex and highly sophisticated mechanisms in newer model automobiles. Technicians require special training to learn how they function.

Automobile-radiator mechanics clean radiators using caustic solutions. They locate and solder leaks and install new radiator cores. In addition, some radiator mechanics repair car heaters and air conditioners and solder leaks in gas tanks.

Alternative fuel technicians are relatively new additions to the field. This specialty has evolved with the nation's efforts to reduce its dependence on foreign oil by exploring alternative fuels, such as ethanol and electricity.

As more automobiles rely on a variety of electronic components, technicians have become more proficient in the basics of electronics, even if they are not electronics specialists. Electronic controls and instruments are located in nearly all the systems of today's cars. Many previously mechanical functions in automobiles are being replaced by electronics, significantly altering the way repairs are performed. Diagnosing and correcting problems with electronic components often involves the use of specialty tools and computers.

Automobile service technicians use an array of tools in their everyday work, ranging from simple hand tools to computerized

A technician in a service center checks a car's oil. *(Stanley Walker, Syracuse Newspapers, The Image Works)*

diagnostic equipment. Technicians supply their own hand tools at an investment of $6,000 to $25,000 or more, depending on their specialty. It is usually the employer's responsibility to furnish the larger power tools, engine analyzers, and other test equipment.

To maintain and increase their skills and to keep up with new technology, automobile technicians must regularly read service and repair manuals, shop bulletins, and other publications. They must also be willing to take part in training programs given by manufacturers or at vocational schools. Those who have voluntary certification must periodically retake exams to keep their credentials.

REQUIREMENTS

High School

In today's competitive job market, aspiring automobile service technicians need a high school diploma to land a job that offers growth possibilities, a good salary, and challenges. There is a big demand in the automotive service industry to fill entry-level positions with well-trained, highly skilled persons. Technology demands more from the technician than it did 10 years ago.

In high school, you should take automotive and shop classes, mathematics, English, and computer classes. Adjustments and repairs to many car components require the technician to make numerous computations, for which good mathematical skills are essential. Good reading skills are also valuable, as a technician must do a lot of reading to stay competitive in today's job market. English classes will prepare you to handle the many volumes of repair manuals and trade journals you will need to remain informed. Computer skills are also vital, as computers are now common in most repair shops. They keep track of customers' histories and parts and often detail repair procedures. Use of computers in repair shops will only increase in the future.

Postsecondary Training

Employers today prefer to hire only those who have completed some kind of formal training program in automobile mechanics—usually a minimum of two years. A wide variety of such programs are offered at community colleges, vocational schools, independent organizations, and manufacturers. Many community colleges and vocational schools around the country offer accredited postsecondary education. These programs are accredited by the National Automotive Technicians Education Foundation and the Accrediting Commission of Career Schools and Colleges of Technology. Postsecondary training programs prepare students through a blend of classroom instruction and hands-on practical experience. They range in length from six months to two years or more, depending on the type of program. Shorter programs usually involve intensive study. Longer programs typically alternate classroom courses with periods of work experience. Some two-year programs include courses on applied mathematics, reading and writing skills, and business practices and lead to an associate's degree.

Some programs are conducted in association with automobile manufacturers. Students combine work experience with hands-on classroom study of up-to-date equipment and new cars provided by manufacturers. In other programs, students alternate time in the classroom with internships in dealerships or service departments. These students may take up to four years to finish their training, but they become familiar with the latest technology and also earn a modest salary.

Certification or Licensing

Automobile service technicians may be certified by ASE in one of the following eight areas—automatic transmission/transaxle, brakes, electrical/electronic systems, engine performance, engine repair, heating and air conditioning, manual drive train and axles, and suspension and steering. Those who become certified in all eight areas are known as master mechanics. Although certification is voluntary, it is a widely recognized standard of achievement for automobile technicians and is highly valued by many employers. Certification also provides the means and opportunity to advance. To maintain their certification, technicians must retake the examination for their specialties every five years. Many employers only hire ASE-accredited technicians and base salaries on the level of the technicians' accreditation.

Other Requirements

To be a successful automobile service technician, you must be patient and thorough in your work; a shoddy repair job may put the driver's life at risk. You must have excellent troubleshooting skills and be able to deduce the cause of system malfunctions.

EXPLORING

Many community centers offer general auto maintenance and mechanics workshops where you can practice working on real cars and learn from instructors. Trade magazines are excellent sources for learning what's new in the industry and can be found at most public libraries or large bookstores. Many public television stations broadcast automobile maintenance and repair programs that can be of help to beginners to see how various types of cars differ.

Working on cars as a hobby provides valuable firsthand experience in the work of a technician. An after-school or weekend part-time job in a repair shop or dealership can give you a feel for the general atmosphere and kinds of problems technicians face on the job. Oil and tire changes, battery and belt replacement, and even pumping gas may be some of the things you will be asked to do on the job; this work will give you valuable experience before you move on to more complex repairs. Experience with vehicle repair work in the armed forces is another way to pursue your interest in this field.

EMPLOYERS

Because the automotive industry is so vast, automobile service technicians have many choices concerning type of shop and geographic location. Automobile repairs are needed all over the country, in large cities as well as rural areas.

The majority of automobile service technicians work for automotive dealers and independent automotive repair shops and gasoline service stations. The field offers a variety of other employment options as well. The U.S. Department of Labor estimates that more than 16 percent of automobile service technicians are self-employed. Other employers include franchises such as PepBoys and Midas

Books to Read

Curcio, Vincent. *Chrysler: The Life and Times of an Automotive Genius*. New York: Oxford University Press, 2005.

Hollembeak, Barry. *Today's Technician: Automotive Electricity and Electronics*. 4th ed. Stamford, Conn: Thomson Delmar Learning, 2006.

Knowles, Don. *Today's Technician: Automotive Suspension and Steering Systems*. 4th ed. Stamford, Conn: Thomson Delmar Learning, 2006.

Lee, Richard S., and Mary Price Lee. *Careers for Car Buffs & Other Freewheeling Types*. 2d ed. New York: McGraw-Hill, 2003.

Matchett, Steve. *The Mechanic's Tale: Life in the Pit-Lanes of Formula One*. London, U.K.: Orion Media, 2002.

Owen, Clifton E. *Today's Technician: Automotive Brake Systems*. 3d ed. Stamford, Conn: Thomson Delmar Learning, 2003.

Schwaller, Anthony E. *Total Automotive Technology*. 4th ed. Stamford, Conn: Thomson Delmar Learning, 2004.

Turner Publishing Company. *Ford Motor Company: The First 100 Years*. Paducah, Ky.: Turner Publishing Company, 2007.

Van Valkenburgh, Paul. *Race Car Engineering & Mechanics*. New York: HP Books, 2004.

that offer routine repairs and maintenance, and automotive service departments of automotive and home supply stores. Some automobile service technicians maintain fleets for taxicab and automobile leasing companies or for government agencies with large automobile fleets.

Technicians with experience and/or ASE certification certainly have more career choices. Some master mechanics may go on to teach at technical and vocational schools or at community colleges. Others put in many years working for someone else and go into business for themselves after they have gained the experience to handle many types of repairs and oversee other technicians.

STARTING OUT

The best way to start out in this field is to attend one of the many postsecondary training programs available throughout the country. Trade and technical schools usually provide job placement assistance for their graduates. Schools often have contacts with local employers who need to hire well-trained people. Frequently, employers post job openings at nearby trade schools with accredited programs. Job openings are frequently listed on the Internet through regional and national automotive associations or career networks.

A decreasing number of technicians learn the trade on the job as apprentices. Their training consists of working for several years under the guidance of experienced mechanics. Fewer employers today are willing to hire apprentices due to the time and money it takes to train them. Those who do learn their skills on the job will inevitably require some formal training if they wish to advance and stay in step with the changing industry.

Intern programs sponsored by car manufacturers or independent organizations provide students with excellent opportunities to actually work with prospective employers. Internships can provide students with valuable contacts who will be able to recommend future employers once they have completed their training. Many students may even be hired by the shop at which they interned.

ADVANCEMENT

With today's complex automobile components requiring hundreds of hours of study and practice to master, more repair shops prefer to hire specialists. Generalist automobile technicians advance as they gain experience and become specialists. Other technicians advance to diesel repair, where the pay may be higher. Those with good communications and planning skills may advance to shop foreman or service manager at large repair shops or to sales workers at dealerships. Master mechanics with good business skills often go into business for themselves and open their own shops.

EARNINGS

Salary ranges of automobile service technicians vary depending on the level of experience, type of shop the technician works in, and geographic location. Generally, technicians who work in small-town, family-owned gas stations earn less than those who work at dealerships and franchises in metropolitan areas.

According to the U.S. Department of Labor, automobile service technicians had median annual salaries of $33,780 ($16.24 an hour) in 2006. The lowest paid 10 percent made less than $19,070 ($9.17 an hour), and the highest paid 10 percent made more than $56,620 ($27.22 an hour). Since most technicians are paid on an hourly basis and frequently work overtime, their salaries can vary significantly. In many repair shops and dealerships, technicians can earn higher incomes by working on commission. Master technicians who work on commission can earn more than $100,000 annually. Employers often guarantee a minimum level of pay in addition to commissions.

Benefit packages vary from business to business. Most technicians receive health insurance and paid vacation days. Additional benefits may include dental, life, and disability insurance and a pension plan. Employers usually pay for a technician's work clothes and may pay a percentage on hand tools purchased. An increasing number of employers pay for all or most of an employee's certification training, if he or she passes the test. A technician's salary can increase through yearly bonuses or profit sharing if the business does well.

WORK ENVIRONMENT

Depending on the size of the shop and whether it's an independent or franchised repair shop, dealership, or private business, automobile technicians work with anywhere from two to 20 other technicians. Most shops are well lighted and well ventilated. They can frequently be noisy with running cars and power tools. Minor hand and back injuries are the most common problems of technicians. When reaching in hard-to-get-at places or loosening tight bolts, technicians often bruise, cut, or burn their hands. With caution and experience, most technicians learn to avoid hand injuries. Working for long periods in cramped or bent positions often results in a stiff back or neck. Technicians also lift many heavy objects that can cause injury if not handled carefully; however, this is becoming less of a problem with new cars, as automakers design smaller and lighter parts to improve fuel economy. Some technicians may experience allergic reactions to solvents and oils used in cleaning, maintenance, and repair. Shops must comply with strict safety procedures set by the Occupational Safety and Health Administration and Environmental Protection Agency to help employees avoid accidents and injuries.

The U.S. Department of Labor reports that most technicians work a standard 40-hour week, but 30 percent of all technicians work more than 40 hours a week. Some technicians make emergency repairs to stranded automobiles on the roadside during odd hours.

OUTLOOK

With an estimated 221 million vehicles in operation today, automobile service technicians should feel confident that a good percentage will require servicing and repair. Skilled and highly trained technicians will be in particular demand. Less-skilled workers will face tough competition. The U.S. Department of Labor predicts that this field will grow about as fast as the average for all occupations through 2014, but in some areas, growth could be higher because of a tight labor market. According to the ASE, even if school enrollments were at maximum capacity, the demand for automobile service technicians still would exceed the supply in the immediate future. As a result, many shops are beginning to recruit employees while they are still in vocational or even high school.

Another concern for the industry is the automobile industry's trend toward developing the "maintenance-free" car. Manufacturers are producing high-end cars that require no servicing for their first 100,000 miles. In addition, many new cars are equipped with on-board diagnostics that detect both wear and failure for many of the car's components, eliminating the need for technicians to perform extensive diagnostic tests. Also, parts that are replaced before they completely wear out prevent further damage from occurring to connected parts that are affected by a malfunction or breakdown. Although this will reduce troubleshooting time and the number of overall repairs, the components that need repair will be more costly and require a more experienced (and hence, more expensive) technician.

Most new jobs for technicians will be at independent service dealers, specialty shops, and franchised new car dealers. Because of the increase of specialty shops, fewer gasoline service stations will hire technicians, and many will eliminate repair services completely. Other opportunities will be available at companies or institutions with private fleets (e.g., cab, delivery, and rental companies, and government agencies and police departments).

FOR MORE INFORMATION

For information on accredited training programs, contact
    Accrediting Commission of Career Schools and Colleges of Technology
    2101 Wilson Boulevard, Suite 302
    Arlington, VA 22201
    Tel: 703-247-4212
    Email: info@accsct.org
    http://www.accsct.org

For more information on the automotive service industry, contact
    Automotive Aftermarket Industry Association
    7101 Wisconsin Avenue, Suite 1300
    Bethesda, MD 20814-3415

Tel: 301-654-6664
Email: aaia@aftermarket.org
http://www.aftermarket.org

For industry information and job listings, contact
Automotive Service Association
PO Box 929
Bedford, TX 76095-0929
Tel: 800-272-7467
Email: asainfo@asashop.org
http://www.asashop.org

For information and statistics on automotive dealers, contact
National Automobile Dealers Association
8400 Westpark Drive
McLean, VA 22102-5116
Tel: 800-252-6232
Email: nadainfo@nada.org
http://www.nada.org

For information on certified educational programs and careers,
contact
National Automotive Technicians Education Foundation
101 Blue Seal Drive, Suite 101
Leesburg, VA 20175-5646
Tel: 703-669-6650
http://www.natef.org

For information on certification, contact
National Institute for Automotive Service Excellence
101 Blue Seal Drive, SE, Suite 101
Leesburg, VA 20175-5646
Tel: 877-273-8324
http://www.asecert.org

―――――――――――― **INTERVIEW** ――――――――――――

Michael Fobes is an instructor of automotive technology at Renton Technical College in Renton, Washington. He discussed the field with the editors of Careers in Focus: Mechanics.

Q. How long have you worked in the field of automotive technology?

A. Eight years as a full-time automotive instructor, 20 years as a master automotive technician. I am currently National Institute for Automotive Service Excellence–certified in over 40 areas, including six master certificates (master automobile technician, master heavy truck technician, master engine machinist, master truck equipment technician, master school bus technician, and master collision repair/refinish technician).

Q. Tell us about your program.

A. We are a two-year master National Automotive Technicians Education Foundation-certified program teaching all aspects of automotive repair to work on today's sophisticated and complex machines. Students learn all areas of study and are provided with hands-on training in real-world shop environments using modern state-of-the-art equipment and facilities.

Q. What are the most important qualities for automotive technology majors?

A. With the sophistication of today's automobile, students need strong computer skills, good mechanical and electrical aptitude, and [ability in] math, science, and physics. Students also must learn to excel at customer service, attendance, and punctuality.

Q. What advice would you give automotive technology students as they graduate and look for jobs?

A. Ask your mentors for advice, research the company you're interested in, and talk to current employees of the company. Attend a job skills class, write a resume, and don't take the first offer you are given without searching the field. Know what you like, what you want to do, and look for what makes you happy [i.e., a fast-moving, busy shop; a team approach; a specialty (transmission repair); or an independent shop with job duties across the board].

Q. What advice would you give to high school students who are interested in this career?

A. First and foremost, choose a career that you enjoy. Talk with other technicians, join a car club, visit a college campus with an automotive program that you're interested in, talk to students currently enrolled in that program, and talk with your parents.

Bicycle Mechanics

QUICK FACTS

School Subjects
Physics
Technical/shop

Personal Skills
Following instructions
Mechanical/manipulative

Work Environment
Primarily indoors
Primarily one location

Minimum Education Level
High school diploma

Salary Range
$15,550 to $21,790 to
$31,090+

Certification or Licensing
Voluntary

Outlook
About as fast as the average

DOT
639

GOE
05.03.02

NOC
7445

O*NET-SOC
49-3091.00

OVERVIEW

Bicycle mechanics use hand and power tools to repair, service, and assemble all types of bicycles. They may do routine maintenance and tune-ups or completely rebuild damaged or old bicycles. Bike manufacturers, dealers, retail bike and sporting goods stores, and general merchandise stores may employ bicycle mechanics. The popularity of bicycles and the fact that many riders lack the time to repair their bikes makes for a steady employment outlook for bicycle mechanics. Approximately 8,000 bicycle mechanics work in the United States.

HISTORY

Bicycles have been said to be the most efficient means ever devised to turn human energy into propulsion. The first successful bicycle was built in Scotland around 1839. Like the bicycles built for many years afterward, it had a large front wheel that was pedaled and steered and a smaller wheel in back for balance. In time, advances in design and technology improved the ease with which riders could balance, steer, brake, and get on and off bicycles. The first modern-looking bicycle, with equal-sized front and rear wheels and a loop of chain on a sprocket drive, was built in 1874. By the early 1890s, pneumatic tires and the basic diamond-pattern frame made bicycles stable, efficient, and fairly inexpensive. Bicycle riding became a popular recreation and, in some countries around the world, a major form of transportation. In the 20th century, bicycle performance was further improved by lightweight frames with new designs and improved gear mechanisms, tires, and other components.

After automobiles became the dominant vehicles on American roads, bicycles were usually considered children's toys in the United States. However, the environmental movement of the 1960s and 1970s, and the resulting concern with polluting fossil fuels, saw a resurgence in their popularity among adults that has continued to this day. With the increasing costs associated with cars and environmental concerns, more people are using bikes not only for exercise, racing, or touring but also for short trips to the store, to visit friends, or to go to work.

THE JOB

Repairing bicycles takes mechanical skill and careful attention to detail. Many repairs, such as replacing brake cables, are relatively simple, while others can be very complicated. Mechanics use a variety of tools, including wrenches, screwdrivers, drills, vises, and specialized tools to repair and maintain bikes. There are many different brands of bikes, both domestic and foreign, and each has its own unique characteristics and mechanical problems.

Bicycle mechanics work on both new and used bicycles. They may be required to do emergency repairs or routine tune-ups, or they may need to repair and recondition used bikes so they can be sold. Many new bikes come from the manufacturer unassembled, and mechanics working at a bicycle dealership or shop must assemble them and make adjustments so they operate properly. Many department stores and discount houses that sell bikes contract out this type of assembly work to dealerships or bike shops, and it can be very profitable.

Some of the basic repairs that bicycles need can easily be done by the owner, but many cyclists lack the tools, time, or initiative to learn how to service their bikes. They prefer to take most problems to professional bicycle mechanics. One type of repair is fixing a flat tire. Leaks in *clincher tires* (those with a separate inner tube) can be fixed at home, but many owners choose to take them to a bicycle mechanic. Repairing *sew-up tires* (which have no inner tube) is a more complicated process that generally requires a mechanic. Mechanics can also build wheels, replace and tighten spokes, and "true," or align, the wheels. To build a wheel, the mechanic laces the spokes between the rim and the hub of the wheel and then tightens them individually with a special wrench until the wheel spins without wobbling. A truing machine is used to test the balance of the wheel as it spins.

The gear mechanism on multiple-speed bikes is another common concern for bicycle mechanics. On some bikes, gears are shifted by means of a derailleur, which is located on the back wheel hub or

Bicycle mechanics need excellent hand-eye coordination because they often work with small tools to make fine adjustments. *(Geri Engberg, The Image Works)*

at the bottom bracket assembly where the pedals and chain meet. This derailleur frequently needs adjustment. The mechanic aligns the front and rear gears of the derailleur to reduce wear on both the chain and the gear teeth and adjusts the mechanism to keep constant pressure on the chain. Gear mechanisms vary greatly among different makes of bicycles so mechanics have to keep up with current models and trends.

Bicycle mechanics must be able to spot trouble in a bike and correct problems before they become serious. They may have to straighten a bent frame by using a special vise and a heavy steel rod. They may be asked to adjust or replace the braking mechanism so that the force on the brakes is spread evenly. They may need to take apart, clean, grease, and reassemble the headset, or front hub, and the bottom bracket that houses the axle of the pedal crank.

Mechanics who work in a bike shop sometimes work as salespeople, advising customers on their bike purchases or accessories, including helmets, clothing, mirrors, locks, racks, bags, and more. In some shops, especially those located in resort areas, bike mechanics may also work as bicycle-rental clerks. Where winters are cold and biking is seasonal, bike mechanics may work part of the year on other recreational equipment, such as fitness equipment, snowmobiles, or small engines.

REQUIREMENTS

High School

Completion of high school or other formal education is not necessarily required for a job as a bicycle mechanic, although employers may prefer applicants who are high school graduates. If you are considering this kind of work, you will benefit from taking vocational-technical or shop classes in high school. Such classes will give you the opportunity to work with your hands, follow blueprints or other directions, and build equipment. Science classes, such as physics, will give you an understanding of the principles at work behind the design of equipment as well as help you to understand how it functions. Since you will most likely be working in a retail environment, consider taking business, accounting, or computer classes that will teach you business and related skills. Don't forget to take English or communication classes. These classes will help you develop your communication skills, an asset when dealing with customers, as well as your research and reading skills, an asset when your work includes reviewing maintenance and repair documentation for many different types of bikes.

Postsecondary Training

Bicycle maintenance courses are offered at some technical and vocational schools, and there are at least three privately operated training schools for mechanics. Bicycle manufacturers may also offer factory instruction to mechanics employed by the company's authorized dealers. Completion of many of the courses offered earns the mechanic certificates that may help when seeking a job or when seeking a promotion.

Certification or Licensing

The Barnett Bicycle Institute and the United Bicycle Institute offer certification programs for bicycle mechanics. Contact the institutes for more information.

Other Requirements

For the most part, bike mechanics learn informally on the job. At least two years of hands-on training and experience is required to become a thoroughly skilled mechanic, but because new makes and models of bikes are constantly being introduced, there are always

Did You Know?

- In 1863, the first practical bicycle, the *velocipede*, was invented by Pierre Michaux and Pierre Lallement in France. It was nicknamed the "bone shaker" because the ride was so rough.
- Bicycle racing has been an Olympic sport since 1896.
- Consumers in the United States purchased 18.3 million bicycles in 2004.
- Approximately 42.5 million Americans ride bicycles.
- A 2003 survey of bicycle riders found that most rode for exercise/ health (41 percent) and recreation (37 percent), with only 5 percent citing commuting to work as their principal use.
- Bicycling is a low-impact transportation mode that is great for the environment. It is estimated that the use of bicycles as a replacement for automobiles eliminates the use of more than 238 million gallons of gasoline annually.

Sources: *Bicycle Retailer and Industry News*, National Sporting Goods Association, Bureau of Transportation Statistics, League of American Bicyclists

new things to learn that may require additional training. Many times a bicycle distributor visits bike mechanics at a shop to make sure the mechanic's work is competent before the shop is officially permitted to sell and service a new kind of bike. Because of this steady stream of new information, bicycle mechanics must have a desire to study and add to their knowledge.

Bicycle mechanics also need excellent hand-eye coordination and a certain degree of physical endurance. They may work with small tools to make fine adjustments. Often, much of their work is performed while they stand, bend, or kneel. Mechanics must be independent decision makers, able to decide on proper repair strategies, but they should also be able to work comfortably with others. Frequently, they will need to interact with customers and other workers.

EXPLORING

Many people become interested in bicycle repair because they own and maintain their own bikes. Taking general maintenance and tune-up classes that some bike shops offer for bicycle owners is a good way for you to explore your interest in working with bikes. Visit with the bicycle mechanics at these shops and ask them for their insights. How did they start in this line of work? What do they enjoy most about it? What is the most challenging aspect of the job? If a local shop does not offer classes, consider taking courses at a private school such as the United Bicycle Institute or the Barnett Bicycle Institute (contact information is at the end of this article).

Bike shops sometimes hire inexperienced students as assistants to work on a part-time basis or during the summer when their business is most brisk. Such a job is probably the best way to find out about this type of work.

Various magazines available at larger newsstands, bookstores, or public libraries are devoted to recreational cycling and serious bicycle racing. These magazines often cover the technical aspects of how bicycles are constructed and operated, and they may provide helpful information to anyone interested in bike repair. Bicycle associations can provide additional information regarding classes, industry news, and employment.

EMPLOYERS

There are approximately 8,000 bicycle mechanics working in the United States, and they are employed nationwide. They may work in local bicycle shops, for large sporting goods stores, or for bicycle manufacturers. Resorts and some retail stores also hire people with these skills. Bicycle mechanics may also be required to repair other types of equipment or serve as sales clerks.

STARTING OUT

If you are a beginner with no experience, start out by contacting local bike shops or bike manufacturers to find one that is willing to hire trainees. Check the Yellow Pages for a list of bicycle dealers in your area. Bike dealers may also be willing to provide on-the-job training. In addition, the want ads of your local newspaper are a source of information on job openings. Also, try joining a local bicycling club that will allow you to network with other enthusiasts who may know of open positions.

People who have learned bike repair and have accumulated the tools they need may be able to do repair work independently, perhaps using ads and referrals to gradually build a small business.

ADVANCEMENT

There are few opportunities for advancement for bicycle mechanics unless they combine their interest in bikes with another activity. For example, after a few years on the job, they may be able to start managing the bike shop where they work. Some mechanics move on to jobs with the bicycle department of a large department or sporting goods store and from there move up to department manager or regional sales manager. Another possibility is to become a sales representative for a bicycle manufacturer or distributor.

Some bicycle mechanics are merely working their way through college. Others want to own and operate their own bike stores. If they gain enough experience and save or borrow enough money to cover start-up costs, they may be able to establish a successful new business. College courses in business, management, and accounting are recommended for aspiring shop owners. Bicycle businesses tend to do best in progressive communities where there are publicly funded bike paths and people actively look for alternatives to America's automobile culture.

EARNINGS

Many bicycle mechanics work a standard 40-hour week. In some areas of the country, mechanics may find that their hours increase in the spring, when people bring their bikes out of storage, and decrease when the weather gets colder. Workers in this field are typically paid on an hourly basis, with 2006 salaries ranging from $7.48 per hour ($15,550 per year) for the lowest 10 percent, comprising trainees and inexperienced mechanics, to $14.95 or more an hour ($31,090 a year) for the top 10 percent. According to the U.S. Department of Labor, the median salary for bicycle repairers in 2006 was $10.48 an hour, or $21,790 a year.

Benefits vary depending on the shop or facility where employed and the number of hours worked. Some jobs may include standard benefits.

WORK ENVIRONMENT

Bicycle mechanics do much of their work indoors standing at a workbench. They work constantly with their hands and various tools to perform the prescribed tasks. It is a job that requires attention to detail and, in some cases, the ability to diagnose and troubleshoot problems. Because of the wide variety of bicycles on the market today, mechanics must be familiar with many different types of bicycles, and their problems and repair procedures. Although it is sometimes greasy and dirty work, it is, in general, not very strenuous. Most heavy work, such as painting, brazing, and frame straightening, is done in larger bike shops and specialty shops.

Once the job is mastered, workers may find it somewhat repetitious and not very challenging. It may also be frustrating in cases where bicycles are so old or in such bad shape that they are virtually irreparable. Most often, bicycle mechanics choose this profession because they are cycling enthusiasts themselves. If this is the case, it may be very enjoyable for them to be able to work with bicycles and interact with customers who are fellow cyclists.

Mechanics work by themselves or with a few coworkers as they service bikes, but in many shops they also deal with the public, working the register or helping customers select and purchase bicycles and accessories. The atmosphere around a bike shop can be hectic, especially during peak seasons in shops where mechanics must double as clerks. As is true in any retail situation, bicycle mechanics may sometimes have to deal with irate or rude customers.

OUTLOOK

Cycling continues to gain in popularity. People are bicycling for fun, fitness, as a means of transportation, and for the thrill of racing. Bikes don't burn gas or pollute the environment, and they are relatively cheap and versatile. With personal fitness and the preservation of the environment as two of the nation's biggest trends and concerns, the bicycling industry looks to a positive future. The U.S. Department of Labor predicts employment for bicycle mechanics to grow about as fast as the average for all occupations through 2014.

Bicycle repair work is also relatively immune to fluctuations in the economy. In times of economic boom, people buy more new bikes and mechanics are kept busy assembling, selling, and servicing them. During economic recessions, people take their old bikes to mechanics for repair.

FOR MORE INFORMATION

For biking news and to read online articles from the magazine Adventure Cyclist, *contact*

Adventure Cycling Association
150 East Pine Street
PO Box 8308
Missoula, MT 59802-4515
Tel: 800-755-2453
Email: info@adventurecycling.org
http://www.adv-cycling.org

For information on courses in bicycle repair and mechanics, contact
Barnett Bicycle Institute
2755 Ore Mill Drive, #14
Colorado Springs, CO 80904-3159
Tel: 719-632-5173
http://www.bbinstitute.com

For news and information about upcoming races and events, contact
League of American Bicyclists
1612 K Street, NW, Suite 800
Washington, DC 20006-2850
Tel: 202-822-1333
Email: bikeleague@bikeleague.org
http://www.bikeleague.org

For more information on the industry, contact
National Bicycle Dealers Association
777 West 19th Street, Suite O
Costa Mesa, CA 92627-6130
Tel: 949-722-6909
Email: info@nbda.com
http://www.nbda.com

For information on beginning to advanced courses in repair, frame building, and mechanic certification, contact
United Bicycle Institute
401 Williamson Way
PO Box 128
Ashland, OR 97520-1250
Tel: 541-488-1121
Email: ask@bikeschool.com
http://www.bikeschool.com

━━━ INTERVIEW ━━━

Robert St. Cyr is the general manager of the Bike Barn, a bicycle repair facility located on the campus of the University of California-Davis. He discussed bicycle repair with the editors of Careers in Focus: Mechanics.

Q. Please tell us about the Bike Barn.

A. The Bike Barn was established in 1971 as a centrally located, on-campus bicycle repair shop that offered free tool usage, low-cost repairs, replacement parts, and rental bikes. At that time, none of the local shops were able to meet these needs of the students. The shop is an old dairy barn built in 1910. The shop continues to meet these needs, adding the selling of used bicycles and repair classes to the list. Currently, the Bike Barn repairs 10,000 bikes annually and maintains a rental fleet of 200 bicycles.

Q. Tell us about your duties as general manager.

A. As general manager, I have a wide variety of duties. I am the primary decision maker, establishing all policies and procedures. I perform repairs, train employees in the discipline of bicycle mechanics, and teach student managers how to run a commercial, not-for-profit business. Administratively, I conduct interviews, hire, discipline, and release employees. I create the budget, attend budget hearings, and work with student senators for funding and repairs and improvements to the building and shop. I am responsible for ensuring the building receives the repairs and maintenance needed. I supervise a staff of 13–18 student employees. (Generally, they are between the ages of 18 and 22. All of my employees are required to be currently enrolled at the university.) I perform all of the parts ordering, interact with vendors and sales representatives, and maintain the inventory. In addition, I attend trade shows and teach bicycle safety and repair classes.

Q. Do your employees go on to pursue careers in bicycle repair, or is this just a good job while they're in college?

A. I have been the general manager for 10 years and have hired and trained around 100 employees. Most leave the shop for jobs outside the bicycle industry. Some have become bicycle racers; one directs a large bicycle supply company. Many go on to earn graduate and doctoral degrees. Some have become medical doctors, scientists, optometrists, psychiatrists, and mechanical engineers. The job provides the employees with a good foundation that helps them succeed as they put their degrees to work. They gain customer relation skills, problem solving skills, and decision making skills. Because the bicycle industry tends to be more a labor of love then a lucrative career, many, sadly, leave the bike world to pursue more lucrative careers

Q. What do you like most and least about your job?

A. The best part is getting to work with such bright, intelligent, young people. They learn so quickly, so it is a pleasure to teach them. The worst part is saying goodbye once the student graduates.

Q. What are the three most important professional qualities for bicycle mechanics?

A. Honesty, integrity, and love.

Honesty: Customers can usually tell when you're not telling them the truth about the work that you have performed on their bike.

Integrity: Do the job right, to the best of your ability.

Love: Enjoy what you do because many people are envious of how cool your job is. Share that passion with others.

Q. What are some of the most offbeat repairs that you've encountered in your time at the Bike Barn?

A. • Flat repair on a 36" unicycle—the tire was very tall!
   • Rod brakes on a vintage Dutch bicycle.
   • Cranks that wobbled so much, there were holes worn through the frame from the crank whacking the chain stay.
   • Wheel and flat repairs on a vintage Schwinn bicycle that had a flower garden growing in the rear basket—it was very heavy!

Biomedical Equipment Technicians

OVERVIEW

Biomedical equipment technicians handle the complex medical equipment and instruments found in hospitals, clinics, and research facilities. This equipment is used for medical therapy and diagnosis and includes heart-lung machines, artificial kidney machines, patient monitors, chemical analyzers, and other electrical, electronic, mechanical, or pneumatic devices.

Technicians' main duties are to inspect, maintain, repair, and install this equipment. They disassemble equipment to locate malfunctioning components, repair or replace defective parts, and reassemble the equipment, adjusting and calibrating it to ensure that it operates according to manufacturers' specifications. Other duties of biomedical equipment technicians include modifying equipment according to the directions of medical or supervisory personnel, arranging with equipment manufacturers for necessary equipment repair, and safety-testing equipment to ensure that patients, equipment operators, and other staff members are safe from electrical or mechanical hazards. Biomedical equipment technicians work with hand tools, power tools, measuring devices, and manufacturers' manuals.

Technicians may work for equipment manufacturers as salespeople or as service technicians, or for a health care facility specializing in the repair or maintenance of specific equipment, such as that used in radiology, nuclear medicine, or patient monitoring. In the United States, approximately 29,000 people work as biomedical equipment technicians.

QUICK FACTS

School Subjects
Biology
Technical/shop

Personal Skills
Mechanical/manipulative
Technical/scientific

Work Environment
Primarily indoors
Primarily one location

Minimum Education Level
Associate's degree

Salary Range
$23,700 to $40,580 to $66,160+

Certification or Licensing
Recommended

Outlook
About as fast as the average

DOT
639

GOE
05.03.03

NOC
N/A

O*NET-SOC
49-9062.00, 51-9082.00

HISTORY

Today's complex biomedical equipment is the result of advances in three different areas of engineering and scientific research. The first, of course, is our ever-increasing knowledge of the human body and of the disease processes that afflict it. Although the accumulation of medical knowledge has been going on for thousands of years, most of the discoveries leading to the development of medical technology have occurred during the last three hundred years. During the past one hundred years especially, we have learned a great deal about the chemical and electrical nature of the human body.

The second contribution to biomedical technology's development is the field of instrumentation—the design and building of precision measuring devices. Throughout the history of medicine, physicians and medical researchers have tried to learn about and to monitor the workings of the human body with whatever instruments were available to them. However, it was not until the industrial revolution of the 18th and 19th centuries that instruments were developed that could detect the human body's many subtle and rapid processes.

The third area is mechanization and automation. Biomedical equipment often relies on mechanisms, such as pumps, motors, bellows, control arms, etc. These kinds of equipment were initially developed and improved during the industrial revolution; however, it was not until the 1950s that the field of medical technology began incorporating the use of automation. During the 1950s, researchers developed machines for analyzing the various components of blood and for preparing tissue specimens for microscopic examination. Probably the most dramatic development of this period was the introduction of the heart-lung machine by John Haysham Gibbon of Philadelphia in 1953, a project he had been working on since 1937.

Since the 1950s, the growth of biomedical technology has been especially dramatic. Thirty years ago, even the most advanced hospitals had only a few pieces of electronic medical equipment; today such hospitals have thousands. And, to service this equipment, the biomedical equipment technician has become an important member of the health care delivery team.

In a sense, biomedical equipment technicians represent the newest stage in the history of technicians. The first technicians were skilled assistants who had learned a trade and gone to work for an engineer or scientist. The second generation learned a technology, such as electronics. The most recent generation of technicians needs integrated instruction and competence in at least two fields of science and technology. For the biomedical equipment technician, the fields may vary, but they will most often be electronics and human physiology.

THE JOB

Biomedical equipment technicians are an important link between technology and medicine. They repair, calibrate, maintain, and operate biomedical equipment working under the supervision of researchers, biomedical engineers, physicians, surgeons, and other professional health care providers.

Biomedical equipment technicians may work with thousands of different kinds of equipment. Some of the most frequently encountered are the following: patient monitors; heart-lung machines; kidney machines; blood-gas analyzers; spectrophotometers; X-ray units; radiation monitors; defibrillators; anesthesia apparatus; pacemakers; blood pressure transducers; spirometers; sterilizers; diathermy equipment; patient-care computers; ultrasound machines; and diagnostic scanning machines, such as the CT (computed tomography) scan machine, PET (positron emission tomography) scanner, and MRI (magnetic resonance imaging) machines.

Repairing faulty instruments is one of the chief functions of biomedical equipment technicians. They investigate equipment problems, determine the extent of malfunctions, make repairs on instruments that have had minor breakdowns, and expedite the repair of instruments with major breakdowns, for instance, by writing an analysis of the problem for the factory. In doing this work, technicians rely on manufacturers' diagrams, maintenance manuals, and standard and specialized test instruments, such as oscilloscopes and pressure gauges.

Installing equipment is another important function of biomedical equipment technicians. They inspect and test new equipment to make sure it complies with performance and safety standards as described in the manufacturer's manuals and diagrams, and as noted on the purchase order. Technicians may also check on proper installation of the equipment, or, in some cases, install it themselves. To ensure safe operations, technicians need a thorough knowledge of the regulations related to the proper grounding of equipment, and they need to carry out all steps and procedures to ensure safety.

Maintenance is the third major area of responsibility for biomedical equipment technicians. In doing this work, technicians try to catch problems before they become more serious. To this end, they take apart and reassemble devices, test circuits, clean and oil moving parts, and replace worn parts. They also keep complete records of all machine repairs, maintenance checks, and expenses.

In all three of these areas, a large part of technicians' work consists of consulting with physicians, administrators, engineers, and other related professionals. For example, they may be called upon to assist hospital administrators as they make decisions about the repair, replacement, or purchase of new equipment. They consult with medical and research staffs to determine that equipment is functioning safely and properly. They also consult with medical and engineering staffs when called upon to modify or develop equipment. In all of these activities, they use their knowledge of electronics, medical terminology, human anatomy and physiology, chemistry, and physics.

In addition, biomedical equipment technicians are involved in a range of other related duties. Some biomedical equipment technicians maintain inventories of all instruments in the hospital, their condition, location, and operators. They reorder parts and components, assist in providing people with emergency instruments, restore unsafe or defective instruments to working order, and check for safety regulation compliance.

Other biomedical equipment technicians help physicians, surgeons, nurses, and researchers conduct procedures and experiments. In addition, they must be able to explain to staff members how to operate these machines, the conditions under which a certain apparatus may or may not be used, how to solve small operating problems, and how to monitor and maintain equipment.

In many hospitals, technicians are assigned to a particular service, such as pediatrics, surgery, or renal medicine. These technicians become specialists in certain types of equipment. However, unlike electrocardiograph technicians or dialysis technicians, who specialize in one kind of equipment, most biomedical equipment technicians must be thoroughly familiar with a large variety of instruments. They might be called upon to prepare an artificial kidney or to work with a blood-gas analyzer. Biomedical equipment technicians also maintain pulmonary function machines. These machines are used in clinics for ambulatory patients, hospital laboratories, departments of medicine for diagnosis and treatment, and rehabilitation of cardiopulmonary patients.

While most biomedical equipment technicians are trained in electronics technology, there is also a need for technicians trained in plastics to work on the development of artificial organs and for people trained in glass blowing to help make the precision parts for specialized equipment.

Many biomedical equipment technicians work for medical instrument manufacturers. These technicians consult and assist in the construction of new machinery, helping to make decisions concerning materials and construction methods to be used in the manufacture of the equipment.

REQUIREMENTS

High School

There are a number of classes you can take in high school to help you prepare for this work. Science classes, such as chemistry, biology, and physics, will give you the science background you will need for working in a medical environment. Take shop classes that deal with electronics, drafting, or blueprint reading. These classes will give you experience working with your hands, following printed directions, using electricity, and working with machinery. Mathematics classes will help you become comfortable working with numbers and formulas. Don't neglect your English studies. English classes will help you develop your communication skills, which will be important to have when you deal with a variety of different people in your professional life.

Postsecondary Training

To become qualified for this work, you will need to complete postsecondary education that leads either to an associate's degree from a two-year institution or a bachelor's degree from a four-year college or university. Most biomedical equipment technicians choose to receive an associate's degree. Biomedical equipment technology is a relatively new program in some schools and may also be referred to as *medical electronics technology* or *biomedical engineering technology*. No matter what the name of the program, however, you should expect to receive instruction in such areas as anatomy, physiology, electrical and electronic fundamentals, chemistry, physics, and biomedical equipment construction and design. In addition, you will study safety methods in health care facilities and medical equipment troubleshooting, as it will be your job to be the problem solver. You should also expect to continue taking communication or English classes since communications skills will be essential to your work. In addition to the classroom work, many programs often provide you with practical experience in repairing and servicing equipment in a clinical or laboratory setting under the supervision of an experienced equipment technician. In this way, you learn about electrical components and circuits, the design and construction of common pieces of machinery, and computer technology as it applies to biomedical equipment.

By studying various pieces of equipment, you learn a problem-solving technique that applies not only to the equipment studied, but also to equipment you have not yet seen, and even to equipment that has not yet been invented. Part of this problem-solving technique includes learning how and where to locate sources of information.

Some biomedical equipment technicians receive their training in the armed forces. During the course of an enlistment period of four years or less, military personnel can receive training that prepares them for entry-level or sometimes advanced-level positions in the civilian workforce.

Certification or Licensing
The Board of Examiners for Biomedical Equipment Technicians, which is affiliated with the Association for the Advancement of Medical Instrumentation (AAMI), maintains certification programs for biomedical equipment technicians. The following categories are available: biomedical equipment technician, radiology equipment specialist, and clinical laboratory equipment specialist. Contact the AAMI for more information. Although certification is not required for employment, it is highly recommended. Technicians with certification have demonstrated that they have attained an overall knowledge of the field and are dedicated to their profession. Many employers prefer to hire technicians who have this certification.

Other Requirements
Biomedical equipment technicians need mechanical ability and should enjoy working with tools. Because this job demands quick decision-making and prompt repairs, technicians should work well under pressure. You should also be extremely precise and accurate in your work, have good communications skills, and enjoy helping others—an essential quality for anyone working in the health care industry.

EXPLORING
You will have difficulty gaining any direct experience in biomedical equipment technology until you are in a training program or working professionally. Your first hands-on opportunities generally come in the clinical and laboratory phases of your education. You can, however, visit school and community libraries to seek out books written about careers in medical technology. You can also join a hobby club devoted to chemistry, biology, radio equipment, or electronics.

Perhaps the best way to learn more about this job is to set up, with the help of teachers or guidance counselors, a visit to a local health care facility or to arrange for a biomedical technician to speak to interested students, either on site or at a career exploration seminar hosted by the school. You may be able to ask the technician about his or her educational background, what a day on the job is like, and what new technologies are on the horizon. Try to visit a school offer-

Books to Read

Carr, Joseph J., and John M. Brown. *Introduction to Biomedical Equipment Technology.* 4th ed. Upper Saddle River, N.J.: Prentice Hall, 2000.

Dyro, Joseph F. *Clinical Engineering Handbook.* San Diego: Academic Press, 2004.

Khandpur, R. S. *Biomedical Instrumentation: Technology and Applications.* New York: McGraw-Hill Professional, 2004.

Prutchi, David. *Design and Development of Medical Electronic Instrumentation: A Practical Perspective of the Design, Construction, and Test of Medical Devices.* Hoboken, N.J.: Wiley-Interscience, 2004.

Stiefel, Robert H. *Medical Equipment Management Manual.* Arlington, Va.: Association for the Advancement of Medical Instrumentation, 2005.

ing a program in biomedical equipment technology and discuss your career plans with an admissions counselor there. The counselor may also be able to provide you with helpful insights about the career and your preparation for it.

Finally, because this work involves the health care field, consider getting a part-time job or volunteering at a local hospital. Naturally, you won't be asked to work with the biomedical equipment, but you will have the opportunity to see professionals on the job and experience being in the medical environment. Even if your duty is only to escort patients to their tests, you may gain a greater understanding of this work.

EMPLOYERS

Many schools place students in part-time hospital positions to help them gain practical experience. Students are often able to return to these hospitals for full-time employment after graduation. Other places of employment include research institutes and biomedical equipment manufacturers. Government hospitals and the military also employ biomedical equipment technicians.

STARTING OUT

Most schools offering programs in biomedical equipment technology work closely with local hospitals and industries, and school career services officers are usually informed about openings when they become available. In some cases, recruiters may visit a school periodically to conduct interviews. Also, many schools place students in part-time hospital jobs to help them gain practical experience. Students are often able to return to these hospitals for full-time employment after graduation.

Another effective method of finding employment is to write directly to hospitals, research institutes, or biomedical equipment manufacturers. Other good sources of leads for job openings include state employment offices and newspaper want ads.

ADVANCEMENT

With experience, biomedical equipment technicians can expect to work with less supervision, and in some cases they may find themselves supervising less-experienced technicians. They may advance to positions in which they serve as instructors, assist in research, or have administrative duties. Although many supervisory positions are open to biomedical equipment technicians, some positions are not available without additional education. In large metropolitan hospitals, for instance, the minimum educational requirement for biomedical engineers, who do much of the supervising of biomedical equipment technicians, is a bachelor's degree; many engineers have a master's degree as well.

EARNINGS

Salaries for biomedical equipment technicians vary in different institutions and localities and according to the experience, training, certification, and type of work done by the technician. According to the U.S. Department of Labor, the median annual salary for medical equipment repairers was $40,580 in 2006. The top 10 percent in this profession made $66,160 a year, while the lowest 10 percent made $23,700 per year. In general, biomedical equipment technicians who work for manufacturers have higher earnings than those who work for hospitals. Naturally, those in supervisory or senior positions also command higher salaries. Benefits, such as health insurance and vacation days, vary with the employer.

WORK ENVIRONMENT

Working conditions for biomedical equipment technicians vary according to employer and type of work done. Hospital employees generally work a 40-hour week; their schedules sometimes include weekends and holidays, and some technicians may be on call for emergencies. Technicians working for equipment manufacturers may have to do extensive traveling to install or service equipment.

The physical surroundings in which biomedical equipment technicians work may vary from day to day. Technicians may work in a lab or treatment room with patients or consult with engineers, administrators, and other staff members. Other days, technicians may spend most of their time at a workbench repairing equipment.

OUTLOOK

Because of the expanding healthcare field and increasing use of electronic medical devices and other sophisticated biomedical equipment, there is a steady demand for skilled and trained biomedical equipment technicians. The U.S. Department of Labor predicts that employment for this group will grow about as fast as the average for all occupations through 2014.

In hospitals the need for more biomedical equipment technicians exists not only because of the increasing use of biomedical equipment but also because hospital administrators realize that these technicians can help hold down costs. Biomedical equipment technicians do this through their preventive maintenance checks and by taking over some routine activities of engineers and administrators, thus releasing those professionals for activities that only they can perform. Through the coming decades, cost containment will remain a high priority for hospital administrators, and as long as biomedical equipment technicians can contribute to that effort, the demand for them should remain strong.

For the many biomedical equipment technicians who work for companies that build, sell, lease, or service biomedical equipment, job opportunities should also continue to grow.

The federal government employs biomedical equipment technicians in its hospitals, research institutes, and the military. Employment in these areas will depend largely on levels of government spending. In the research area, spending levels may vary; however, in health care delivery, spending should remain high for the near future.

FOR MORE INFORMATION

For information on student memberships, biomedical technology programs, and certification, contact

Association for the Advancement of Medical Instrumentation
1110 North Glebe Road, Suite 220
Arlington, VA 22201-4795

Tel: 800-332-2264
Email: certifications@aami.org
http://www.aami.org

For *industry information, contact*
Medical Equipment and Technology Association Board
Email: information@mymeta.org
http://www.mymeta.org

Boilermakers and Boilermaker Mechanics

OVERVIEW

Boilermakers and *boilermaker mechanics* construct, assemble, and repair boilers, vats, tanks, and other large metal vessels designed to hold liquids and gases. Following blueprints, they lay out, cut, fit, bolt, weld, and rivet together heavy metal plates, boiler tubes, and castings. Boilermaker mechanics maintain and repair boilers and other vessels made by boilermakers. There are approximately 19,000 boilermakers working in the United States.

HISTORY

Boilers first became important during the industrial revolution, when steam power emerged as a practical way to drive various kinds of machinery. A *boiler* is an apparatus that heats a liquid, usually water, and converts it to vapor. Boilers were first made and used in England at the beginning of the 18th century. Manufacturers first used iron and then began using steel in boilers because steel could withstand more heat and pressure in use. During the 19th and 20th centuries, a series of design changes and improved alloys made boilers useful in a wide variety of industrial applications.

Because boilers are often operated at extremely high pressures, faulty construction, bad repairs, or improper operation can be very dangerous. Explosions were not uncommon in the early years of the industry before safety measures were instituted and construction methods improved. During the late 19th century, regulations were put in place in some localities to prevent accidents caused by careless construction. Workers in the industry began organizing in the 1880s. By 1893, the two unions representing workers in boilermaking and similar trades met in Chicago to unite into what was then called the International Brotherhood of Boiler Makers, Iron Ship Builders, Blacksmiths, Forgers, and Helpers.

It was not until 1908, however, that rules and regulations were developed to apply to any sizable area. Massachusetts created a Board of Boiler Rules in that year, and Ohio followed with its own set of rules in 1911. By 1934, 19 states and 15 cities had such codes. Today, as a result of the combined efforts of industry, labor unions, and government, safety codes are practically universal. The American Society of Mechanical Engineers and the International Brotherhood of Boilermakers, Iron Ship Builders, Blacksmiths, Forgers, and Helpers have been leaders in the promotion and enforcement of the codes of safe manufacture and maintenance.

THE JOB

Some boilermakers and boilermaker mechanics work at or near the site where the boiler, tank, or vat is installed. Such sites include petroleum refineries, schools, and other institutions with large heating plants, factories where boilers are used to generate power to run machines, factories that make and store products such as chemicals or beer in large tanks, and atomic energy plants. Others work in shops or factories where boilers and other large vessels are manufactured.

Boilermakers who do layout work usually work in a shop or factory. These workers follow drawings, blueprints, and patterns to mark pieces of metal plate and tubing indicating how the metal will be cut and shaped by other workers into the sections of vessels. Once the sections are fabricated, other workers at the shop, called *fitters*, temporarily put together the plates and the framework of the vessels. They check the drawings and other specifications and bolt or tack-weld pieces together to be sure that the parts fit properly.

In doing the final assembly at the site, boilermakers first refer to blueprints and mark off dimensions on the base that has been prepared for the finished vessel. They use measuring devices, straightedges, and transits. They attach rigging equipment such as hoists, jacks, and rollers to any prefabricated sections of the vessel that are so large they must be lifted into place with cranes. After crane operators move the sections to the correct positions, the boilermakers fine-tune the alignment of the parts. They use levels and check plumb lines and then secure the sections in place with wedges and turnbuckles. With cutting torches, files, and grinders, they remove irregularities and precisely adjust the fit and finally weld and rivet the sections together. They may also attach other tubing, valves, gauges, or other parts to the vessel and then test the container for leaks and defects.

Boilermakers also work in shipbuilding and in repairing the hulls, bulkheads, and decks of iron ships. In a typical repair, boilermakers first remove damaged metal plates by drilling out rivets and cutting off rivet heads with a chipping hammer. Then they take measurements of the damaged plates or make wooden patterns of them so that new plates can be made. They install the new plates, reaming and aligning rivet holes, then fastening on the plates by driving in rivets. Sometimes similar work is done on ships' boilers, condensers, evaporators, loaders, gratings, and stacks.

Field construction boilermakers work outdoors and move from one geographic location to another. They join construction teams in erecting and repairing pressure vessels, air pollution equipment, blast furnaces, water treatment plants, storage tanks, and stacks and liners. They can be involved in the erection of a 750,000-gallon water storage tank, the placement of a nuclear power plant reactor dome, or the construction of components on a hydroelectric power station.

Boilermaker mechanics maintain and repair boilers and other vessels. They routinely clean or direct others to clean boilers, and they inspect fittings, valves, tubes, controls, and other parts. When necessary, they check the vessels to identify specific weaknesses or sources of trouble. They update components, such as burners and boiler tubes, to make them as efficient as possible. They dismantle the units to replace worn or defective parts, using hand and power tools, gas torches, and welding equipment. Sometimes repairs require that they use metalworking machinery, such as power shears and presses to cut and shape parts to specification. They strengthen joints and supports, and they put patches on weak areas of metal plates. Like fabrication and installation work, all repairs must be done in compliance with state and local safety codes.

REQUIREMENTS

High School

A high school diploma is required for all applicants to the boiler-making trade. In the past, people have become boilermakers through on-the-job training, but apprenticeships are now strongly recommended. To gain an apprenticeship, an applicant must score well on an aptitude test. You can prepare yourself for this test and the career by taking math classes and shop classes throughout high school. Courses that give you the opportunity to learn blueprint reading, welding, and metalworking are especially helpful.

Postsecondary Training

Formal apprenticeships usually last four years. An apprentice receives practical training while working as a helper under the supervision of an experienced boilermaker. In addition to working, trainees attend classes in the technical aspects of the trade. Apprentices study subjects such as blueprint reading, layout, welding techniques, mechanical drawing, the physics and chemistry of various metals, and applied mathematics. While on the job, apprentices practice the knowledge they have acquired in the classroom. They develop such skills as using rigging and hoisting equipment, welding, riveting, and installing auxiliary devices and tubes onto vessels.

Other Requirements

Mechanical aptitude and manual dexterity are important characteristics for prospective boilermakers. Because the work can be very strenuous, stamina is needed for jobs that require a great deal of bending, stooping, squatting, or reaching. Before they begin work, boilermakers may need to pass a physical examination showing that they are in good enough health to do the work safely. On the job, they must be able to work well despite noisy surroundings, odors, working at heights or in small, enclosed spaces, and other discomforts and dangers. It is also important that they be cautious and careful in their work and that they closely follow safety rules.

EXPLORING

You may be able to observe boilermakers or workers who use similar skills as they work on construction projects or repair and maintenance jobs. For example, welders and equipment operators lifting heavy objects with elaborate rigging can sometimes be seen working at sites where large buildings are being erected. High school shop courses such as blueprint reading and metalworking can give you an idea of some of the activities of boilermakers. With the help of shop teachers or guidance counselors, you may be able to arrange to talk with people working in the trade. Information may also be obtained by contacting the local union-management committee in charge of apprenticeships for boilermakers.

EMPLOYERS

Approximately 19,000 boilermakers work in the United States. Of that number, nearly 70 percent work in the construction industry. Approximately 14 percent work in manufacturing, employed primarily in boiler manufacturing shops, iron and steel plants, petroleum refineries, chemical plants, and shipyards. Still others work for boiler repair firms, for railroads, and in navy shipyards and federal power facilities.

STARTING OUT

There are a limited number of apprenticeships available in boilermaking; only the best applicants are accepted, and there may be a waiting period before the apprenticeship starts. Sometimes workers begin as helpers in repair shops and enter formal apprenticeships later. These helper jobs are often advertised in newspapers. Vocational and technical schools and sometimes high schools with metal shop courses may also help their graduates locate such positions. Other good approaches are to apply directly to employers and to contact the local office of the state employment service.

ADVANCEMENT

Upon completing their training programs, apprentices qualify as journeymen boilermakers. With experience and the right kind of leadership abilities, boilermakers may be able to advance to supervisory positions. In fabrication shops, layout workers and fitters who start as helpers can learn the skills they need in about two years. In time, they may move up to become shop supervisors, or they may decide to become boilermakers who work on-site to assemble vessels.

EARNINGS

According to the U.S. Department of Labor, the median hourly wage for boilermakers in 2006 was $22.58. For full-time work at 40 hours per week, this wage translates into a median annual income of $46,960. The department also reported that the lowest paid 10 percent earned less than $14.62 per hour, or less than approximately $30,410 per year for full-time work. At the other end of the pay scale, the highest paid 10 percent made more than $34.22 per hour (approximately $71,170 annually).

According to the International Brotherhood of Boilermakers, annual earnings vary greatly because of the temporary, cyclical nature of the work. Apprentices start at about 60 percent of journeyman wages. Earnings also vary according to the part of the country where boilermakers work, the industry that employs them, and their level of skill and experience. Boilermakers tend to make more than boilermaker mechanics. Among employees in boiler-fabrication shops, layout workers generally earn more while fitters earn less. Both layout workers and fitters normally work indoors; therefore, their earnings are not limited by seasonal variations in weather.

Most boilermakers are members of unions, and union contracts set their wages and benefits. The largest union is the International Brotherhood of Boilermakers, Iron Ship Builders, Blacksmiths, Forgers, and Helpers. Other boilermakers are members of the Industrial Union of Marine and Shipbuilding Workers of America; the United Steelworkers of America; the International Association of Machinists and Aerospace Workers; and the International Union, United Automobile, Aerospace, and Agricultural Implement Workers of America. Among the fringe benefits established under union contracts are health insurance, pension plans, and paid vacation time.

WORK ENVIRONMENT

Boilermaking tends to be more hazardous than many other occupations. Boilermakers often work with dangerous tools and equipment; they must manage heavy materials; and they may climb to heights to do installation or repair work. Despite great progress in preventing accidents, the rate of on-the-job injuries for boilermakers remains higher than the average for all manufacturing industries. Employer and union safety programs and standards set by the federal government's Occupational Safety and Health Administration (OSHA) are helping to control dangerous conditions and reduce accidents.

The work often requires physical exertion and may be carried on in extremely hot, poorly ventilated, noisy, and damp places. At times it is necessary to work in cramped quarters inside boilers, vats, or tanks. At other times, workers must handle materials and equipment several stories above ground level. Sometimes installation workers work on jobs that require them to remain away from home for considerable periods of time.

To protect against injury, boilermakers and mechanics use a variety of special clothing and equipment, such as hard hats, safety glasses and shoes, harnesses, and respirators. A 40-hour week is average, but in some jobs, deadlines may require overtime.

OUTLOOK

Employment of boilermakers is expected to grow about as fast as the average for all occupations through 2014, according to the U.S. Department of Labor. One reason for this lagging growth is the current trend of repairing and retrofitting, rather than replacing, boilers. In addition, the smaller boilers currently being used require less on-site assembly. Finally, the automation of production technologies and the increasing use of imported boilers will cut down on the need for boilermakers. An increasing number of boilermakers will be employed by utilities, as these organizations seek to upgrade their boiler systems to comply with the Federal Clean Air Act.

During economic downturns, boilermakers, including layout workers and fitters, may be laid off because many industries stop expanding their operations and install very few new boilers. On the other hand, boilermaker mechanics are less affected by downturns because they work more on maintaining and repairing existing equipment, which requires their services regardless of economic conditions.

Despite average growth, there will be openings for boilermakers every year as experienced workers leave the field. Workers who have completed apprenticeships will have the best opportunities for good jobs.

FOR MORE INFORMATION

For information about boilermaker apprenticeships, contact
Boilermakers National Joint Apprenticeship Program
1017 North 9th Street
Kansas City, KS 66101-2624
Tel: 913-342-2100
Email: hpsloubnap@msn.com
http://www.bnap.com

For additional career information, contact
International Brotherhood of Boilermakers, Iron Ship Builders,
Blacksmiths, Forgers and Helpers, AFL-CIO
753 State Avenue, Suite 570
Kansas City, KS 66101-2511
Tel: 913-371-2640
http://www.boilermakers.org

Communications Equipment Technicians

QUICK FACTS

School Subjects
Mathematics
Technical/shop

Personal Skills
Following instructions
Mechanical/manipulative

Work Environment
Primarily indoors
Primarily multiple locations

Minimum Education Level
Some postsecondary training

Salary Range
$22,760 to $52,430 to
$68,310+

Certification or Licensing
Required for certain positions

Outlook
Decline

DOT
822

GOE
05.02.01

NOC
7246

O*NET-SOC
49-2021.00, 49-2022.00,
49-2022.03

OVERVIEW

Communications equipment technicians install, test, maintain, troubleshoot, and repair a wide variety of telephone and radio equipment used to transmit communications—voices, data, graphics, and video—across long distances. This does not include, however, equipment that handles entertainment broadcast to the public via radio or television signals. Most communications equipment technicians work in telephone company offices or on customers' premises. In the United States, approximately 222,000 people work as communications equipment technicians.

HISTORY

Alexander Graham Bell patented the first practical telephone in 1876. By 1878, a commercial telephone company that switched calls between its local customers was operating in New Haven, Connecticut. For many years, telephone connections were made by operators who worked at central offices of telephone companies. A company customer who wanted to speak with another customer had to call the operator at a central office, and the operator would connect the two customer lines together by inserting a metal plug into a socket.

Today, automatic switching equipment has replaced operators for routine connections like this, and telephones carry much more than voice messages between local customers. Vast quantities of information are sent across phone lines in the form of visual images and computer data. Furthermore, telephone systems today are part of larger interconnected telecommunications systems. These systems link together telephones with other equipment that sends information via microwave and television transmissions, fiber optics cables, undersea cables, and signals bounced off satellites in space. High-speed computerized switching and routing equipment makes it possible for telecommunications systems to handle millions of calls and other data signals at the same time.

THE JOB

Although specific duties vary, most communications equipment technicians share some basic kinds of activities. They work with electrical measuring and testing devices and hand tools; read blueprints, circuit diagrams, and electrical schematics (diagrams); and consult technical manuals. The following paragraphs describe just a few of the many technicians who work in this complex industry.

Central office equipment installers, also called *equipment installation technicians,* are specialists in setting up and taking down the switching and dialing equipment located in telephone company central offices. They install equipment in newly established offices, update existing equipment, add on to facilities that are being expanded, and remove old, outdated apparatus.

Central office repairers, also called *switching equipment technicians* or *central office technicians,* work on the switching equipment that automatically connects lines when customers dial calls. They analyze defects and malfunctions in equipment, make fine adjustments, and test and repair switches and relays. These workers use various special tools, gauges, meters, and ordinary hand tools.

PBX systems technicians or *switching equipment technicians* work on PBXs, or private branch exchanges, which are direct lines that businesses install to bypass phone company lines. PBX systems can handle both voice and data communications and can provide specialized services such as electronic mail and automatic routing of calls at the lowest possible cost.

PBX installers install these systems. They may assemble customized switchboards for customers. *PBX repairers* maintain and repair PBX systems and associated equipment. Many of these workers are also now installing voice-over Internet protocol systems—which allow users to make voice calls using a broadband Internet connection.

Maintenance administrators test customers' lines within the central office to find causes and locations of malfunctions reported by customers. They report the nature of the trouble to maintenance crews and coordinate their activities to clear up the trouble. Some

A technician troubleshoots a problem with a circuit box. *(David R. Frazier, The Image Works)*

maintenance administrators work in cable television company offices, diagnosing subscribers' problems with cable television signals and dispatching repairers if necessary. They use highly automated testboards and other equipment to analyze circuits. They enter data into computer files and interpret computer output about trouble areas in the system.

Many workers in this group are concerned with other kinds of communications equipment that are not part of telephone systems. Among these are *radio repairers and mechanics,* who install and repair radio transmitters and receivers. Sometimes they work on other electronics equipment at microwave and fiber optics installations. *Avionics technicians* work on electronic components in aircraft communication, navigation, and flight control systems. *Signal maintainers* or *track switch maintainers* work on railroads. They install, inspect, and maintain the signals, track switches, gate crossings, and communications systems throughout rail networks. *Instrument repairers* work in repair shops, where they repair, test, and modify a variety of communications equipment.

REQUIREMENTS

High School
Most employers prefer to hire candidates with at least some post-secondary training in electronics. So to prepare for this career, you

should take computer courses, algebra, geometry, English, physics, and shop classes in high school. Useful shop courses are those that introduce you to principles of electricity and electronics, basic machine repair, reading blueprints and engineering drawings, and using hand tools.

Postsecondary Training

Most telecommunications employers prefer to hire technicians who have already learned most of the necessary skills, so consider getting training in this area either through service in the military or from a postsecondary training program. Programs at community or junior colleges or technical schools in telecommunications technology, electronics, electrical, or electromechanical technology, or even computer maintenance or related subjects, may be appropriate for people who want to become communications equipment technicians. Most programs last two years, although certificates in specific areas often can be obtained through a one-year program. Useful classes are those that provide practical knowledge about electricity and electronics and teach the use of hand tools, electronic testing equipment, and computer data terminals. Classes in digital and fiber optic technology are also beneficial.

Applicants for entry-level positions may have to pass tests of their knowledge, general mechanical aptitude, and manual dexterity. Once hired, employees often go through company training programs. They may study practical and theoretical aspects of electricity, electronics, and mathematics that they will need to know for their work. Experienced workers also may attend training sessions from time to time. They need to keep their knowledge up to date as new technology in the rapidly changing telecommunications field affects the way they do their jobs.

Certification or Licensing

Some workers in this field must obtain a license. Federal Communications Commission regulations require that anyone who works with radio transmitting equipment must have a Global Maritime Distress and Safety System (GMDSS) license. In order to receive a license, applicants need to pass a written test on radio laws and operating procedures and take a Morse code examination.

Certification for technicians is available from the National Association of Radio and Telecommunications Engineers and the Society of Cable Telecommunications Engineers. To receive certification, you'll need a certain amount of education and experience in telecommunications, and you'll have to pass an examination.

Other Requirements

You'll need strong mechanical and electrical aptitudes, as well as manual dexterity. Keep in mind, too, that you'll need to be able to distinguish between colors because many wires are color-coded. You should also have problem-solving abilities and the ability to work without a lot of direct supervision. Math and computer skills are also very important; you'll also need to be able to interpret very technical manuals and blueprints. You'll be expected to keep accurate records, so you'll need to be organized.

EXPLORING

In high school, you can begin to find out about the work of communications equipment technicians by taking whatever electronics, computer, and electrical shop courses are available, and also other shop courses that help you become familiar with using various tools. Teachers or guidance counselors may be able to help you arrange a visit to a telephone company central office, where you can see telephone equipment and observe workers on the job. It may be possible to obtain a part-time or summer-helper job at a business that sells and repairs electronics equipment. Such a job could provide the opportunity to talk to workers whose skills are similar to those needed by many communications equipment technicians. Serving in the armed forces in a communications section can also provide a way to learn about this field and gain some useful experience.

EMPLOYERS

Approximately 222,000 people work as communications equipment technicians in the United States. Local and long-distance telephone companies and manufacturers of telephone and other electronic communications equipment employ communications equipment technicians. Work is also available with electrical repair shops and cable television companies.

STARTING OUT

Beginning technicians can apply directly to the employment office of the local telephone company. Many times, it is necessary for newly hired workers to take a position in a different part of the company until an opening as a technician becomes available. However, telephone companies have been reducing the number of technicians they need in recent years, and competition for these positions is especially heavy.

Information on job openings in this field may be available through the offices of the state employment service and through classified advertisements in newspapers. Because many communications equipment technicians are members of unions such as the Communications Workers of America (CWA) and the International Brotherhood of Electrical Workers, job seekers can contact their local offices for job leads and assistance, or visit the CWA Web site. The Personal Communications Industry Association also offers free job listings on its Wireless Jobnet online. Graduates of technical programs may be able to find out about openings at local companies through the school's career services office or through contacts with teachers and administrators.

ADVANCEMENT

The advancement possibilities for communications equipment technicians depend on the area of the telecommunications industry in which they work. Because of changes in equipment and technology, workers who hope to advance will need to have received recent training or update their skills through additional training. This training may be offered through employers or can be obtained through technical institutes or telecommunications associations.

Advancement opportunities in telephone companies may be limited because of the fact that many telephone companies are reducing their workforces and will have less need for certain types of workers in the future. This will result in fewer positions to move into and increased competition for more advanced positions. However, some workers may be able to advance to supervisory or administrative positions.

Many workers can advance through education resulting in an associate's or bachelor's degree. Workers who have completed two- or four-year programs in electrical or telecommunications engineering programs have the best opportunity to advance and can become engineering technicians and technologists, engineers, or telecommunications specialists.

EARNINGS

Earnings vary among communications equipment workers depending on their area of specialization, the size of their employer, and their location. The U.S. Department of Labor reports that median hourly earnings for telecommunication equipment installers and repairers were $25.21 in 2006. A technician earning this amount and working full-time at 40 hours a week would have a yearly income of approximately $52,430. The lowest paid 10 percent of telecommunications equipment technicians earned less than $14.96 per hour (approximately $31,110 yearly); the highest paid 10 percent earned more than $32.84 per hour (approximately $68,310 annually).

The Department of Labor also reports that the 2006 median hourly wage for radio mechanics was $18.12. The annual income for a technician working full-time at this pay rate would be approximately $37,690. At the low end of the pay scale, 10 percent made less than $10.94 hourly (approximately $22,760 per year); at the high end, 10 percent made more than $28.54 hourly (approximately $59,360 annually).

Most workers in this group who are employed by telephone companies are union members, and their earnings are set by contracts between the union and the company. Many currently employed communications equipment technicians have several years of experience and are at the higher end of the pay scale. Most workers in this field receive extra pay for hours worked at night, on weekends, or over 40 hours a week. Benefits vary but generally include paid vacations, paid holidays, sick leaves, and health insurance. In addition, some companies offer pension and retirement plans.

WORK ENVIRONMENT

Communications equipment technicians usually work 40 hours a week. They may have to work at night, on weekends, and on holidays because telecommunications systems must give uninterrupted service and trouble can occur at any time.

Central telephone offices are clean, well lighted, and well ventilated. Communications equipment technicians may also work on site, which may require some crawling around on office floors and some bending. Even if these workers are running cables, they aren't likely to be doing much heavy lifting; machinery assists them in some of the more strenuous work. These workers may work alone, or they may supervise the work of others. Some communications equipment technicians also work directly with clients.

The work can be stressful, as technicians are often expected to work quickly to remedy urgent problems with communication equipment. Some technicians who work for large companies with clients nationwide must also travel as part of their jobs.

OUTLOOK

The U.S. Department of Labor predicts that employment for communications equipment technicians will decline through 2014.

Nevertheless, job availability will depend on the technician's area of specialization. For example, technicians working as central office and PBX installers should find numerous job opportunities, in part because growing use of the Internet places new demands on communications networks. On the other hand, employment for radio mechanics and other installers is expected to decline as pre-wired buildings, the replacement of two-way radio systems with wireless systems, and extremely reliable equipment translate into less need for maintenance and repair. New technology relies on transmission through telecommunications networks rather than central-office switching equipment. There are far fewer mechanical devices that break, wear out, and need to be periodically cleaned and lubricated. These networks contain self-diagnosing features that detect problems and, in some cases, route operations around a trouble spot until repairs can be made. When problems occur, it is usually easier to replace parts rather than repair them. Competition for existing positions will be keen, and workers with the best qualifications stand the best chance of obtaining available jobs.

FOR MORE INFORMATION

To learn about issues affecting jobs in telecommunications, contact or visit the CWA's Web site.
Communications Workers of America (CWA)
501 Third Street, NW
Washington, DC 20001-2797
Tel: 202-434-1100
http://www.cwa-union.org

For information on union membership, contact
International Brotherhood of Electrical Workers
1125 15th Street, NW
Washington, DC 20001-3886
Tel: 202-833-7000
http://ibew.org

For information on certification, contact
National Association of Radio and Telecommunications
    Engineers
167 Village Street
Medway, MA 02053-1135
Tel: 800-896-2783
Email: narte@narte.org
http://www.narte.org

For information on educational programs and job opportunities in wireless technology (cellular, PCS, and satellite), contact
PCIA: The Wireless Infrastructure Association
500 Montgomery Street, Suite 700
Alexandria, VA 22314-1561
Tel: 800-759-0300
http://www.pcia.com

For information on certification, contact
Society of Cable Telecommunications Engineers
140 Phillips Road
Exton, PA 19341-1318
http://www.scte.org

For information about conferences, special programs, and membership, contact
Women in Cable Telecommunications
14555 Avion Parkway, Suite 250
Chantilly, VA 20151-1117
Tel: 703-234-9810
http://www.wict.org

Diesel Mechanics

OVERVIEW

Diesel mechanics repair and maintain diesel engines that power trucks, buses, ships, construction and roadbuilding equipment, farm equipment, and some automobiles. They may also maintain and repair nonengine components, such as brakes, electrical systems, and heating and air conditioning. Approximately 270,000 diesel mechanics work in the United States.

HISTORY

In 1892, Rudolf Diesel patented an engine that despite its weight and large size was more efficient than the gasoline engine patented by Gottlieb Daimler less than a decade earlier. While Daimler's engine became the standard for automobiles, Diesel found his engine had practical use for industry. The diesel engine differs from the gasoline engine in that the ignition of fuel is caused by compression of air in the engine's cylinders rather than by a spark. Diesel's engines were eventually used to power pipelines, electric and water plants, automobiles and trucks, and marine craft. Equipment used in mines, oil fields, factories and trans-oceanic shipping also came to rely on diesel engines. With the onset of World War I, diesel engines became standard in submarines, tanks, and other heavy equipment. Suddenly, diesel mechanics were in big demand and the armed forces established training programs. Combat units supported by diesel-powered machines often had several men trained in diesel mechanics to repair breakdowns. The war proved to industry that diesel engines were tough and efficient, and many companies found applications for diesel-powered machines in the following years.

At the turn of the century, trucks were wooden wagons equipped with gasoline engines. As they became bigger, transported more goods, and traveled farther, fuel efficiency became a big concern. In 1930, the trucking industry adopted the diesel engine, with its efficiency and durability, as its engine for the future. Many diesel mechanics began their training as automobile mechanics, and learned diesel through hands-on experience. World War II brought a new demand for highly trained diesel mechanics, and again the armed forces trained men in diesel technology. After the war, diesel mechanics found new jobs in diesel at trucking companies that maintained large fleets of trucks, and at construction companies that used diesel-powered equipment. It wasn't until the 1970s that diesel engines in consumer passenger cars began to gain popularity. Before then, the disadvantages of diesel—its heaviness, poor performance, and low driving comfort—made diesel a second choice for many consumers. But the fuel crisis of the 1970s brought diesel a greater share of the automotive market, creating more demand for mechanics who could repair and maintain diesel engines.

Today, job growth and security for diesel mechanics is closely tied to the trucking industry. In the 1980s and 1990s, the trucking industry experienced steady growth as other means of transportation, such as rail, were used less frequently. Now, many businesses and manufacturers have found it cost efficient to maintain less inventory. Instead, they prefer to have their materials shipped on an as-needed basis. This low-inventory system has created a tremendous demand on the trucking industry, and diesel mechanics are essential to helping the industry meet that demand.

THE JOB

Most diesel mechanics work on the engines of heavy trucks, such as those used in hauling freight over long distances, or in heavy industries such as construction and mining. Many are employed by companies that maintain their own fleet of vehicles. The diesel mechanic's main task is preventive maintenance to avoid breakdowns, but they also make engine repairs when necessary. Diesel mechanics also frequently perform maintenance on other nonengine components, such as brake systems, electronics, transmissions, and suspensions.

Through periodic maintenance, diesel mechanics keep vehicles or engines in good operating condition. They run through a checklist of standard maintenance tasks, such as changing oil and filters, checking cooling systems, and inspecting brakes and wheel bearings for wear. They make the appropriate repairs or adjustments and replace parts that are worn. Fuel injection units, fuel pumps, pistons, crankshafts, bushings, and bearings must be regularly removed, reconditioned, or replaced.

As more diesel engines rely on a variety of electronic components, mechanics have become more proficient in the basics of electronics. Previously technical functions in diesel equipment (both engine and nonengine parts) are being replaced by electronics, significantly altering the way mechanics perform maintenance and repairs. As new technology evolves, diesel mechanics may need additional training to use tools and computers to diagnose and correct problems with electronic parts. Employers generally provide this training.

Diesel engines are scheduled for periodic rebuilding usually every 18 months or 100,000 miles. Mechanics rely upon extensive records they keep on each engine to determine the extent of the rebuild. Records detail the maintenance and repair history that helps mechanics determine repair needs and prevent future breakdowns. Diesel mechanics use various specialty instruments to make precision measurements and diagnostics of each engine component. Micrometers and various gauges test for engine wear. Ohmmeters, ammeters, and voltmeters test electrical components. Dynamometers and oscilloscopes test overall engine operations.

Engine rebuilds usually require several mechanics, each specializing in a particular area. They use ordinary hand tools such as ratchets and sockets, screwdrivers, wrenches, and pliers; power tools such as pneumatic wrenches; welding and flame-cutting equipment; and machine tools like lathes and boring machines. Diesel mechanics typically supply their own hand tools at an investment of $6,000 to $25,000, depending upon their specialty. It is the employer's responsibility to furnish the larger power tools, engine analyzers, and other diagnostic equipment.

In addition to trucks and buses, diesel mechanics also service and repair construction equipment such as cranes, bulldozers, earth moving equipment, and road construction equipment. The variations in transmissions, gear systems, electronics, and other engine components of diesel engines may require additional training.

To maintain and increase their skills and to keep up with new technology, diesel mechanics must regularly read service and repair manuals, industry bulletins, and other publications. They must also be willing to take part in training programs given by manufacturers or at vocational schools. Those who have certification must periodically retake exams to keep their credentials. Frequent changes in technology demand that mechanics keep up to date with the latest training.

A mechanic repairs a diesel engine. *(David R. Frazier, The Image Works)*

REQUIREMENTS

High School

A high school diploma is the minimum requirement to land a job that offers growth possibilities, a good salary, and challenges. In addition to automotive and shop classes, high school students should take mathematics, English, and computer classes. Adjustments and repairs to many car components require the mechanic to make numerous computations, for which good mathematical skills will be essential. Diesel mechanics must be voracious readers in order to stay competitive; there are many must-read repair manuals and trade journals. Computer skills are also important, as computers are common in most repair shops.

Postsecondary Training

Employers prefer to hire those who have completed some kind of formal training program in diesel mechanics, or in some cases automobile mechanics—usually a minimum of two years' education in either case. A wide variety of such programs are offered at community colleges, vocational schools, independent organizations, and manufacturers. Most accredited programs include periods of internship.

Some programs are conducted in association with truck and heavy equipment manufacturers. Students combine work experience with hands-on classroom study of up-to-date equipment provided by manufacturers. In other programs students alternate time in the classroom with internships at manufacturers. Although these students may take up to four years to finish their training, they become familiar with the latest technology and also earn modest salaries as they train.

Certification or Licensing

One indicator of quality for entry-level mechanics recognized by everyone in the industry is certification by the National Institute for Automotive Service Excellence. There are eight areas of certification available in medium/heavy-duty truck repair: gasoline engines; diesel engines; drive train; brakes; suspension and steering; electrical/electronic systems; heating, ventilation, and air conditioning; and preventive maintenance inspection. There are seven areas of certification available in school bus repair: body systems and special equipment, diesel engines, drive train, brakes, suspension and steering, electrical/electronic systems, and air conditioning systems and controls. Applicants must have at least two years of experience in the field and pass the examinations related to their specialty. To maintain their certification, mechanics must retake the examination for their specialties every five years. The Association of Diesel Specialists also offers voluntary certification to diesel mechanics.

Other Requirements

Diesel mechanics must be patient and thorough in their work. They need to have excellent troubleshooting skills and must be able to logically deduce the cause of system malfunctions. Diesel mechanics also need a Class A driver's license.

Typical Classes for Diesel Mechanics Majors

Introduction to Computer and Computer-Aided Design Operations
Basic Brake Systems
Basic Electrical Systems
Introduction to Diesel Engines
Basic Hydraulics
Introduction to Industrial Maintenance
Power Train Systems
Heating, Ventilation, and Air Conditioning Troubleshooting and
    Repair
Auto Power Shift and Hydrostatic Transmissions
Advanced Diesel Tune-up and Troubleshooting
Advanced Hydraulics
Failure Analysis
Electronic Controls
Natural Gas Compression
Tracks and Undercarriages

EXPLORING

Many community centers offer general auto maintenance workshops where students can get additional practice working on real cars and learn from instructors. Trade magazines such as *Land Line* (http://www.landlinemag.com) and *Overdrive* (http://www.overdriveonline.com) are an excellent source for learning what's new in the trucking industry and can be found at libraries and some larger bookstores. Working part time at a repair shop or dealership can prepare students for the atmosphere and challenges a mechanic faces on the job.

Many diesel mechanics begin their exploration on gasoline engines because spare diesel engines are hard to come by for those who are just trying to learn and experiment. Diesel engines are very similar to gasoline engines except for their ignition systems and size. Besides being larger, diesel engines are distinguished by the absence of common gasoline engine components such as spark plugs, ignition wires, coils, and distributors. Diesel mechanics use the same hand tools as automobile mechanics, however. In this way, learning technical aptitude on automobiles will be important for the student who wishes eventually to learn to work on diesel engines.

EMPLOYERS

Diesel mechanics may find employment in a number of different areas. Many work for dealers that sell semi trucks and other diesel-powered equipment. About 17 percent of the country's 270,000 diesel mechanics work for local and long distance trucking companies. Others maintain the buses and trucks of public transit companies, schools, or governments or service buses, trucks, and other diesel-powered equipment at automotive repair and maintenance shops, motor vehicle and parts wholesalers, or automotive equipment rental and leasing agencies. Diesel mechanics can find work all over the country, in both large and small cities. Job titles may range from bus maintenance technician to hydraulic system technician, clutch rebuilder, and heavy-duty maintenance mechanic. A small number of diesel mechanics may find jobs in the railway and industrial sectors and in marine maintenance.

STARTING OUT

The best way to begin a career as a diesel mechanic is to enroll in a postsecondary training program and obtain accreditation. Trade and technical schools nearly always provide job placement assistance for their graduates. Such schools usually have contacts with local employers who need to hire well-trained people. Often, employers post job openings at accredited trade schools in their area.

Although postsecondary training programs are more widely available and popular today, some mechanics still learn the trade on the job as apprentices. Their training consists of working for several years under the guidance of experienced mechanics. Trainees usually begin as helpers, lubrication workers, or service station attendants, and gradually acquire the skills and knowledge necessary for many service or repair tasks. However, fewer employers today are willing to hire apprentices because of the time and cost it takes to train them. Those who do learn their skills on the job inevitably require some formal training if they wish to advance and stay in step with the changing industry.

Intern programs sponsored by truck manufacturers or independent organizations provide students with opportunities to actually work with prospective employers. Internships can provide students with valuable contacts who will be able to recommend future employers once students have completed their classroom training. Many students may even be hired by the company for which they interned.

ADVANCEMENT

Typically, the first step a mechanic must take to advance is to receive certification. Although certification is voluntary, it is a widely recognized standard of achievement for diesel mechanics and the way many advance. The more certification a mechanic has, the more his or her worth to an employer, and the higher he or she advances.

With today's complex diesel engine and truck components requiring hundreds of hours of study and practice to master, more employers prefer to hire certified mechanics. Certification assures the employer that the employee is skilled in the latest repair procedures and is familiar with the most current diesel technology. Those with good communication and planning skills may advance to shop supervisor or service manager at larger repair shops or companies that keep large fleets. Others with good business skills go into business for themselves and open their own shops or work as freelance mechanics. Some master mechanics may teach at technical and vocational schools or at community colleges.

EARNINGS

Diesel mechanics' earnings vary depending upon their region, industry (trucking, construction, railroad), and other factors. Technicians in the West and East tend to earn more than those in other regions, although these distinctions are gradually disappearing.

According to the U.S. Department of Labor, the median hourly pay for all diesel mechanics in 2006 was $18.11, or approximately $37,660 annually, for full-time employment. The department also reported that the lowest paid 10 percent of diesel mechanics earned approximately $11.71 an hour, or $24,370 a year. The highest paid 10 percent earned more than $26.50 an hour, amounting to $55,120 a year. Mechanics who work for companies that must operate around the clock, such as bus lines, may work at night, on weekends, or on holidays and receive extra pay for this work. Some industries, such as construction, are subject to seasonal variations in employment levels.

The highest paid diesel mechanics work in motor vehicle manufacturing. They earned a mean wage of $26.97 an hour, or $55,890 a year, in 2006. Those who worked for general freight trucking companies earned a mean hourly wage of $17.19, or $35,760 a year, and those who specialized in automotive repair and maintenance earned an average of $17.79 an hour, or $37,000 a year.

Mechanics working for construction companies during peak summer building seasons earn up to $1,000 a week.

Many diesel mechanics are members of labor unions, and their wage rates are established by contracts between the union and the employer. Benefits packages vary from business to business. Mechanics can expect health insurance and paid vacation from most employers. Other benefits may include dental and eye care, life and disability insurance, and a pension plan. Employers usually cover a mechanic's work clothes through a clothing allowance and may pay a percentage of hand-tools purchases. An increasing number of employers pay all or most of an employee's certification training if he or she passes the test. A mechanic's salary can increase by yearly bonuses or profit sharing if the business does well.

WORK ENVIRONMENT

Depending on the size of the shop and whether it is a trucking or construction company, government, or private business, diesel mechanics work with anywhere from two to 20 other mechanics. Most shops are well lighted and well ventilated. They can be frequently noisy due to running trucks and equipment. Hoses are attached to exhaust pipes and led outside to avoid carbon monoxide poisoning.

Minor hand and back injuries are the most common problem for diesel mechanics. When reaching in hard-to-get-at places or loosening tight bolts, mechanics often bruise, cut, or burn their hands. With caution and experience, most mechanics learn to avoid hand injuries. Working for long periods in cramped or bent positions often results in a stiff back or neck. Diesel mechanics also lift many heavy objects that can cause injury if not handled cautiously; however, most shops have small cranes or hoists to lift the heaviest objects. Some may experience allergic reactions to the variety of solvents and oils frequently used in cleaning, maintenance, and repair. Shops must comply with strict safety procedures to help employees avoid accidents. Most mechanics work between 40- and 50-hour workweeks, but may be required to work longer hours when the shop is busy or during emergencies. Some mechanics make emergency repairs to stranded, roadside trucks or to construction equipment.

OUTLOOK

With diesel technology getting better (smaller, smarter, and less noisy), more light trucks and other vehicles and equipment are switching to diesel engines. Diesel engines are already more fuel-efficient than gasoline engines. Also, the increased reliance by businesses on quick deliveries has increased the demand on trucking companies. Many businesses maintain lower inventories of materials, instead preferring to have items shipped more frequently. The increase in diesel-powered vehicles, together with a trend toward increased cargo transportation via trucks, will create jobs for highly skilled diesel mechanics. Less skilled workers will face tough competition. The U.S. Department of Labor predicts that employment will grow about as fast as the average for all occupations through 2014.

Diesel mechanics enjoy good job security. Fluctuations in the economy have little effect on employment in this field. When the economy is bad, people service and repair their trucks and equipment rather than replace them. Conversely, when the economy is good, more people are apt to service their trucks and equipment regularly as well as buy new trucks and equipment.

The most jobs for diesel mechanics will open up at trucking companies who hire mechanics to maintain and repair their fleets. Construction companies are also expected to require an increase in diesel mechanics to maintain their heavy machinery, such as cranes, earthmovers, and other diesel-powered equipment.

FOR MORE INFORMATION

For information on certification, contact
Association of Diesel Specialists
10 Laboratory Drive
PO Box 13966
Research Triangle Park, NC 27709-3966
Tel: 919-406-8804
Email: info@diesel.org
http://www.diesel.org

For information on the automotive service industry and continuing education programs, contact
Automotive Aftermarket Industry Association
7101 Wisconsin Avenue, Suite 1300
Bethesda, MD 20814-3415
Tel: 301-654-6664
Email: aaia@aftermarket.org
http://www.aftermarket.org

For information on training, accreditation, and testing, contact
Inter-Industry Conference on Auto Collision Repair
5125 Trillium Boulevard
Hoffman Estates, IL 60192-3600
Tel: 800-422-7872
http://www.i-car.com

For information on careers and accredited programs, contact
National Automotive Technicians Education Foundation
101 Blue Seal Drive, Suite 101
Leesburg, VA 20175-5646
Tel: 703-669-6650
http://www.natef.org

For information on becoming a certified mechanic, contact
National Institute for Automotive Service Excellence
101 Blue Seal Drive, Suite 101
Leesburg, VA 20175-5646
Tel: 877-273-8324
http://www.asecert.org

Elevator Installers and Repairers

QUICK FACTS

School Subjects
Mathematics
Technical/shop

Personal Skills
Following instructions
Mechanical/manipulative

Work Environment
Primarily indoors
Primarily multiple locations

Minimum Education Level
Apprenticeship

Salary Range
$36,990 to $63,620 to
$87,660+

Certification or Licensing
Required (certification)
Required by certain states
(licensing)

Outlook
About as fast as the average

DOT
825

GOE
05.02.01

NOC
7318

O*NET-SOC
47-4021.00

OVERVIEW

Elevator installers and repairers, also called *elevator constructors* or *elevator mechanics,* are skilled crafts workers who assemble, install, and repair elevators, escalators, dumbwaiters, and similar equipment. They may also be responsible for modernizing this equipment. Approximately 22,000 elevator installers and repairers are employed in the United States.

HISTORY

The use of mechanical devices for lifting loads dates back at least to the time of the ancient Romans, who used platforms attached to pulleys in constructing buildings. In the 17th century, a crude passenger elevator known as the "flying chair" was invented. These early elevators were operated by human, animal, or waterpower.

By the early 19th century, steam was used to power machines that raised elevators. For about the first half of the century, elevators were almost always used for lifting freight. This was because the hemp ropes that supported and hauled the elevators were not strong enough to be safe for passenger use. In 1852, Elisha G. Otis designed and installed the first elevator with a safety device that prevented it from falling if the rope broke. Five years later, Otis's first safety elevator for carrying passengers was put into use in a store in New York City, and it was immediately declared a success.

Steam-powered elevators were used until the 1880s, when elevators powered by electricity were introduced. Subsequent design changes brought a series of improvements such as push-button operation, taller shafts, and faster speeds, so that the elevators could be used even in skyscrapers, and power doors and automatic operation, which made elevators more economical than they had been when human operators were necessary. Today's elevators often are controlled electronically and may be capable of moving up and down at 2,000 feet per minute.

Jesse W. Reno invented the escalator, or moving stairway, in 1891. Early escalators, like modern ones, were electrically powered and resembled an inclined endless belt held in position by two tracks. Moving sidewalks and ramps are based on the same principle.

Almost as long as these machines have been in use in buildings to move people and their belongings, there has been a need for workers who specialize in assembling, installing, and maintaining them.

THE JOB

Elevator installers and repairers may service and update old equipment that has been in operation for many years. Or they may work on new systems, which may be equipped with state-of-the-art microprocessors capable of monitoring a whole elevator system and automatically operating it with maximum possible efficiency. Installing and repairing elevators requires a good understanding of electricity, electronics, and hydraulics.

Installers begin their work by examining plans and blueprints that describe the equipment to be installed. They need to determine the layout of the components, including the framework, guide rails, motors, pumps, cylinders, plunger foundations, and electrical connections. Once the layout is clear, they install the guide rails (for guiding the elevator as it moves up and down) on the walls of the shaft. Then they run electrical wiring in the shaft between floors and install controls and other devices on each floor and at a central control panel. They assemble the parts of the car at the bottom of the shaft. They bolt or weld together the steel frame and attach walls, doors, and parts that keep the car from moving from side to side as it travels up and down the shaft. They also install the entrance doors and doorframes on each floor.

Installers set up and connect the equipment that moves the cars. In cable elevator systems, steel cables are attached to each car and, at their other end, to a large counterweight. Hoisting machinery, often located at the top of the shaft, moves the cables around a pulley, thus moving the elevator car up or down and the counterweight in the opposite direction. In hydraulic systems, the car rests on a hydraulic cylinder that is raised and lowered by a pump, thus moving the elevator car up and down like an automobile on a lift. New technology also is being developed to run elevators without cables, using magnetic fields instead. Regardless of the type of elevator involved, after the various parts of the elevator system are in place, the elevator installers test the operation of the system and make any necessary adjustments so that the installation meets building and safety code requirements.

In hotels, restaurants, hospitals, and other institutions where food is prepared, elevator installers may work on dumbwaiters, which are small elevators for transporting food and dishes from one part of a building to another. They may also work on escalators, installing wiring, motors, controls, the stairs, the framework for the stairs, and the tracks that keep the stairs in position. Increasingly, installers are working on APMs, or automated people movers, the sort of "moving sidewalks" you might see at an airport.

After elevator and escalator equipment is installed, it needs regular adjustment and maintenance to ensure that the system continues to function in a safe, reliable manner. Elevator repairers routinely inspect the equipment, perform safety tests using meters and gauges, clean parts that are prone to getting dirty, make adjustments, replace worn components, and lubricate bearings and other moving parts.

Repairers also do minor emergency repairs, such as replacing defective parts. Finding the cause of malfunctions often involves troubleshooting. For this reason, repairers need a strong mechanical aptitude. In addition, repairers may work as part of crews that do major repair and modernization work on older equipment.

Elevator installers and repairers use a variety of hand tools, power tools, welding equipment, and electrical testing devices such as digital multimeters, logic probes, and oscilloscopes.

REQUIREMENTS

High School

Employers prefer to hire high school graduates who are at least 18 years of age and in good physical condition. Mechanical aptitude, an interest in machines, and some technical training related to the field are other important qualifications. While you are in high school, therefore, take such classes as machine shop, electronics, and blueprint reading. Mathematics classes will teach you to work with numbers, and applied physics courses will give you a basis for understanding the workings of this equipment. Also, take English classes to enhance your verbal and writing skills. In this work, you will be interacting with a variety of people and communication skills will be a necessity.

Postsecondary Training

Union elevator installers and repairers receive their training through the National Elevator Industry (NEI) Educational Program, administered on a local level by committees made up of local employers who belong to the National Elevator Industry Inc., and local branches of the International Union of Elevator Constructors. The programs consist of on-the-job training under the supervision of experienced workers, together with classroom instruction in related subjects. In the work portion of the program, trainees begin with the simplest tasks and gradually progress to more difficult activities. In the classroom, they learn about installation procedures, basic electrical theory, electronics, and job safety.

Union trainees spend their first six months in the industry in a probationary status. Those who complete the period successfully go on to become elevator constructor helpers. After an additional four to five years of required field and classroom education, they become eligible to take a validated mechanic exam. Upon passing this exam, workers become fully qualified journeyman installers and repairers. They may be able to advance more quickly if they already have a good technical background, acquired by taking courses at a postsecondary technical school or junior college.

Certification or Licensing

Certification through the NEI Educational Program's training curriculum is required of new workers in this field. The National Association of Elevator Contractors offers the following voluntary certifications: certified elevator technician and certified accessibility and private residence lift technician. Additionally, most states and municipalities require that elevator installers and repairers pass a licensing examination. This is not true of all areas at this time, but the trend toward mandatory licensure is growing.

Other Requirements

Elevator installers and repairers must be in good physical shape because this job will periodically require them to carry heavy equipment or tools and work in small areas or in awkward positions. Elevator installers and repairers should also enjoy learning. To be successful in this field, they must constantly update their knowledge regarding new technologies, and continuing education through seminars, workshops, or correspondence courses is a must. Elevator installers and repairers need good hand-eye coordination. These workers should not be afraid of heights or confined areas, since some of their work may take place in elevator shafts. Also, because elevator installers and repairers frequently work with electrical wiring and wires are typically color-coded based on their function, they need to have accurate color vision.

While union membership is not necessarily a requirement for employment, most elevator installers and repairers are members of the International Union of Elevator Constructors.

EXPLORING

High school courses such as electrical shop, machine shop, and blueprint reading can give you a hands-on sense of tasks that are similar to everyday activities of elevator installers and repairers. A part-time or summer job as a helper at a commercial building site may provide you with the opportunity to observe the conditions that these workers encounter on the job. If you or your guidance counselor can arrange for a tour of an elevator manufacturing firm, this experience will allow you to see how the equipment is built. One of the best ways to learn about the work may be to talk to a professional recommended by local representatives of the International Union of Elevator Constructors.

EMPLOYERS

Approximately 22,000 elevator installers and repairers are employed in the United States, and contractors specializing in work with elevators employ the majority. Other elevator installers and repairers work for one of the more than 60 large elevator manufacturers such as Otis Elevator Company or ThyssenKrupp Elevator, for government agencies, or for small, local elevator maintenance contractors. Some larger institutions (such as hospitals, which run 24 hours a day) employ their own elevator maintenance and repair crews.

STARTING OUT

If you are seeking information about trainee positions in this field, you can contact the National Elevator Industry Educational Program or the International Union of Elevator Constructors for brochures. The local office of your state's employment service may also be a source of information and job leads.

ADVANCEMENT

When an installer/repairer has completed the approximately five-year training program, met any local licensure requirements, and successfully passed a validated mechanic's exam, he or she is considered fully qualified—a journeyman. After gaining further experience, installers and repairers who work for elevator contracting firms may be promoted to positions such as mechanic-in-charge or supervisor, coordinating the work done by other installers. Other advanced positions include *adjusters,* highly skilled professionals who check equipment after installation and fine-tune it to specifications, and *estimators,* who figure the costs for supplies and labor for work before it is done. Those who work for an elevator manufacturer may move into sales positions, jobs related to product design, or management. Other experienced workers become inspectors employed by the government to inspect elevators and escalators to ensure that they comply with specifications and safety codes.

EARNINGS

Earnings depend on a variety of factors, such as experience and geographical location. Workers who are not fully qualified journeymen earn less than full-time professionals; for example, probationary workers start at about 50 percent of the full wage, and trainees earn about 70 percent of full wage. According to the U.S. Department of Labor, the median hourly wage for fully qualified elevator installers and repairers was $30.59 in 2006. This hourly wage translates into a yearly income of approximately $63,320 for full-time work. The department also reported that the lowest paid 10 percent of installers and repairers made about $17.79 per hour (approximately $36,990 annually), while the highest paid 10 percent earned more than $42.14 per hour (approximately $87,660 annually). In addition to regular wages, union elevator installers and repairers receive other benefits, including health insurance, pension plans, paid holidays and vacations, and some tuition-free courses in subjects related to their work. A recent change in the union contract called for the institution of a 401(k) retirement program.

WORK ENVIRONMENT

The standard workweek for elevator installers and repairers is 40 hours. Some workers put in overtime hours (for which they are paid extra), and some repairers are on call for 24-hour periods to respond to emergency situations. Most repair work is done indoors, so little time is lost because of bad weather. It frequently is necessary to lift heavy equipment and parts and to work in very hot or cold, cramped, or awkward places.

OUTLOOK

The U.S. Department of Labor predicts that employment for elevator installers and repairers will grow about as fast as the average for all occupations through 2014. Few new jobs are expected, however, because this occupation is so small. There will also be little need for replacement workers—the turnover in this field is relatively low because the extensive training people go through to gain these jobs results in high wages, which prompts workers to remain in the field. In addition, job outlook is somewhat dependent on the construction industry, particularly for new workers. Because installation of elevators is part of the interior work in new buildings, elevator installers are employed to work on sites about a year after construction begins, so job availability in this field lags behind boom periods in the construction industry by about a year. Slowdowns in the building industry will eventually catch up to elevator installers, again lagging by about a year as installers complete previously assigned jobs Due to the growing elderly population in the United States, professionals will also be needed to install and service stair lifts and elevators in homes.

Changes in the union contract that increased the retirement age for elevator installers and repairers brought many older workers back into the workforce in 1998. The NEI Educational Program expects that new openings will become available in future years as these older workers retire. In addition, as the technology in the industry becomes more complex, employers will increasingly seek workers who are technically well trained.

FOR MORE INFORMATION

For information on benefits, scholarships, and job opportunities, contact

International Union of Elevator Constructors
7154 Columbia Gateway Drive
Columbia, MD 21046-2132
Tel: 410-953-6150
Email: contact@iuec.org
http://www.iuec.org

For industry news and information on certification and continuing education, contact
National Association of Elevator Contractors
1298 Wellbrook Circle, Suite A
Conyers, GA 30012-8031
Tel: 800-900-6232
Email: info@naec.org
http://www.naec.org

For education, scholarship, and career information aimed at women in the construction industry, contact
National Association of Women in Construction
327 South Adams Street
Fort Worth, TX 76104-1002
Tel: 800-552-3506
Email: nawic@nawic.org
http://www.nawic.org

For industry information, contact
National Elevator Industry
1677 County Route 64
PO Box 838
Salem, NY 12865-0838
Tel: 518-854-3100
Email: info@neii.org
http://www.neii.org

For information on training in the elevator industry, contact
National Elevator Industry Educational Program
11 Larsen Way
Attleboro Falls, MA 02763-1068
Tel: 800-228-8220
http://www.neiep.org

Farm Equipment Mechanics

QUICK FACTS

School Subjects
Agriculture
Technical/shop

Personal Skills
Mechanical/manipulative
Technical/scientific

Work Environment
Indoors and outdoors
Primarily multiple locations

Minimum Education Level
Some postsecondary training

Salary Range
$19,340 to $29,460 to
$43,210+

Certification or Licensing
None available

Outlook
More slowly than the average

DOT
620

GOE
05.03.01

NOC
7312

O*NET-SOC
49-3041.00

OVERVIEW

Farm equipment mechanics maintain, adjust, repair, and overhaul equipment and vehicles used in planting, cultivating, harvesting, moving, processing, and storing plant and animal farm products. Among the specialized machines with which they work are tractors, harvesters, combines, pumps, tilling equipment, silo fillers, hay balers, and sprinkler irrigation systems. They work for farm equipment repair shops, farm equipment dealerships, and on large farms that have their own shops. Approximately 33,000 farm equipment mechanics work in the United States.

HISTORY

The purpose of the mechanical devices used in farming has always been to increase production and decrease the need for human labor. In prehistoric times, people used simple wood and stone implements to help turn soil, plant seeds, and harvest crops more efficiently than they could with their bare hands. With the introduction of metal tools and the domestication of animals that could pull plows and vehicles, people were able to produce much more. Until the 19th century, farmers around the globe relied on human labor, animal power, and relatively simple equipment to accomplish all the tasks involved in agriculture.

Modern mechanized agriculture was developed in the 1800s. Initially, steam power was used for farm equipment. In the early part of the 20th century, gasoline-powered engines appeared. Shortly after, diesel engines were introduced to power various kinds of farm machinery. The use of motor-driven machines on farms had far-reaching effects. Machines improved agricultural productivity while lessening the need for human labor. As a result of increased use of farm machinery, the number of people working on farms has steadily decreased in many countries of the world.

In recent decades, farm machines have become large and complex, using electronic, computerized, and hydraulic systems. Agriculture is now a business operation that requires extremely expensive equipment capable of doing specialized tasks quickly and efficiently. Farmers cannot afford for their equipment to break down. They are now almost completely reliant on the dealers who sell them their equipment to be their source for the emergency repairs and routine maintenance services that keep the machines functioning well. Farm equipment mechanics are the skilled specialists who carry out these tasks, usually as employees of equipment dealers or of independent repair shops.

THE JOB

The success of today's large-scale farming operations depends on the reliability of many complex machines. It is the farm equipment mechanic's responsibility to keep the machines in good working order and to repair or to overhaul them when they break down.

When farm equipment is not working properly, mechanics begin by diagnosing the problem. Using intricate testing devices, they are able to identify what is wrong. A compression tester, for example, can determine whether cylinder valves leak or piston rings are worn, and a dynamometer can measure engine performance. The mechanic will also examine the machine, observing and listening to it in operation and looking for clues such as leaks, loose parts, and irregular steering, braking, and gear shifting. It may be necessary to dismantle whole systems in the machine to diagnose and correct malfunctions.

When the problem is located, the broken, worn-out, or faulty components are repaired or replaced, depending on the extent of their defect. The machine or piece of equipment is reassembled, adjusted, lubricated, and tested to be sure it is again operating at its full capacity.

Farm equipment mechanics use many tools in their work. Besides hand tools such as wrenches, pliers, and screwdrivers and precision instruments such as micrometers and torque wrenches, they may use welding equipment, power grinders and saws, and other power tools. In addition, they do major repairs using machine tools such as drill presses, lathes, and milling and woodworking machines.

A farm equipment mechanic inspects a planter after installing new bearings and chains. *(Steve Warmowski/Journal Courier, The Image Works)*

As farm equipment becomes more complex, mechanics are increasingly expected to have strong backgrounds in electronics. For instance, newer tractors have large, electronically controlled engines and air-conditioned cabs, as well as transmissions with many speeds.

Much of the time, farmers can bring their equipment into a shop, where mechanics have all the necessary tools available. But during planting or harvesting seasons, when timing may be critical for the farmers, mechanics are expected to travel to farms for emergency repairs in order to get the equipment up and running with little delay.

Farmers usually bring movable equipment into a repair shop on a regular basis for preventive maintenance services such as adjusting and cleaning parts and tuning engines. Routine servicing not only ensures less emergency repairs for the mechanics, but it also assures farmers that the equipment will be ready when it is needed. Shops in the rural outskirts of metropolitan areas often handle maintenance and repairs on a variety of lawn and garden equipment, especially lawn mowers.

If a mechanic works in a large shop, he or she may specialize in specific types of repairs. For example, a mechanic may overhaul gasoline or diesel engines, repair clutches and transmissions, or concentrate on the air-conditioning units in the cabs of combines and large tractors. Some mechanics, called *farm machinery set-up mechanics,* uncrate, assemble, adjust, and often deliver machinery to farm locations. Mechanics also do body work on tractors and other machines, repairing damaged sheet-metal body parts.

Some mechanics may work exclusively on certain types of equipment, such as hay balers or harvesters. Other mechanics work on equipment installed on farms. For example, *sprinkler-irrigation equipment mechanics* install and maintain self-propelled circle-irrigation systems, which are like giant motorized lawn sprinklers. *Dairy equipment repairers* inspect and repair dairy machinery and equipment such as milking machines, cream separators, and churns.

Most farm equipment mechanics work in the service departments of equipment dealerships. Others are employed by independent repair shops. A smaller number work on large farms that have their own shops.

REQUIREMENTS

High School

Take technical/shop courses that will introduce you to machinery repair, electrical work, and welding. Mechanical drawing classes can also prepare you for the work. Computer courses will be valuable; computers are used increasingly in farm machinery, as well as in the administrative office of a machine repair and sales business. Science courses that include units in soil and agronomy will help you to understand the needs of the agriculture industry. As a member of the National FFA Organization (formerly the Future Farmers of America), you may be involved in special projects that include working with farm machinery.

Postsecondary Training

After graduating from high school, most farm equipment mechanics go on to complete a one- or two-year program in agricultural or farm mechanics at a vocational school or community college. If you can't find such a program, study in diesel mechanics or appropriate experience through the military are also options. Topics that you will learn about include the maintenance and repair of diesel and gasoline engines, hydraulic systems, welding, and electronics. Your education doesn't stop there, however. After completing one of these programs, you will be hired as a trainee or helper and continue to learn on the job, receiving training from experienced mechanics.

Some farm equipment mechanics learn their trade through apprenticeship programs. These programs combine three to four years of on-the-job training with classroom study related to farm equipment repair and maintenance. Apprentices are usually chosen from among shop helpers.

To stay up-to-date on technological changes that affect their work, mechanics and trainees may take special short-term courses conducted by equipment manufacturers. In these programs, which usually last a few days, company service representatives explain the design and function of new models of equipment and teach mechanics how to maintain and repair them. Some employers help broaden their mechanics' skills by sending them to local vocational schools for special intensive courses in subjects such as air-conditioning repair, hydraulics, or electronics.

Other Requirements

Farm machinery is usually large and heavy. Mechanics need the strength to lift heavy machine parts such as transmissions. They also need manual dexterity to be able to handle tools and small components. Farm equipment mechanics are usually expected to supply their own hand tools. After years of accumulating favorite tools, experienced mechanics may have collections that represent an investment of thousands of dollars. Employers generally provide all the large power tools and test equipment needed in the shop.

EXPLORING

Many people who go into farm equipment work have grown up with mechanical repair—they have experimented with lawn mowers, old cars, and other machinery, and they have used a lot of farm equipment. If you do not live on a farm, you may be able to find part-time or summer work on a farm. You can also get valuable mechanical experience working at a gasoline service station, automobile repair shop, or automotive supply house. Attending farm shows is a good way to learn about farm equipment and manufacturers. At shows, you may have the opportunity to talk to equipment manufacturers' representatives and learn more about new developments in the industry. In addition, consider joining a chapter of the National FFA Organization. This organization is open to students aged 12 to 21 enrolled in agricultural programs and offers a wide variety of activities, including career-development programs.

EMPLOYERS

Approximately 33,000 farm equipment mechanics are employed in the United States. Farm equipment mechanics work in all parts of the country, but there are more job opportunities in the "farm belt"—the Midwestern states. Work is available with independent repair and service businesses, large farm equipment sales companies, and large independent and commercial farms. Some mechanics are self-employed, running their own repair businesses in rural areas. Most independent repair shops employ fewer than five mechanics, while in dealers' service departments there may be 10 or more mechanics on the payroll.

STARTING OUT

Many people who become trainees in this field have prior experience in related occupations. They may have worked as farmers, farm laborers, heavy-equipment mechanics, automobile mechanics, or air-conditioning mechanics. Although people with this kind of related experience are likely to begin as helpers, their training period may be considerably shorter than the training for beginners with no such experience.

When looking for work, you should apply directly to local farm equipment dealers or independent repair shops. Graduates of vocational schools can often get help finding jobs through their schools' career services office. State employment service offices are another source of job leads, as well as a source of information on any apprenticeships that are available in the region.

ADVANCEMENT

After they have gained some experience, farm equipment mechanics employed by equipment dealers may be promoted to such positions as shop supervisor, service manager, and eventually manager of the dealership. Some mechanics eventually decide to open their own repair shops (fewer than 4 percent of all mechanics are self-employed). Others become service representatives for farm equipment manufacturers. Additional formal education, such as completion of a two-year associate's degree program in agricultural mechanics or a related field, may be required of service representatives.

EARNINGS

Farm equipment mechanics had median hourly earnings of $14.16 in 2006, according to the U.S. Department of Labor. This figure translates into a yearly income of approximately $29,460. In addition, the department reports that the lowest paid 10 percent of farm equipment mechanics earned less than $9.30 per hour ($19,340 per year), while the highest paid 10 percent earned $20.77 or more per hour ($43,210 or more per year). Exact earnings figures are difficult to determine because farm equipment mechanics do not generally work consistent 40-hour weeks throughout the year. During the busy planting and harvest seasons, for example, mechanics may work many hours of overtime, for which they are usually paid time-and-a-half rates. This overtime pay can substantially increase their weekly earnings. However, during the winter months, some mechanics may work less or be temporarily laid off, reducing their total income.

Employee benefits may be rare when working for a small shop. A large commercial farm or sales company may offer health insurance plans and sick leave.

WORK ENVIRONMENT

Farm equipment mechanics generally work indoors on equipment that has been brought into the shop. Most modern shops are properly ventilated, heated, and lighted. Some older shops may be less comfortable. During harvest seasons, mechanics may have to leave the shop frequently and travel many miles to farms, where they perform emergency repairs outdoors in any kind of weather. They may often work six to seven days a week, 10 to 12 hours a day during this busy season. In the event of an emergency repair, a mechanic often works independently, with little supervision. Mechanics need to be self-reliant and able to solve problems under pressure. When a farm machine breaks down, the lost time can be very expensive for the farmer. A mechanic must be able to diagnose problems quickly and perform repairs without delay.

Grease, gasoline, rust, and dirt are part of the farm equipment mechanic's life. Although safety precautions have improved in recent years, mechanics are often at risk of injury when lifting heavy equipment and parts with jacks or hoists. Other hazards they must routinely guard against include burns from hot engines, cuts from sharp pieces of metal, and exposure to toxic farm chemicals. Following good safety practices can reduce the risks of injury to a minimum.

OUTLOOK

The U.S. Department of Labor reports that employment of farm equipment mechanics will grow more slowly than the average for all occupations through 2014 because of the efficiency and dependability of modern farm equipment. To be competitive in the job market, a farm equipment mechanic may need a few years of college training along with some practical experience.

Advancements in technology have revolutionized farm equipment. Those working with farm equipment will have to have an understanding of computers, electronics, and highly sophisticated devices and, therefore, more specialized training.

FOR MORE INFORMATION

For AEM press releases, equipment sales statistics, agricultural reports, and other news of interest to farm mechanics, contact
Association of Equipment Manufacturers (AEM)
6737 West Washington Street, Suite 2400
Milwaukee, WI 53214-5647
Tel: 414-272-0943
Email: info@aem.org
http://www.aem.org

At the FEMA Web site, you can learn about its publications, read industry news, and find out about upcoming farm shows.
Farm Equipment Manufacturers Association (FEMA)
1000 Executive Parkway, Suite 100
St. Louis, MO 63141-6369
Tel: 314-878-2304
Email: info@farmequip.org
http://www.farmequip.org

For information on student chapters and the many activities available, contact
National FFA Organization
6060 FFA Drive
PO Box 68960
Indianapolis, IN 46268-0960
Tel: 317-802-6060
Email: membership@ffa.org
http://www.ffa.org

Fluid Power Technicians

QUICK FACTS

School Subjects
Mathematics
Technical/shop

Personal Skills
Mechanical/manipulative
Technical/scientific

Work Environment
Primarily indoors
Primarily multiple locations

Minimum Education Level
Some postsecondary training

Salary Range
$38,500 to $45,000 to
$50,000+

Certification or Licensing
Voluntary

Outlook
About as fast as the average

DOT
600

GOE
05.03.03

NOC
2132

O*NET-SOC
49-9069.99

OVERVIEW

Fluid power technicians work with equipment that utilizes the pressure of a liquid or gas in a closed container to transmit, multiply, or control power. Working under the supervision of an engineer or engineering staff, they assemble, install, maintain, and test fluid power equipment, which is found in almost every facet of American daily life.

HISTORY

Machinery that operates using fluid power has been in use for thousands of years. In Roman times, water flowing past a rotating paddle wheel produced power for milling. Early leather bellows, hand-operated by blacksmiths, were the first known devices to use compressed air. In Italy, in the 16th century, a more sophisticated bellows was invented that used falling water to compress air. Shortly thereafter, Denis Papin, a French physicist, used power from a waterwheel to compress air in a similar manner.

The 19th century brought the first practical application of an air-driven, piston-operated hammer, invented in Great Britain by George Law. In the mid-1800s, water-cooled reciprocating compressors were introduced in the United States and resulted in the development of large compressed-air units that factory workers used to operate industrial tools. In 1875, American engineer and industrialist George Westinghouse created and utilized a continuous automatic compressed-air brake system for trains.

In the latter part of the 19th century and the early part of the 20th, experiments in fluid dynamics by Osborne Reynolds and Ludwig Prandtl led to a new understanding of the way fluid behaves in certain circumstances. These findings laid the groundwork for modern fluid power mechanics. The 20th and 21st centuries have witnessed a significant increase in the use of fluid power for many different applications.

Fluid power workers are now employed in any number of industries, from aerospace to materials handling. Fluid power is also routinely used and depended upon in daily life. Anyone who has ever ridden in a car, for example, has relied upon fluid power to operate its hydraulic braking system. With fluid power so widely used, many businesses throughout the United States employ men and women who are trained in its various aspects. Fluid power technicians, with their specialized skills and knowledge, have become a mainstay of industrial support groups that work with this type of machinery.

THE JOB

Many different machines use some kind of fluid power system, including equipment used in industries such as agriculture, manufacturing, defense, and mining. We come across fluid power systems every day when we use automatic door closers, bicycle pumps, and spray guns. Even automobile transmissions incorporate fluid power.

There are two types of fluid power machines. The first kind—hydraulic machines—use water, oil, or another liquid in a closed system to transmit the energy needed to do work. For example, a hydraulic jack, which can be used to lift heavy loads, is a cylinder with a piston fitted inside it. When a liquid is pumped into the bottom of the cylinder, the piston is forced upward, lifting the weight on the jack. To lower the weight, the liquid is released through a valve, returning the pressure in the system to normal.

Pneumatic machines, the other type of fluid power systems, are activated by the pressure of air or another gas in a closed system. Pavement-breaking jackhammers and compressed-air paint sprayers are common examples of pneumatic machines.

Fluid power systems are a part of most machines used in industry, so fluid power technicians work in many different settings. Most often, however, they work in factories where fluid power systems are used in manufacturing. In such a factory, for example, they might maintain and service pneumatic machines that bolt together products on an automated assembly line.

In their work, fluid power technicians analyze blueprints, drawings, and specifications; set up various milling, shaping, grinding, and drilling machines; make precision parts; use sensitive measuring instruments to make sure the parts are exactly the required size; and use hand and power tools to put together components of the fluid power system they are assembling or repairing.

Technicians may also be responsible for testing fluid power systems. To determine whether a piece of equipment is working properly, they connect the unit to test equipment that measures such factors as fluid pressure, flow rates, and power loss from friction or wear. Based on their analysis of the test results, they may advise changes in the equipment setup or instrumentation.

Some technicians work for companies that research better ways to develop and use fluid power systems. They may work in laboratories as part of research and development teams who set up fluid power equipment and test it under operating conditions. Other technicians work as sales and service representatives for companies that make and sell fluid power equipment to industrial plants. These technicians travel from one plant to another, providing customers with specialized information and assistance with their equipment. Some technicians repair and maintain fluid power components of heavy equipment used in construction, on farms, or in mining. Because fluid power technology is important in the flight controls, landing gear, and brakes of airplanes, many technicians are also employed in the aircraft industry.

REQUIREMENTS

High School

If you are considering a career in fluid power, you should take as many courses as possible in computer science and mathematics. Physics, shop, drafting, and English will also provide a solid background for this type of work.

Postsecondary Training

In the past, you could become a fluid power technician with only a high school diploma and, perhaps, some related technical experience. Technicians were trained in fluid power technology by their employers or by taking short courses or workshops. Today, however, most employers prefer to hire fluid power technicians who have at least two years of post-high school training, such as that offered by community and technical colleges.

There are relatively few technical training programs that focus primarily on fluid power technology—fewer than 40 in the entire

United States. A student enrolled in one of these programs might expect to take classes on very specialized topics, such as fluid power math, process and fabrication fundamentals, hydraulic components and accessories, pneumatic components and circuits, and advanced systems calculations. If it is not possible to attend one of the schools that offer programs in fluid power, training in a related field, such as mechanical or electrical technology, can provide adequate preparation for employment.

Certification or Licensing

Certification for fluid power technicians is voluntary. Offered through the Fluid Power Certification Board, the certification process is administered by the International Fluid Power Society. Applicants must pass a three-hour, written examination and a three-hour job performance test before receiving technician certification. This certification may be beneficial to technicians in finding jobs, obtaining more advanced positions, or receiving higher pay.

Other Requirements

Technicians must be able to understand and analyze mechanical systems. In order to do this well, you should have both mechanical aptitude and an analytical mindset. Because you will often work as a member of a team, an ability to work well and communicate easily with others is important. Finally, you should enjoy challenges and the process of troubleshooting problems.

EXPLORING

Your school or public library should have books that explain the field of fluid power. If you happen to live near one of the schools that offer a degree in fluid power technology, it may be possible to arrange a meeting with instructors or students in the program. Talking with a fluid power technician can be an excellent way of learning about the job firsthand. Finally, taking certain classes, such as machine shop, physics, or electronics, might help you gauge your enjoyment and ability level for this work.

EMPLOYERS

The largest consumers of fluid power products are the aerospace, construction equipment, agricultural equipment, machine tool, and material handling industries, according to the National Fluid Power Association, an industry trade organization. Fluid power also provides power for auxiliary systems on planes, ships, trains, and trucks.

STARTING OUT

Most fluid power technicians obtain their jobs through their community and technical college career services offices. In addition, organizations such as the International Fluid Power Society and the Fluid Power Educational Foundation have lists of their corporate members that can be used to start a job search. Some openings might be listed in the employment sections of newspapers.

ADVANCEMENT

Some technicians advance simply by becoming more knowledgeable and skilled in their work and eventually receive more responsibility. Another route for technicians is to become a fluid power specialist by taking additional training and upgrading their certification. A specialist designs and applies systems, and can instruct newer employees on the basics of fluid power systems.

Some technicians go into sales and marketing, using their experience and knowledge to provide customers with technical assistance. Another option is to become a fluid power consultant, who works with different companies to analyze, design, or improve fluid power systems.

EARNINGS

Salaries for fluid power technicians vary according to geographic location and industry. A Fluid Power Educational Foundation survey from the late 1990s reports that college graduates (of both two- and four-year programs) earned starting salaries of $38,500. An estimated national average wage for technicians might be in the mid-$40,000s. Those who move into consulting or other advanced positions can earn even more. Most workers in this field receive a full benefits package, often including vacation days, sick leave, medical and life insurance, and a retirement plan.

WORK ENVIRONMENT

Because fluid power technicians work in any number of different industries, their work environments vary. Many work in industrial settings and must spend much of their time on the manufacturing floor. In this case, they may have to become accustomed to noise and heat generated by the machinery, although the industry is addressing the noise level issue. Others work in laboratories or testing facilities. Those involved in sales and marketing or in installing and repairing equipment may travel to different customer locations.

The work is frequently dirty, as technicians often have to handle machinery that has been used and may be leaking fluid. Also, working on large machinery and components requires physical strength and may require being in areas where safety regulations must be followed.

Many workers in this field find their jobs enjoyable and satisfying. Because they deal with different problems and solutions all the time, the work is challenging, interesting, and not repetitive. It can also be gratifying to figure out how to make a machine run properly or improve upon its performance through testing and experimenting.

OUTLOOK

Because fluid power is used in so many different industries, the need for technicians is growing rapidly. Currently, in fact, demand exceeds the supply of trained workers. In the last decade, electrohydraulic and electropneumatic technologies opened up new markets, such as active suspensions on automobiles, and reestablished older markets, such as robotics. Therefore, the fluid power industry is expected to continue growing and the outlook for technicians should remain strong through the next decade.

FOR MORE INFORMATION

For industry information, contact
Fluid Power Distributors Association
PO Box 1420
Cherry Hill, NJ 08034-0054
Tel: 856-424-8998
http://www.fpda.org

For a list of schools offering courses in fluid power technology and information about available scholarships, contact
Fluid Power Educational Foundation
3333 North Mayfair Road, Suite 211
Milwaukee, WI 53222-3219
Tel: 414-778-3364
Email: info@fpef.org
http://www.fpef.org

For information on certification, contact
International Fluid Power Society
PO Box 1420
Cherry Hill, NJ 08034-0054

Tel: 856-489-8983
Email: info@ifps.org
http://www.ifps.org

For career information, a list of educational programs that offer training in fluid power technology, and an overview of the fluid power industry, contact
National Fluid Power Association
3333 North Mayfair Road, Suite 211
Milwaukee, WI 53222-3219
Tel: 414-778-3344
Email: nfpa@nfpa.com
http://www.nfpa.com

INTERVIEW

Jim Fischer is a fluid power instructor at the Granite Falls Campus of Minnesota West Community & Technical College. He discussed the field with the editors of Careers in Focus: Mechanics.

Q. Please tell us about your program.

A. Minnesota West Community & Technical College, Granite Falls Campus offers a two-year fluid power technology program that has a 67-credit diploma and a 72-credit AAS degree. Visit our Web site, http://www.mnwest.edu, for more information.

Q. What types of students study fluid power technology in your program?

A. Students who like math and working with mechanical things like fluid power. We also have students who are people oriented who choose careers in the sales aspect of fluid power. Their backgrounds vary depending on career choice [application engineering, sales, customer service, service and repair, fabrication, and research and development].

Q. What advice would you give fluid power technology students as they graduate and look for jobs?

A. Fluid power graduates should be prepared to put themselves in the shoes of the employer to understand their needs. When they do, they will do better at interviewing and being a good employee when they start their career. They are encouraged to be patient and work hard, and they will have a rewarding career.

Q. What is the future employment outlook in the field? Have certain areas of this field been especially promising in recent years?

A. The future is great in fluid power. The integration of electronics for control and fluid power equipment for power transmission has opened up many applications. The machines that incorporate this technology need skilled people to design, build, and repair this equipment.

General Maintenance Mechanics

QUICK FACTS

School Subjects
Mathematics
Technical/shop

Personal Skills
Mechanical/manipulative
Technical/scientific

Work Environment
Indoors and outdoors
Primarily one location

Minimum Education Level
High school diploma

Salary Range
$19,140 to $31,910 to
$50,840+

Certification or Licensing
Voluntary

Outlook
About as fast as the average

DOT
620

GOE
05.03.01

NOC
7311

O*NET-SOC
49-9042.00, 49-9043.00

OVERVIEW

General maintenance mechanics, sometimes called *maintenance technicians* or *building engineers,* repair and maintain machines, mechanical equipment, and buildings, and work on plumbing, electrical, and controls. They also do minor construction or carpentry work and routine preventive maintenance to keep the physical structures of businesses, schools, factories, and apartment buildings in good condition. They also maintain and repair specialized equipment and machinery found in cafeterias, laundries, hospitals, offices, and factories. There are approximately 1.3 million general maintenance mechanics employed in the United States, working in almost every industry.

HISTORY

Before machines came to dominate the manufacturing of goods, craftsworkers had to learn many different kinds of skills. Blacksmiths, for example, had to know about forging techniques, horseshoeing, making decorative metalwork, and many other aspects of their trade. Carriage makers had to be familiar with carpentry, metalworking, wheelmaking, upholstering, and design. The industrial revolution set in motion many new trends, however, including a shift toward factory-type settings with workers who specialized in specific functions. This shift occurred partly because new machine production methods required a high degree of discipline and organization. Another reason for the change was that, because the new technology was so complex, no one person could be expected to master a whole field and keep up with changes that developed in it.

In a way, today's general maintenance mechanics recall crafts workers of the era before specialization. They are jacks-of-all-trades. Typically, they have a reasonable amount of skill in a variety of fields, including construction, electrical work, carpentry, plumbing, machining, direct digital controls, as well as other trades. They are responsible for keeping buildings and machines in good working order. To do this, they must have a broad understanding of mechanical tools and processes as well as the ability to apply their knowledge to solving problems.

THE JOB

General maintenance mechanics perform almost any task that may be required to maintain a building or the equipment in it. They may be called on to replace faulty electrical outlets, fix air-conditioning motors, install water lines, build partitions, patch plaster or drywall, open clogged drains, dismantle, clean, and oil machinery, paint windows, doors, and woodwork, repair institutional-size dishwashers or laundry machines, and see to many other problems. Because of the diverse nature of the responsibilities of maintenance mechanics, they have to know how to use a variety of materials and be skilled in the use of most hand tools and ordinary power tools. They also must be able to recognize when they cannot handle a problem and must recommend that a specialized technician be called.

General maintenance mechanics work in many kinds of settings. Mechanics who work primarily on keeping industrial machines in good condition may be called *factory maintenance workers* or *mill maintenance workers,* while those mechanics who concentrate on the maintenance of a building's physical structure may be called *building maintenance workers and technicians.*

Once a problem or defect has been identified and diagnosed, maintenance mechanics must plan the repairs. They may consult blueprints, repair manuals, and parts catalogs to determine what to do. They obtain supplies and new parts from a storeroom or order them from a distributor. They install new parts in place of worn or broken ones, using hand tools, power tools, and sometimes electronic test devices and other specialized equipment. In some situations, maintenance mechanics may fix an old part or even fabricate a new part. To do this, they may need to set up and operate machine tools, such as lathes or milling machines, and operate gas- or arc-welding equipment to join metal parts together.

One of the most important kinds of duties general maintenance mechanics perform is routine preventive maintenance to correct defects before machinery breaks down or a building begins to deteriorate. This type of maintenance keeps small problems from turning into large, expensive ones. Mechanics often inspect machinery on a regular schedule, perhaps following a checklist that includes such items as inspecting belts, checking fluid levels, replacing filters, oiling moving parts, and so forth. They keep records of the repair work done and the inspection dates. Repair and inspection records can be important evidence of compliance with insurance requirements and government safety regulations.

New buildings often have computer-controlled systems, so mechanics who work in them must have basic computer skills. For example, newer buildings might have light sensors that are electronically controlled and automatically turn lights on and off. The maintenance mechanic has to understand how to make adjustments and repairs.

In small establishments, one mechanic may be the only person working in maintenance, and thus may be responsible for almost any kind of repair. In large establishments, however, tasks may be divided among several mechanics. For example, one mechanic may be assigned to install and set up new equipment, while another may handle preventive maintenance.

REQUIREMENTS

High School

Many employers prefer to hire helpers or mechanics who are high school graduates, but a diploma is not always required. High school courses that will prepare you for this occupation include mechanical drawing, metal shop, electrical shop, woodworking, blueprint reading, general science, computer science, and applied mathematics.

Postsecondary Training

Some mechanics learn their skills by working as helpers to people employed in building trades, such as electricians or carpenters. Other mechanics attend trade or vocational schools that teach many of the necessary skills. Becoming fully qualified for a mechanic's job usually requires one to four years of on-the-job training or classroom instruction or some combination of both.

Certification or Licensing

Some certification and training programs are open to maintenance mechanics. BOMI International, for example, offers the designation of systems maintenance technician (SMT) to applicants who have completed courses in boilers, heating systems, and applied mathematics; refrigeration systems and accessories; air handling, water treatment, and plumbing systems; electrical systems and illumination; and building control systems. Technicians who have achieved SMT status can go on and become certified as systems maintenance administrators (SMAs) by taking further classes in building design and maintenance, energy management, and supervision. The Association for Facilities Engineering offers the certified plant engineer and certified plant maintenance manager designations to applicants who pass an examination and satisfy job experience requirements. While not necessarily required for employment, employees with certification may become more valuable assets to their employers and may have better chances at advancement.

Other Requirements

General maintenance mechanics need to have good manual dexterity and mechanical aptitude. People who enjoy taking things apart and putting them back together are good candidates for this career. Since some of the work, such as reaching, squatting, and lifting, requires physical strength and stamina, reasonably good health is necessary. Mechanics also need the ability to analyze and solve problems and to work effectively on their own without constant supervision.

EXPLORING

Shop classes can give you a good indication of your mechanical aptitude and of whether or not you would enjoy maintenance work. The best way to experience the work these mechanics do, however, is to get a summer or part-time job as a maintenance helper in a factory, apartment complex, or similar setting. If such a job is not available, you might try talking with a maintenance mechanic to get a fuller, more complete picture of his or her responsibilities.

EMPLOYERS

General maintenance mechanics are employed in factories, hospitals, schools, colleges, hotels, offices, stores, malls, gas and electric companies, government agencies, and apartment buildings throughout the United States. Statistics from the U.S. Department of Labor indicate that there are approximately 1.3 million people in the field. Approximately 20 percent are employed in manufacturing industries. Others are employed in service industries, such as elementary and secondary schools, colleges and universities,

Earnings by Specialty, 2006

Industry	Mean Annual Earnings
Scheduled air transportation	$52,440
Telecommunications resellers	$51,890
Motor vehicle manufacturing	$50,150
Tobacco manufacturing	$49,940
Wired telecommunications carriers	$49,750
Local government	$34,020
Elementary and secondary schools	$33,930
Activities related to real estate	$29,600
Lessors of real estate	$28,740
Traveler accommodation	$27,250

Source: U.S. Department of Labor

hospitals and nursing homes, and hotels, office and apartment buildings, government agencies, and utility companies.

STARTING OUT

General maintenance mechanics usually start as helpers to experienced mechanics and learn their skills on the job. Beginning helpers are given the simplest jobs, such as changing light bulbs or making minor drywall repairs. As general maintenance mechanics acquire skills, they are assigned more complicated work, such as troubleshooting malfunctioning machinery.

Job seekers in this field usually apply directly to potential employers. Information on job openings for mechanic's helpers can often be found through newspaper classified ads, school career services offices, and the local offices of the state employment service. Graduates of trade or vocational schools may be able to get referrals and information from their school's career services office. Union offices may also be a good place to learn about job opportunities.

ADVANCEMENT

Some general maintenance mechanics employed in large organizations may advance to supervisory positions. Another possibility is to move into one of the traditional building trades and become a craftworker, such as a plumber or electrician. In smaller organizations, opportunities for promotion are limited, although increases in pay may result from an employee's good performance and increased value to the employer.

EARNINGS

Earnings for general maintenance mechanics vary widely depending on skill, geographical location, and industry. The U.S. Department of Labor reports that general maintenance mechanics and repairers earned median annual salaries of $31,910 in 2006. Earnings ranged from less than $19,140 to more than $50,840.

Almost all maintenance mechanics receive a benefits package that includes health insurance, paid vacation, sick leave, and a retirement plan. Mechanics earn overtime pay for work in excess of 40 hours per week.

WORK ENVIRONMENT

General maintenance mechanics work in almost every industry and in a wide variety of facilities. In most cases, they work a 40-hour week. Some work evening or night shifts or on weekends; they may also be on call for emergency repairs. In the course of a single day, mechanics may do a variety of tasks in different parts of a building or in several buildings, and they may encounter different conditions in each spot. Sometimes they have to work in hot or cold conditions, on ladders, in awkward or cramped positions, among noisy machines, or in other uncomfortable places. Sometimes they must lift heavy weights. On the job, they must stay aware of potential hazards such as electrical shocks, burns, falls, and cuts and bruises. By following safety regulations and using tools properly, they can keep such risks to a minimum.

The mechanic who works in a small establishment may be the only maintenance worker and is often responsible for doing his or her job with little direct supervision. Those who work in larger establishments usually report to a maintenance supervisor who assigns tasks and directs their activities.

OUTLOOK

Employment of general maintenance mechanics is expected to grow about as fast as the average for all occupations through 2014, according to the U.S. Department of Labor. Although the rate of construction of new apartment and office buildings, factories, hotels, schools, and stores is expected to be slower than in the past, most of these facilities still require the services of maintenance mechanics. This is a large occupation with a high turnover rate. In addition to newly created jobs, many openings will arise as experienced mechanics transfer to other occupations or leave the labor force.

General maintenance mechanics who work for manufacturing companies may be subject to layoffs during bad economic times, when their employers are under pressure to cut costs. Most mechanics, however, are not usually as vulnerable to layoffs related to economic conditions.

FOR MORE INFORMATION

For information on certification, contact
Association for Facilities Engineering
8160 Corporate Park Drive, Suite 125
Cincinnati, OH 45242-3307
Tel: 513-489-2473
http://www.afe.org

This organization provides education programs for commercial property professionals, including building engineers and technicians.
BOMA International
1201 New York Avenue, NW, Suite 300
Washington, DC 20005-3999
Tel: 202-408-2662
Email: info@boma.org
http://www.boma.org

For information on professional certifications, contact
BOMI International
1521 Ritchie Highway
Arnold, MD 21012-2747
Tel: 800-235-2664
Email: service@bomi-edu.org
http://www.bomi-edu.org

For information on general maintenance careers in building maintenance and construction, contact
Mechanical Contractors Association of America
1385 Piccard Drive
Rockville, MD 20850-4329
Tel: 301-869-5800
http://www.mcaa.org/careers

Industrial Machinery Mechanics

OVERVIEW

Industrial machinery mechanics, often called *machinery maintenance mechanics* or *industrial machinery repairers,* inspect, maintain, repair, and adjust industrial production and processing machinery and equipment to ensure its proper operation in various industries. There are approximately 220,000 industrial machinery mechanics employed in the United States.

HISTORY

Before 1750 and the beginning of the industrial revolution in Europe, almost all work was done by hand. Families grew their own food, wove their own cloth, and bought or traded very little. Gradually the economic landscape changed. Factories mass-produced products that had once been created by hand. The spinning jenny, a multiple-spindle machine for spinning wool or cotton, was one of the first machines of the industrial revolution. After it came a long procession of inventions and developments, including the steam engine, power loom, cotton gin, steamboat, locomotive, telegraph, and Bessemer converter. With these machines came the need for people who could maintain and repair them.

Mechanics learned that all machines are based on six configurations: the lever, the wheel and axle, the pulley, the inclined plane, the wedge, and the screw. By combining these elements in more complex ways, the machines could do more work in less time than people or animals could do. Thus, the role of machinery mechanics became vital in keeping production lines running and businesses profitable.

The industrial revolution continues even today, although now it is known as the Age of Automation. As machines become more numerous and more complex, the work of the industrial machinery mechanic becomes even more necessary.

THE JOB

The types of machinery on which industrial machinery mechanics work are as varied as the types of industries operating in the United States today. Mechanics are employed in metal stamping plants, printing plants, chemical and plastics plants, and almost any type of large-scale industrial operation that can be imagined. The machinery in these plants must be maintained regularly. Breakdowns and delays with one machine can hinder a plant's entire operation, which is costly for the company.

Preventive maintenance is a major part of mechanics' jobs. They inspect the equipment, oil and grease moving components, and clean and repair parts. They also keep detailed maintenance records on the equipment they service. They often follow blueprints and engineering specifications to maintain and fix equipment.

When breakdowns occur, mechanics may partially or completely disassemble a machine to make the necessary repairs. They replace worn bearings, adjust clutches, and replace and repair defective parts. They may have to order replacement parts from the machinery's manufacturer. If no parts are available, they may have to make the necessary replacements, using milling machines, lathes, or other tooling equipment. After the machine is reassembled, they may have to make adjustments to its operational settings. They often work with the machine's regular operator to test it. When repairing electronically controlled machinery, mechanics may work closely with electronic repairers or electricians who maintain the machine's electronic parts.

Often these mechanics can identify potential breakdowns and fix problems before any real damage or delays occur. They may notice that a machine is vibrating, rattling, or squeaking, or they may see that the items produced by the machine are flawed. Many types of new machinery are built with programmed internal evaluation systems that check the accuracy and condition of equipment. This assists mechanics in their jobs, but it also makes them responsible for maintaining the check-up systems.

Machinery installations are becoming another facet of a mechanic's job. As plants retool and invest in new equipment, they rely on mechanics to properly situate and install the machinery. In many plants, millwrights traditionally did this job, but as employers

Books to Read

Braga, Newton C. *Mechatronics for the Evil Genius*. New York: McGraw-Hill/TAB Electronics, 2005.

Cutcher, Dave. *Electronic Circuits for the Evil Genius*. New York: McGraw-Hill/TAB Electronics, 2004.

Fox, Robert W., Alan T. McDonald, and Philip J. Pritchard. *Introduction to Fluid Mechanics*. Hoboken, N.J.: Wiley, 2005.

Hibbeler, Russell C. *Mechanics of Materials*. 6th ed. Upper Saddle River, N.J.: Prentice Hall, 2004.

Iannini, Robert E. *Electronic Gadgets for the Evil Genius: 28 Build-It-Yourself Projects*. New York: McGraw-Hill/TAB Electronics, 2004.

Mims, Forrest M, III. *Getting Started in Electronics*. Niles, Ill.: Master Publishing Inc., 2003.

Petroski, Henry. *The Evolution of Useful Things*. New York: Vintage Books, 1994.

Predko, Myke. *123 Robotics Experiments for the Evil Genius*. New York: McGraw-Hill/TAB Electronics, 2004.

Scherz, Paul. *Practical Electronics for Inventors*. New York: McGraw-Hill/TAB Electronics, 2006.

increasingly seek workers with multiple skills, industrial machinery mechanics are taking on new responsibilities.

Industrial machinery mechanics use a wide range of tools when doing preventive maintenance or making repairs. For example, they may use simple tools such as a screwdriver and wrench to repair an engine or a hoist to lift a printing press off the ground. Sometimes they solder or weld equipment. They use power and hand tools and precision measuring instruments. In some shops, mechanics troubleshoot the entire plant's operations. Others may become experts in electronics, hydraulics, pneumatics, or other specialties.

REQUIREMENTS

High School

While most employers prefer to hire those who have completed high school, opportunities do exist for those without a diploma as long as they have had some kind of related training. While you are in high school, take courses in mechanical drawing, general mathematics, algebra, and geometry. Other classes that will help prepare you for this career are physics, computer science, and electronics. Any class that gives you experience in blueprint reading adds to your qualifications.

Postsecondary Training

In the past, most industrial machinery mechanics learned the skills of the trade informally by spending several years as helpers in a particular factory. Currently, as machinery has become more complex, more formal training is necessary. Today many mechanics learn the trade through apprenticeship programs sponsored by a local trade union. Apprenticeship programs usually last four years and include both on-the-job and related classroom training. In addition to the use and care of machine and hand tools, apprentices learn the operation, lubrication, and adjustment of the machinery and equipment they will maintain. In class they learn shop mathematics, blueprint reading, safety, hydraulics, welding, and other subjects related to the trade.

Students may also obtain training through vocational or technical schools. Useful programs are those that offer machine shop courses and provide training in electronics and numerical control machine tools.

Industrial machinery mechanics should have mechanical aptitude and manual dexterity. (*Corbis*)

Certification and Licensing
ISA—The Instrumentation, Systems, and Automation Society offers certification for industrial maintenance mechanics. Contact the society for more information.

Other Requirements
Students interested in this field should possess mechanical aptitude and manual dexterity. Good physical condition and agility are necessary because as a mechanic you will sometimes have to lift heavy objects, crawl under large machines, or climb to reach equipment located high above the factory floor.

Mechanics are responsible for valuable equipment and are often called upon to exercise considerable independent judgment. Because of technological advances, you should be willing to learn the requirements of new machines and production techniques. When a plant purchases new equipment, the equipment's manufacturer often trains plant employees in proper operation and maintenance. Technological change requires mechanics to be adaptable and to have inquiring minds.

EXPLORING
If you are interested in this field, you should take as many shop courses as you can. Exploring and repairing machinery such as automobiles and home appliances will also sharpen your skills. In addition, try landing part-time work or a summer job in an industrial plant that gives you the opportunity to observe industrial repair work being done.

EMPLOYERS
Approximately 220,000 industrial machinery mechanics are employed in the United States. These mechanics work in a wide variety of plants and are employed in every part of the country, although employment is concentrated in industrialized areas. According to the U.S. Department of Labor, two-thirds of all industrial machinery mechanics work in manufacturing industries such as chemicals, motor vehicles, food processing, textile mill products, primary metals, and fabricated metal products. Others work for public utilities, government agencies, and mining companies.

STARTING OUT
Jobs can be obtained by directly applying to companies that use industrial equipment or machinery. The majority of mechanics work

for manufacturing plants. These plants are found in a wide variety of industries, including the automotive, plastics, textile, electronics, packaging, food, beverage, and aerospace industries. Chances for job openings may be better at a large plant. New workers are generally assigned to work as helpers or trainees.

Prospective mechanics also may learn of job openings or apprenticeship programs through local unions. Industrial mechanics may be represented by one of several unions, depending on their industry and place of employment. These unions include the International Union, United Automobile, Aerospace, and Agricultural Implement Workers of America; the United Steelworkers of America; the United Auto Workers; the International Union of Electronic, Electrical, Salaried, Machine, and Furniture Workers–Communications Workers of America; the United Brotherhood of Carpenters and Joiners of America; and the International Association of Machinists and Aerospace Workers. According to the U.S. Department of Labor, approximately 25 percent of all industrial machinery mechanics are members of a union. Private and state employment offices are other good sources of job openings.

ADVANCEMENT

Those who begin as helpers or trainees usually become journeymen in four years. Although opportunities for advancement beyond this rank are somewhat limited, industrial machinery mechanics who learn more complicated machinery and equipment can advance to higher paying positions. The most highly skilled mechanics may be promoted to master mechanics. Those who demonstrate good leadership and interpersonal skills can become supervisors. Skilled mechanics also have the option of becoming machinists, numerical control tool programmers, precision metalworkers, packaging machinery technicians, and robotics technicians. Some of these positions do require additional training, but the skills of a mechanic readily transfer to these areas.

EARNINGS

In 2006, median hourly earnings for industrial machinery mechanics were $19.74 (or $41,050 annually), according to the U.S. Department of Labor. The lowest paid 10 percent earned less than $12.84 an hour (or $26,710 annually). The highest 10 percent earned $29.85 or more per hour (or $62,080 annually). Apprentices generally earn lower wages and earn incremental raises as they advance in their training. Earnings vary based on experience, skills, type of industry, and geographic location. Those working in union plants generally earn more than those in nonunion plants. Most industrial machinery mechanics are provided with benefit packages, which can include paid holidays and vacations; medical, dental, and life insurance; and retirement plans.

WORK ENVIRONMENT

Industrial machinery mechanics work in all types of manufacturing plants, which may be hot, noisy, and dirty or relatively quiet and clean. Mechanics frequently work with greasy, dirty equipment and need to be able to adapt to a variety of physical conditions. Because machinery is not always accessible, mechanics may have to work in stooped or cramped positions or on high ladders.

Although working around machinery poses some danger, this risk is minimized with proper safety precautions. Modern machinery includes many safety features and devices, and most plants follow good safety practices. Mechanics often wear protective clothing and equipment, such as hard hats and safety belts, glasses, and shoes.

Mechanics work with little supervision and need to be able to work well with others. They need to be flexible and respond to changing priorities, which can result in interruptions that pull a mechanic off one job to repair a more urgent problem. Although the standard workweek is 40 hours, overtime is common. Because factories and other sites cannot afford breakdowns, industrial machinery mechanics may be called to the plant at night or on weekends for emergency repairs.

OUTLOOK

The U.S. Department of Labor predicts that employment for industrial machinery mechanics will grow more slowly than the average for all occupations through 2014. Some industries will have a greater need for mechanics than others. Much of the new automated production equipment that companies are purchasing has its own self-diagnostic capabilities and is more reliable than older equipment. Although this machinery still needs to be maintained, most job openings will stem from the replacement of transferring or retiring workers.

Certain industries are extremely susceptible to changing economic factors and reduce production activities in slow periods. During these periods, companies may lay off workers or reduce hours. Mechanics are less likely to be laid off than other workers as machines need to be maintained regardless of production levels. Slower production periods and temporary shutdowns are often used to overhaul equipment. Nonetheless, employment opportunities are generally better at companies experiencing growth or stable levels of production.

Because machinery is becoming more complex and automated, mechanics need to be more highly skilled than in the past. Mechanics who stay up to date with new technologies, particularly those related to electronics and computers, should find favorable employment opportunities over the next decade.

FOR MORE INFORMATION

For information on certification, careers, and student membership, contact
ISA—The Instrumentation, Systems, and Automation Society
67 Alexander Drive
Research Triangle Park, NC 27709
Tel: 919-549-8411
Email: info@isa.org
http://www.isa.org

For information about apprentice programs, contact the UAW.
International Union, United Automobile, Aerospace, and Agricultural Implement Workers of America (UAW)
8000 East Jefferson Avenue
Detroit, MI 48214-3963
Tel: 313-926-5000
http://www.uaw.org

For information about the machining industry and career opportunities, contact
National Tooling and Machining Association
9300 Livingston Road
Fort Washington, MD 20744-4914
Tel: 800-248-6862
http://www.ntma.org

For industry information, contact
Precision Machined Products Association
6700 West Snowville Road
Brecksville, OH 44141-3212
Tel: 440-526-0300
http://www.pmpa.org

Instrumentation Technicians

OVERVIEW

Instrumentation technicians are skilled craftsworkers who do precision work and are involved in the field of measurement and control. Technicians inspect, test, repair, and adjust instruments that detect, measure, and record changes in industrial environments. They work with theoretical or analytical problems, helping engineers improve instrument and system performance.

HISTORY

The use of instruments as a means for people to monitor and control their environment and to guide their activities is as old as the sundial. As modern technology progresses, we still find ourselves in need of precise information that is sometimes difficult for a person to physically obtain.

For instance, with the advent of the steam engine in the 19th century, a train operator had to know how much pressure was inside a boiler. A gauge was designed to measure this safely. The early 20th century saw the development of the internal combustion engine and powered flight. With these developments, engineers and technicians designed and made instruments such as speedometers, altimeters, and tachometers to provide vital data for the safe operation of these engines and auxiliary equipment.

Since World War II, instrumentation technology has become a fast-growing field, responding to challenging needs as people explore space, research our oceans, perform biomedical studies, and advance nuclear technology. Today, instrumentation technology involves both

QUICK FACTS

School Subjects
Mathematics
Physics
Technical/shop

Personal Skills
Mechanical/manipulative
Technical/scientific

Work Environment
Primarily indoors
Primarily one location

Minimum Education Level
Associate's degree

Salary Range
$29,830 to $44,720 to $68,700+

Certification or Licensing
Voluntary

Outlook
About as fast as the average

DOT
003

GOE
02.08.04, 05.03.03

NOC
2243

O*NET-SOC
17-3023.02, 17-3024.00, 17-3027.00, 49-9062.00, 49-9069.00

measurement and control, and technicians are critical to their accurate operation. For instance, instrumentation technicians at nuclear reactors assure that the devices inside accurately measure heat, pressure, and radiation, and their rates of change. If any of these factors is not at its specific level, other instruments make the necessary adjustments. This allows the plant to operate safely and efficiently.

THE JOB

Instrumentation technicians work with complex instruments that detect, measure, and record changes in industrial environments. As part of their duties, these technicians perform tests, develop new instruments, and install, repair, inspect, and maintain the instruments. Examples of such instruments include altimeters, pressure gauges, speedometers, and radiation detection devices.

Some instrumentation technicians operate the laboratory equipment that produces or records the effects of certain conditions on the test instruments, such as vibration, stress, temperature, humidity, pressure, altitude, and acceleration. Other technicians sketch, build, and modify electronic and mechanical fixtures, instruments, and related apparatuses.

As part of their duties, technicians might verify the dimensions and functions of devices assembled by other technicians and craftsworkers, plan test programs, and direct technical personnel in carrying out these tests. Instrumentation technicians also perform mathematical calculations on instrument readings and test results so they can be used in graphs and written reports.

Instrumentation technicians work with three major categories of instruments: *pneumatic and electropneumatic equipment,* which includes temperature and flow transmitters and receivers and devices that start or are started by such things as pressure springs, diaphragms, and bellows; *hydraulic instrumentation,* which includes hydraulic valves, hydraulic valve operators, and electrohydraulic equipment; and *electrical and electronic equipment,* which includes electrical sensing elements and transducers, electronic recorders, electronic telemetering systems, and electronic computers.

In some industries, a technician might work on equipment from each category, while in other industries, a technician might be responsible for only one specific type of task. The different levels of responsibility depend also on the instrumentation technician's level of training and experience.

Instrumentation technicians may hold a variety of different positions. *Mechanical instrumentation technicians,* for example, handle routine mechanical functions. They check out equipment before operation, calibrate it during operation, rebuild it using standard replacement parts, mount interconnecting equipment from blueprints, and perform routine repairs using common hand tools. They must be able to read both instrumentation and electronic schematic diagrams. *Instrumentation repair technicians* determine the causes of malfunctions and make repairs. Such repairs usually involve individual pieces of equipment, as distinguished from entire systems. This job requires experience, primarily laboratory-oriented, beyond that of mechanical instrumentation technicians.

Troubleshooting instrumentation technicians make adjustments to instruments and control systems, calibrate equipment, set up tests, diagnose malfunctions, and revise existing systems. Their work is performed either on-site or at a workbench. Advanced training in mathematics, physics, and graphics is required for this level of work. Technicians who are involved in the design of instruments are called *instrumentation design technicians*. They work under the supervision of a design engineer. Using information prepared by engineers, they build models and prototypes and prepare sketches, working drawings, and diagrams. These technicians also test out new system designs, order parts, and make mock-ups of new systems.

Technicians in certain industries have more specialized duties and responsibilities. *Biomedical equipment technicians* work with instruments used during medical procedures. They receive special training in the biomedical area in which their instruments are used.

Calibration technicians, also known as *standards laboratory technicians,* work in the electronics industry and in aerospace and aircraft manufacturing. As part of their inspection of systems and instruments, they measure parts for conformity to specifications, and they help develop calibration standards, devise formulas to solve problems in measurement and calibration, and write procedures and practical guides for other calibration technicians.

Electromechanical technicians work with automated mechanical equipment controlled by electronic sensing devices. They assist mechanical engineers in the design and development of such equipment, analyze test results, and write reports. The technician follows blueprints, operates metalworking machines, builds instrument housings, installs electrical equipment, and calibrates instruments and machinery. Technicians who specialize in the assembly of prototype instruments are known as *development technicians. Fabrication technicians* specialize in the assembly of production instruments.

Nuclear instrumentation technicians work with instruments at a nuclear power plant. These instruments control the various systems within the nuclear reactor, detect radiation, and sound alarms in case of equipment failure. *Instrument sales technicians* work for equipment manufacturing companies. They analyze customer needs, outline specifications for equipment cost and function, and sometimes do emergency troubleshooting.

REQUIREMENTS

High School

Math and science courses such as algebra, geometry, physics, and chemistry are essential prerequisites to becoming an instrumentation technician. In addition, machine and electrical shop courses will help you become familiar with electrical, mechanical, and electronic technology. Classes in mechanical drawing and computer-aided drafting are also beneficial. Instrumentation technicians also need good writing and communication skills, so be sure to take English, composition, and speech classes.

Postsecondary Training

The basic requirement for an entry-level job is completion of a two-year technical program or equivalent experience in a related field. Such equivalent experience may come from work in an electronics or manufacturing firm or any job that provides experience working with mechanical or electrical equipment.

Technical programs beyond high school can be found in community colleges as well as technical schools. Programs are offered in many different disciplines in addition to instrumentation technology. Programs may be in electronics or in electrical, mechanical, biomedical, or nuclear technology.

Most programs allow technicians to develop hands-on and laboratory skills as well as learn theory. Classes are likely to include instruction on electronic circuitry, computer science, mathematics, and physics. Courses in basic electronics, electrical theory, and graphics are also important. Technical writing is helpful as most technicians will prepare technical reports. Industrial economics, applied psychology, and plant management courses are helpful to those who plan to move into customer service or design.

Certification or Licensing

Instrumentation technicians who graduate from a recognized technical program may become certified by the National Institute for Certification in Engineering Technologies, although this is usually not a required part of a job. Certification is available at various levels, each combining a written exam in one of more than 25 specialty fields with a specified amount of job-related experience. Instrumentation technicians who specialize in biomedical equipment repair can receive voluntary certification from the Board of Examiners for Biomedical Equipment Technicians. ISA—The Instrumentation, Systems, and Automation Society also offers certification for technicians who are involved in automation, control, maintenance, and manufacturing.

Other Requirements

To be an instrumentation technician, you need mathematical and scientific aptitude and the patience to methodically pursue complex questions. A tolerance for following prescribed procedures is essential, especially when undertaking assignments requiring a very precise, unchanging system of problem solving. Successful instrumentation technicians are able to provide solutions quickly and accurately even in stressful situations.

EXPLORING

As a way to test your abilities and learn more about calibration work, try building small electronic equipment. Kits for building radios and other small appliances are available in some electronics shops. This will give you a basic understanding of electronic components and applications.

Some communities and schools also have clubs for people interested in electronics. They may offer classes that teach basic skills in construction, repair, and adjustment of electrical and electronic products. Model building, particularly in hard plastic and steel, will give you a good understanding of how to adapt and fit parts together. It may also help develop your hand skills if you want to work with precision instruments.

Visits to industrial laboratories, instrument shops, research laboratories, power installations, and manufacturing companies that rely on automated processes can expose you to the activities of instrumentation technicians. During such visits, you might be able to speak with technicians about their work or with managers about possible openings in their company. Also, you might look into getting a summer or part-time job as a helper on an industrial maintenance crew.

EMPLOYERS

Employers of instrumentation technicians include oil refineries, chemical and industrial laboratories, electronics firms, aircraft and aeronautical manufacturers, and biomedical firms. Companies involved in space exploration, oceanographic research, and national defense systems also employ instrumentation technicians. In addition, they work in various capacities in such industries as automotives, food, metals, ceramics, pulp and paper, power, textiles, pharmaceuticals, mining, metals, and pollution control.

STARTING OUT

Many companies recruit students prior to their graduation. Chemical and medical research companies especially need maintenance and operations technicians and usually recruit at schools where training in these areas is strong. Similarly, many industries in search of design technicians recruit at technical institutes and community colleges where the program is likely to meet their needs.

Students may also get assistance in their job searches through their schools' career services office, or they may learn about openings through ads in the newspapers. Prospective employees can also apply directly to a company in which they are interested.

ADVANCEMENT

Entry-level technicians develop their skills by learning tasks on their employers' equipment. Those with good academic records may, upon completion of an employer's basic program, move to an advanced level in sales or another area where a general understanding of the field is more important than specific laboratory skills. Technicians who have developed proficiency in instrumentation may choose to move to a supervisory or specialized position that requires knowledge of a particular aspect of instrumentation.

EARNINGS

Earnings for instrumentation technicians vary by industry, geographic region, educational background, experience, and level of responsibility. According to the U.S. Department of Labor, median annual earnings of electromechanical technicians were $44,720 in 2006. Salaries ranged from less than $29,830 to more than $68,700. Electrical and electronic engineering technicians had median annual earnings of $50,660 in 2006, and mechanical engineering technicians earned $45,850. Medical equipment repairers earned average salaries of $40,580. Employee benefits vary, but can include paid vacations and holidays, sick leave, insurance benefits, 401(k) plans, profit sharing, pension plans, and tuition assistance programs.

WORK ENVIRONMENT

Working conditions vary widely for instrumentation technicians. An oil refinery plant job is as different from space mission instrumentation work as a nuclear reactor instrumentation job is different from work in the operating room of a hospital. All these jobs use similar principles, however, and instrumentation technicians can master new areas by applying what they have learned previously. For technicians who would like to travel, the petroleum industry, in particular, provides employment opportunities in foreign countries.

Instrumentation technicians' tasks may range from the routine to the highly complex and challenging. A calm, professional approach to work is essential. Calibration and adjustment require the dexterity and control of a watchmaker. Consequently, a person who is easily excited or impatient is not well suited to this kind of employment.

OUTLOOK

Employment opportunities for most instrumentation technicians will grow about as fast as the average for all occupations through 2014. Opportunities will be best for graduates of postsecondary technical training programs. As technology becomes more sophisticated, employers will continue to look for technicians who are skilled in new technology and require a minimum of additional job training.

Most developments in automated manufacturing techniques, including robotics and computer-controlled machinery, rely heavily on instrumentation devices. The emerging fields of air and water pollution control are other areas of growth. Scientists and technicians measure the amount of toxic substances in the air or test water with the use of instrumentation.

Oceanography, including the search for undersea deposits of oil and minerals, is another expanding field for instrumentation technology, as is medical diagnosis, including long-distance diagnosis by physicians through the use of sensors, computers, and telephone lines.

One important field of growth is the teaching profession. As demand rises for skilled technicians, qualified instructors with combined knowledge of theory and application will be needed. Opportunities already exist, not only in educational institutions but also in those industries that have internal training programs.

FOR MORE INFORMATION

For a list of accredited technology programs, contact
Accreditation Board for Engineering and Technology Inc.
111 Market Place, Suite 1050
Baltimore, MD 21202-4012
Tel: 410-347-7700
http://www.abet.org

For information on educational programs and medical instrument certification, contact
Association for the Advancement of Medical Instrumentation
1110 North Glebe Road, Suite 220
Arlington, VA 22201-4795
Tel: 800-332-2264
Email: certifications@aami.org
http://www.aami.org

For information on careers and accredited programs, contact
Institute of Electrical and Electronics Engineers
1828 L Street, NW, Suite 1202
Washington, DC 20036-5104
Tel: 202-785-0017
Email: ieeeusa@ieee.org
http://www.ieee.org

For information on certification, careers, and student membership, contact
ISA—The Instrumentation, Systems, and Automation Society
67 Alexander Drive
Research Triangle Park, NC 27709
Tel: 919-549-8411
Email: info@isa.org
http://www.isa.org

For information on careers and student clubs, contact
Junior Engineering Technical Society
1420 King Street, Suite 405
Alexandria, VA 22314-2750
Tel: 703-548-5387
Email: info@jets.org
http://www.jets.org

For information on certification, contact
National Institute for Certification in Engineering Technologies
1420 King Street
Alexandria, VA 22314-2794
Tel: 888-476-4238
http://www.nicet.org

Marine Services Technicians

OVERVIEW

Marine services technicians inspect, maintain, and repair marine vessels, from small boats to large yachts. They work on vessels' hulls, engines, transmissions, navigational equipment, and electrical, propulsion, and refrigeration systems. Depending on their specialty, they may also be known as *motorboat mechanics, marine electronics technicians,* or *fiberglass technicians.* Marine services technicians may work at boat dealerships, boat repair shops, boat engine manufacturers, or marinas. Naturally, jobs are concentrated near large bodies of water and coastal areas.

HISTORY

Ever since there have been boats and other water vessels, it has been necessary to have people who can repair and maintain them. In colonial times in the United States, those who took care of vessels were not called technicians, but they did many of the same routine tasks performed today, with less developed tools and equipment. Marine services technicians have had to keep up with developments in vessel design and material, from wood and iron to fiberglass.

In the past, those who repaired water vessels found work mainly with merchant boats and ships and with military vessels. As the standard of living in the United States has increased, more people have been able to afford pleasure boats, from small motorcraft to luxury yachts. Marine services technicians rely on the pleasure boat industry today for much of their work.

QUICK FACTS

School Subjects
Mathematics
Technical/shop

Personal Skills
Following instructions
Mechanical/manipulative

Work Environment
Indoors and outdoors
One location with some
  travel

Minimum Education Level
Some postsecondary training

Salary Range
$20,680 to $33,210 to
  $50,750+

Certification or Licensing
Required for certain positions

Outlook
About as fast as the average

DOT
806

GOE
05.03.01

NOC
7335

O*NET-SOC
49-3051.00

THE JOB

Marine services technicians work on the more than 16 million boats and other watercraft owned by people in the United States. They test and repair boat engines, transmissions, and propellers; rigging, masts, and sails; and navigational equipment and steering gear. They repair or replace defective parts and sometimes make new parts to meet special needs. They may also inspect and replace internal cabinets, refrigeration systems, electrical systems and equipment, sanitation facilities, hardware, and trim.

Workers with specialized skills often have more specific titles. For example, *motorboat mechanics* work on boat engines—those that are inboard, outboard, and inboard/outboard. Routine maintenance tasks include lubricating, cleaning, repairing, and adjusting parts.

Motorboat mechanics often use special testing equipment, such as engine analyzers, compression gauges, ammeters, and voltmeters, as well as other computerized diagnostic equipment. Technicians must know how to disassemble and reassemble components and refer to service manuals for directions and specifications. Motorboat workers often install and repair electronics, sanitation, and air-conditioning systems. They need a set of general and specialized tools, often provided by their employers; many mechanics gradually acquire their own tools, often spending up to thousands of dollars on this investment.

Marine electronics technicians work with vessels' electronic safety and navigational equipment, such as radar, depthsounders, loran (long-range navigation), autopilots, and compass systems. They install, repair, and calibrate equipment for proper functioning. Routine maintenance tasks include checking, cleaning, repairing, and replacing parts. Electronics technicians check for common causes of problems, such as loose connections and defective parts. They often rely on schematics and manufacturers' specification manuals to troubleshoot problems. These workers also must have a set of tools, including hand tools such as pliers, screwdrivers, and soldering irons. Other equipment, often supplied by their employers, includes voltmeters, ohmmeters, signal generators, ammeters, and oscilloscopes.

Technicians who are *field repairers* go to the vessel to do their work, perhaps at the marina dock. *Bench repairers,* on the other hand, work on equipment brought into shops.

Some technicians work only on vessel hulls. These are usually made of either wood or fiberglass. *Fiberglass repairers* work on fiberglass hulls, of which most pleasure crafts today are built. They reinforce damaged areas of the hull, grind damaged pieces with a sander, or cut them away with a jigsaw and replace them using resin-impregnated fiberglass cloth. They finish the repaired sections by sanding, painting with a gel-coat substance, and then buffing.

REQUIREMENTS

High School

Most employers prefer to hire applicants who have a high school diploma. If you are interested in this work, take mathematics classes and shop classes in metals, woodwork, and electronics while you are in high school. These classes will give you experience completing detailed and precise work. Shop classes will also give you experience using a variety of tools and reading blueprints. Take computer classes; you will probably be using this tool throughout your career for such things as diagnostic and design work. Science classes, such as physics, will also be beneficial to you. Finally, don't forget to take English classes. These classes will help you hone your reading and research skills, which will be needed when you consult technical manuals for repair and maintenance information throughout your career.

Postsecondary Training

Many marine services technicians learn their trade on the job. They find entry-level positions as general boatyard workers, doing such jobs as cleaning boat bottoms, and work their way into the position of service technician. Or they may be hired as trainees. They learn how to perform typical service tasks under the supervision of experienced mechanics and gradually complete more difficult work. The training period may last for about three years.

Other technicians decide to get more formal training and attend vocational or technical colleges for classes in engine repair, electronics, and fiberglass work. Some schools, such as Cape Fear Community College in North Carolina and Washington County Community College in Maine, have programs specifically for marine technicians (see For More Information). These schools often offer an associate's degree in areas such as applied science. Classes students take may include mathematics, physics, electricity, schematic reading, and circuit theory. Boat manufacturers and other types of institutions, such as the American Boatbuilders and Repairers Association, Mystic Seaport Museum, and the WoodenBoat School, offer skills training through less formal courses and seminars that often last several days or a few weeks. The military can also provide training in electronics.

Certification or Licensing

Those who test and repair marine radio transmitting equipment must have a general radio-telephone operator license from the Federal

Communications Commission (445 12th Street, SW, Washington, DC 20554-0001, Tel: 888-225-5322, http://www.fcc.gov).

Certification for technicians in the marine electronics industry is voluntary and is administered by the National Marine Electronics Association. There are four grades of certification for workers in this industry: the certified marine electronic technician (CMET) designation for technicians with one year of experience, the advanced CMET designation for those with three years of experience, the senior CMET designation for those with 10 years of experience, and the lifetime CMET designation for those who have passed the advanced CMET exam, have a minimum of 10 years as a senior CMET, and who are approved by a majority vote of the certification committee. Basic certification is by written examination and the employer's verification as to the technician's proficiency in the repair of basic radar, voice SSB, VHF, depth sounders, and autopilots. The higher degrees of certification are earned by meeting all previous grade requirements plus satisfactorily completing a factory training course or having the employer attest to the technician's proficiency in repairing advanced equipment.

Other Requirements

Most technicians work outdoors some of the time, and they are often required to test-drive the vessels they work on. This is considered an added benefit by many workers. Some workers in this field maintain that one of the most important qualities for a technician is a pleasant personality. Boat owners are often very proud of and attached to their vessels, so workers need to have both respect and authority when communicating with customers.

Technicians also need to be able to adapt to the cyclical nature of this business. They are often under a lot of pressure in the summer months, when most boat owners are enjoying the water and calling on technicians for service. On the other hand, they often have gaps in their work during the winter; some workers receive unemployment compensation at this time.

Motorboat technicians' work can sometimes be physically demanding, requiring them to lift heavy outboard motors or other components. Electronics technicians, on the other hand, must be able to work with delicate parts, such as wires and circuit boards. They should have good eyesight, color vision, and good hearing (to listen for malfunctions revealed by sound).

Some marine services technicians may be required to provide their own hand tools. These tools are usually acquired over a period of time, but the collection may cost the mechanic hundreds if not thousands of dollars.

EXPLORING

This field lends itself to a lot of fun ways to explore job opportunities. Of course, having a boat of your own and working on it is one of the best means of preparation. If friends, neighbors, or relatives have boats, take trips with them and see how curious you are about what makes the vessel work. Offer to help do repairs to the boat, or at least watch while repairs are made and routine maintenance jobs are done. Clean up the deck, sand an old section of the hull, or polish the brass. If a boat just isn't available to you, try to find some type of engine to work on. Even working on an automobile engine will give you a taste of what this type of work is like.

Some high schools have co-op training programs through which students can look for positions with boat-related businesses, such as boat dealerships or even marinas. Check with your guidance counselor about this possibility. You also can read trade magazines such as *Boating Industry* (http://www.boating-industry.com) and the online forum *Professional Boatbuilder* (http://www.proboat. com). These periodicals offer information monthly or bimonthly on the pleasure boat industry, as well as on boat design, construction, and repair.

EMPLOYERS

Marine services technicians are employed by boat retailers, boat repair shops, boat engine manufacturers, boat rental firms, resorts, and marinas. The largest marinas are in coastal areas, such as Florida, New York, California, Texas, Massachusetts, and Louisiana; smaller ones are located near lakes and water recreation facilities such as campgrounds. Manufacturers of large fishing vessels also employ technicians for on-site mechanical support at fishing sites and competitive events. These workers often follow professionals on the fishing circuit, traveling from tournament to tournament maintaining the vessels.

STARTING OUT

A large percentage of technicians get their start by working as general boatyard laborers—cleaning boats, cutting grass, painting, and so on. After showing interest and ability, they can begin to work with experienced technicians and learn skills on the job. Some professional organizations, such as Marine Trades Association of New Jersey and Michigan Boating Industries Association, offer scholarships for those interested in marine technician training.

For those technicians who have attended vocational or technical colleges, career services offices of these schools may have information about job openings.

ADVANCEMENT

Many workers consider management and supervisory positions as job goals. After working for a number of years on actual repairs and maintenance, many technicians like to manage repair shops, supervise other workers, and deal with customers more directly. These positions require less physical labor but more communication and management skills. Many workers like to combine both aspects by becoming self-employed; they may have their own shops, attract their own jobs, and still get to do the technical work they enjoy.

Advancement often depends on an individual's interests. Some become marina managers, manufacturers' salespersons, or field representatives. Others take a different direction and work as *boat brokers,* selling boats. *Marine surveyors* verify the condition and value of boats; they are independent contractors hired by insurance companies and lending institutions such as banks.

EARNINGS

According to the U.S. Department of Labor, the median yearly earnings of motorboat mechanics were $33,210 in 2006. The middle 50 percent earned between $26,330 and $41,610. Salaries ranged from less than $20,680 to more than $50,750 a year.

Technicians in small shops tend to receive few fringe benefits, but larger employers often offer paid vacations, sick leave, and health insurance. Some employers provide uniforms and tools and pay for work-related training. Many technicians who enjoy the hands-on work with boats claim that the best benefit is to take repaired boats out for test-drives.

WORK ENVIRONMENT

Technicians who work indoors often are in well-lit and ventilated shops. The work is cleaner than that on cars because there tends to be less grease and dirt on marine engines; instead, workers have to deal with water scum, heavy-duty paint, and fiberglass. In general, marine work is similar to other types of mechanical jobs, where workers encounter such things as noise when engines are being run and potential danger with power tools and chemicals. Also similar to other mechanics' work, sometimes technicians work alone on a job and at other times they work on a boat with other technicians. Unless a technician is self-employed, his or her work will likely be overseen by a supervisor of some kind. For any repair job, the technician may have to deal directly with customers.

Some mechanics, such as those who work at marinas, work primarily outdoors—and in all kinds of weather. In boats with no air conditioning, the conditions in the summer can be hot and uncomfortable. Technicians often have to work in tight, uncomfortable places to perform repairs. Sailboats have especially tight access to inboard engines.

There is often a big demand for service just before Memorial Day and the Fourth of July. In the summer, workweeks can average 60 hours. But in winter the week can involve less than 40 hours of work, with layoffs common at this time of year. In the warmer climates of the United States, work tends to be steadier throughout the year.

OUTLOOK

According to the U.S. Department of Labor, employment opportunities for small engine mechanics, including marine services technicians, are expected to grow about as fast as the average for all occupations through 2014. As boat design and construction become more complicated, the outlook will be best for well-trained technicians. Most marine craft purchases are made by the over-40 age group, which is expected to increase over the next decade. The growth of this population segment should help expand the market for motorboats and increase the demand for qualified mechanics.

The availability of jobs will be related to the health of the pleasure boat industry. According to *Boating Industry*, there are 10,000 marine retailers in the United States and 1,500 boatyards that repair hulls and engines. One interesting demographic trend that will influence job opportunities is the shift of the population to the South and West, where warm-weather seasons are longer and thus attract more boating activity.

An increase in foreign demand for U.S. pleasure vessels will mean more opportunities for workers in this field. U.S. manufacturers are expected to continue to develop foreign markets and establish more distribution channels. However, legislation in the United States may require boat operator licenses and stricter emission standards, which might lead to a decrease in the number of boats sold and maintained here.

FOR MORE INFORMATION

For industry information, contact
American Boatbuilders and Repairers Association
50 Water Street
Warren, RI 02885-3034
Tel: 401-247-0318
http://www.abbra.org

To find out whether there is a marine association in your area, contact
Marine Retailers Association of America
PO Box 1127
Oak Park, IL 60304-0127
Tel: 708-763-9210
Email: mraa@mraa.com
http://www.mraa.com

For information on certification, the industry, and membership, contact
National Marine Electronics Association
7 Riggs Avenue
Severna Park, MD 21146-3819
Tel: 410-975-9425
Email: info@nmea.org
http://www.nmea.org

For educational information, contact the following schools:
Cape Fear Community College
411 North Front Street
Wilmington, NC 28401-3910
Tel: 910-362-7000
http://cfcc.edu

Washington County Community College
Eastport Campus
16 Deep Cove Road
Eastport, ME 04631-3218
Tel: 800-806-0433
Email: admissions@wccc.me.edu
http://www.wccc.me.edu/abeast.html

INTERVIEW

Rick Brichta is the coordinator of the Marine and Small Engine Technology Program at Iowa Lakes Community College in Emmetsburg, Iowa. He discussed the field with the editors of Careers in Focus: Mechanics.

Q. Please tell us about your program.

A. We offer a one-year program in marine and small engines. Iowa Lakes Community College's marine program prepares students to work in the marine field, including work on personal watercraft, Sterndrive [motors], and outboard and inboard engines. Students learn to be prepared to work in all facets of the marine industry.

Q. What type of students pursue study in your program?

A. Students who like to be outdoors or on the water and like fixing boats, personal watercraft, snowmobiles, and so on pursue study in this field.

Q. For what type of jobs does your program prepare students?

A. Careers in the small engine or marine industry, such as positions at marinas, snowmobile dealerships, and marine parts suppliers. Students can also pursue careers in sales.

Q. What advice would you offer graduates of your program?

A. Be honest, fix it right the first time, work hard, and sell your skills and abilities.

Q. Are there any changes in this job market that students should expect?

A. Yes, students should know there is a huge shortage of marine technicians right now all over the nation. The demand for quality marine technicians will grow by 15 percent in another seven years. This means there are real jobs out there and they are not going anywhere [i.e., overseas]. It would be hard to ship a boat or personal watercraft overseas to get repaired. We are in the upward trend in boat registration this year and last year.

Musical Instrument Repairers and Tuners

OVERVIEW

Musical instrument repairers and *tuners* work on a variety of instruments, often operating inside music shops or repair shops to keep the pieces in tune and in proper condition. Those who specialize in working on pianos or pipe organs may travel to the instrument's location to work. Instrument repairers and tuners usually specialize in certain families of musical instruments, such as stringed or brass instruments. Depending on the instrument, they may be skilled in working with wood, metal, electronics, or other materials. There are approximately 6,100 music instrument repairers and tuners employed in the United States.

HISTORY

The world's first musical instrument was the human body. Paleolithic dancers clapped, stamped, chanted, and slapped their bodies to mark rhythm. Gourd rattles, bone whistles, scrapers, hollow branch and conch shell trumpets, wooden rhythm pounders and knockers, and bullroarers followed. By the early Neolithic times, people had developed drums that produced two or more pitches and pottery and cane flutes that gave several notes. The musical bow, a primitive stringed instrument and forerunner of the jaw harp, preceded the bow-shaped harp (about 3000 B.C.) and the long-necked lute (about 2000 B.C.).

The history of the pipe organ stretches back to the third century B.C., when the Egyptians developed an organ that used water power

172

to produce a stream of air. A few centuries later, organs appeared in Byzantium that used bellows (a device that draws air in and then expels it with great force) to send air through the organ pipes. By A.D., all the features of the modern pipe organ were developed.

The first version of the violin, played by scraping a taut bow across several stretched strings, appeared in Europe around 1510. The end of the 16th century saw the development of the violin as it is known today. Over the next 100 years, violin making reached its greatest achievements in the area around Cremona, Italy, where families of master craftsmen, such as the Stradivaris, the Guarneris, and the Amatis, set a standard for quality that never has been surpassed. Today, their violins are coveted by players around the world for their tonal quality.

The modern piano is the end product of a gradual evolution from plucked string instruments, such as the harp, to instruments employing hammers of one kind or another to produce notes by striking the strings. By the late 1700s, the immediate ancestor of the modern piano had been developed. Improvements and modifications (most involving new materials or manufacturing processes) took place throughout the 19th century, resulting in today's piano.

In addition to the stringed instruments, contemporary orchestral instruments also include the woodwind, brass, and percussion families. Woodwinds include the flute, clarinet, oboe, bassoon, and saxophone. Brass instruments include the French horn, trumpet, cornet, trombone, and tuba. All require some professional care and maintenance at some time. The modern electronic organ is a descendent of the pipe organ. In 1934, Laurens Hammond, an American inventor, patented the first practical electronic organ, an instrument that imitates the sound of the pipe organ but requires much less space and is more economical and practical to own and operate. The development of electronic and computer technology produced the first synthesizers and synthesized instruments, which are used widely today.

THE JOB

All but the most heavily damaged instruments usually can be repaired by competent, experienced craftsworkers. In addition, instruments require regular maintenance and inspection to ensure that they play properly and to prevent small problems from becoming major ones.

Stringed-instrument repairers perform extremely detailed and difficult work. The repair of violins, violas, and cellos might be considered the finest woodworking done in the world today. Because their sound quality is so beautiful, some older, rarer violins are worth millions of dollars, and musicians will sometimes fly halfway around the world to have rare instruments repaired by *master restorers*. In many ways, the work of these master craftspeople may be compared to the restoration of fine art masterpieces.

When a violin or other valuable stringed instrument needs repair, its owner takes the instrument to a repair shop, which may employ many repairers. If the violin has cracks in its body, it must be taken apart. The pieces of a violin are held together by a special glue that allows the instrument to be dismantled easily for repair purposes. The glue, which is made from hides and bones and has been used for more than 400 years, is sturdy but does not bond permanently with the wood.

To repair a crack in the back of a violin, the repairer first pops the back off the instrument. After cleaning the crack with warm water, the repairer glues the crack and attaches cleats or studs above the crack on the inside to prevent further splitting. The repairer reassembles the violin and closes the outside of the crack with fill varnish. Lastly, the repairer treats the crack scrupulously with retouch varnish so that it becomes invisible.

The repairer does not complete every step immediately after the previous one. Depending on the age and value of the instrument, a repair job can take three weeks or longer. Glues and varnishes need to set, and highly detailed work demands much concentration. The repairer also needs to do research to isolate the original type of varnish on the instrument and match it precisely with modern materials. The repairer usually has more than one repair job going at any one time.

A major restoration, such as the replacement of old patchwork or the fitting of inside patches to support the instrument, requires even more time. A large project can take two years or longer. A master restorer can put 2,000 or more hours into the repair of a valuable violin that has nothing more than a few cracks in its finish. Since many fine instruments are worth $2 million or more, they need intense work to preserve the superior quality of their sound. The repairer cannot rush the work, must concentrate on every detail, and complete the repair properly or risk other problems later on.

While all instruments are not made by Stradivari, they still need to be kept in good condition to be played well. Owners bring in their violins, violas, and cellos to the repair shop every season for cleaning, inspecting joints, and gluing gaps. The work involves tools similar to woodworker's tools, such as carving knives, planes, and gouges. The violin repairer will often need to play the instrument to check its condition and tune it. Bow rehairers maintain the quality of the taut, vibrating horsehair string that is stretched from end to end of the resilient wooden bow.

Wind-instrument repairers require a similar level of skill to that required of stringed-instrument repairers. However, as the quality of sound is more standard among manufacturers, old instruments do not necessarily play any better than new ones, and these instruments do not command the same value as a fine violin.

The repairer first needs to determine the extent of repairs that the instrument warrants. The process may range from a few minor repairs to bring the instrument up to playing condition to a complete overhaul. After fixing the instrument, the repairer also will clean both the inside and outside and may replate the metal finish on a scuffed or rusty instrument.

For woodwinds such as clarinets and oboes, common repairs include fixing or replacing the moving parts of the instrument, including replacing broken keys with new keys, cutting new padding or corks to replace worn pieces, and replacing springs. If the body of the woodwind is cracked in any sections, the repairer will take the instrument apart and attempt to pin or glue the crack shut. In some situations, the repairer will replace the entire section or joint of the instrument.

Repairing brass instruments such as trumpets and French horns requires skill in metal working and plating. The pieces of these instruments are held together by solder, which the repairer must heat and remove to take the instrument apart for repair work. To fix dents, the repairer will unsolder the piece and work the dent out with hammers and more delicate tools and seal splits in the metal with solder as well. A final buffing and polishing usually removes any evidence of the repair.

If one of the valves of the brass instrument is leaking, the repairer may replate it and build up layers of metal to fill the gaps. At times, the repairer will replace a badly damaged valve with a new valve from the instrument manufacturer, but often the owner will discard the entire instrument because the cost of making a new valve from raw materials is prohibitive. Replacement parts are usually available from the manufacturer, but parts for older instruments are sometimes difficult or impossible to find. For this reason, many repairers save and stockpile discarded instruments for their parts.

A piano tuner adjusts piano action. *(Frank Pedrick, The Image Works)*

Piano technicians and *piano tuners* repair and tune pianos so that when a key is struck it will produce its correctly pitched note of the musical scale. A piano may go out of tune for a variety of reasons, including strings that have stretched or tightened from age, temperature change, relocation, or through use. Tuners use a special wrench to adjust the pins that control the tension on the strings. Piano tuners usually are specially trained for such work, but piano technicians also may perform tuning in connection with a more thorough inspection or overhaul of an instrument.

A piano's performance is also affected by problems in any of the thousands of moving parts of the action or by problems in the sounding board or the frame holding the strings. These are problems that the technician is trained to analyze and correct. They may involve replacing or repairing parts or making adjustments that enable the existing parts to function more smoothly.

The life of a piano—that is, the period of time before it can no longer be properly tuned or adjusted to correct operational problems—is usually estimated at 20 years. Because the harp and strong outer wooden frame are seldom damaged, technicians often rebuild pianos by replacing the sounding board and strings, refurbishing and replacing parts where necessary, and refinishing the outer case.

In all their work, from tuning to rebuilding, piano technicians discover a piano's problems by talking to the owner and playing the instrument themselves. They may dismantle a piano partially on-site to determine the amount of wear to its parts and look for broken parts. They use common hand tools such as hammers, screwdrivers, and pliers. To repair and rebuild pianos, they use a variety of specialized tools for stringing and setting pins.

For *pipe organ technicians*, the largest part of the job is repairing and maintaining existing organs. This primarily involves tuning the pipes, which can be time consuming, even in a moderate-sized organ.

To tune a flue pipe, the technician moves a slide that increases or decreases the length of the speaking (note-producing) part of the pipe, varying its pitch. The technician tunes a reed pipe varying the length of the brass reed inside the pipe.

To tune an organ, the technician tunes either the A or C pipes by matching their notes with those of a tuning fork or electronic note-producing device. He or she then tunes the other pipes in harmony with the A or C notes. This may require a day or more for a moderate-sized organ and much longer for a giant concert organ.

Pipe organ technicians also diagnose, locate, and correct problems in the operating parts of the organ and perform preventive maintenance on a regular basis. To do this, they work with electric wind-generating equipment and with slides, valves, keys, air channels, and other equipment that enables the organist to produce the desired music.

Occasionally, a new organ is installed in a new or existing structure. Manufacturers design and install the largest organs. Each is unique, and the designer carefully supervises its construction and installation. Often, designers individually create moderate-sized organs specifically for the structure, usually churches, in which they will be played. Technicians follow the designer's blueprints closely during installation. The work involves assembling and connecting premanufactured components, using a variety of hand and power tools. Technicians may work in teams, especially when installing the largest pipes of the organ.

Although the electronic organ imitates the sound of the pipe organ, the workings of the two instruments have little in common. The electronic organ consists of electrical and electronic components and circuits that channel electrical current through various oscillators and amplifiers to produce sound when a player presses each key. It is rare for an oscillator or other component to need adjustment in the way an organ pipe needs to be adjusted to tune it. A technician tunes an electronic organ by testing it for electronic malfunction and replacing or repairing the component, circuit board, or wire.

Musical Instrument Repair Schools in North America

Badger State Repair School
Elkhorn, Wisc.
262-723-4062
Available programs: Brass and Woodwind Instrument Repair (48-week course)

Keyano College–Clearwater Campus
Fort McMurray, Alberta, Canada
800-251-1408, ext. 8979
http://www.keyano.ca/prospective_students/programs/certificate_diploma/music_instrument_repair.htm
Available programs: Musical Instrument Repair (diploma)

Minnesota State College-Southeast Technical–Red Wing Campus
Red Wing, Minn.
877-853-8324
http://it.southeastmn.edu/programs/index.asp
Available programs: Band Instrument Repair (diploma); Musical String Instrument Construction (certificate); Musical String Instrument Repair-Guitar (diploma); Musical String Instrument Repair-Violin (diploma)

Renton Technical College
Renton, Wash.
425-235-2352
http://www.rtc.edu
Available programs: Band Instrument Repair Technology (certificate, associate's degree)

Western Iowa Tech Community College
Sioux City, Iowa
800-352-4649
http://www.witcc.com
Available programs: Band Instrument Repair Technology (associate's degree); Electronic Musical Instrument Repair (certificate)

The work of the *electronic organ technician* is closer to that of the television repair technician than it is to that of the pipe organ technician. The technician often begins looking for the source of a problem by checking for loose wires and solder connections. After making routine checks, technicians consult wiring diagrams that enable them to trace and test the circuits of the entire instrument to find malfunctions. For instance, an unusual or irregular voltage in a circuit may indicate a problem. Once the problem has been located, the technician often solves it by replacing a malfunctioning part, such as a circuit board.

These technicians work with common electrician's tools: pliers, wire cutters, screwdriver, soldering iron, and testing equipment. Technicians can make most repairs and adjustments in the customer's home. Because each manufacturer's instruments are arranged differently, technicians follow manufacturers' wiring diagrams and service manuals to locate trouble spots and make repairs. In larger and more complex instruments, such as those in churches and theaters, this may require a day or more of searching and testing.

Other types of repairers work on a variety of less common instruments. *Percussion tuners and repairers* work on drums, bells, congas, timbales, cymbals, and castanets. They may stretch new skins over the instrument, replace broken or missing parts, or seal cracks in the wood.

Accordion tuners and repairers work on free-reed portable accordions, piano accordions, concertinas, harmoniums, and harmonicas. They repair leaks in the bellows of an instrument, replace broken or damaged reeds, and perform various maintenance tasks. Other specialists in instrument repair include fretted-instrument repairers, harp regulators, trombone-slide assemblers, metal-reed tuners, tone regulators, and chip tuners.

Some musical repairers work as *musical instrument designers* and *builders*. They work in musical instrument factories or as freelancers designing and building instruments in their own workshops. Almost any type of instrument can be designed and built, but musical instrument builders most often craft guitars, banjos, violins, and flutes.

In addition to repairing, designing, or building instruments, those who run their own shops perform duties similar to others in the retail business. They order stock from instrument manufacturers, wait on customers, handle their accounting and billing work, and perform other duties.

REQUIREMENTS

High School

No matter what family of instruments interests you, you should start preparing for this field by gaining a basic knowledge of music. Take high school classes in music history, music theory, and choir, chorus, or other singing classes. By learning to read music, developing an ear for scales, and understanding tones and pitches, you will develop an excellent background for this work. Also, explore your interest in instruments (besides your own voice) by taking band or orchestra classes or private music lessons. By learning how to play an instrument, you will also learn how a properly tuned and maintained instrument should sound. If you find yourself interested in instruments with metal parts, consider taking art or shop classes that provide the opportunity to do metal working. These classes will allow you to practice soldering and work with appropriate tools. If you are interested in piano or stringed instruments, consider taking art or shop classes that offer woodworking. In these classes you will learn finishing techniques and use tools that you may relate to the building and maintaining of the bodies of these instruments.

Because instrument repair of any type is precision work, you will benefit from taking mathematics classes such as algebra and geometry. Since many instrument repairers and tuners are self-employed, take business or accounting classes to prepare for this possibility. Finally, take English classes to develop your research, reading, and communication skills. You will often need to consult technical instruction manuals for repair and maintenance work. You will also need strong communication skills that will help you broaden your client base as well as help you explain to your clients what work needs to be done.

Postsecondary Training

There are two main routes to becoming a music instrument repairer and tuner: extensive apprenticeship or formal education through technical or vocational schools. Apprenticeships, however, can be difficult to find. You will simply need to contact instrument repair shops and request a position as a trainee. Once you have found a position, the training period may last from two to five years. You will get hands-on experience working with the instruments as well as having other duties around the shop, such as selling any products offered.

Depending on the family of instruments you want to work with, there are a number of technical or vocational schools that offer either courses or full-time programs in repair and maintenance work. Professional organizations may have information on such schools. The National Association of Professional Band Instrument Repair Technicians, for example, provides a listing of schools offering programs in band instrument repair. The Piano Technicians Guild has information on both full-time programs and correspondence courses. Wind-instrument repairers can learn their craft at one of the handful of vocational schools in the country that offers classes in instrument repair. Entrance requirements vary among schools, but all require at least a high school diploma or GED. Typical classes that are part of any type of instrument repair and tuning education include acoustics, tool care and operation, and small business practices. Depending on what instrument you choose to specialize in, you may also study topics such as buffing, dent removal, plating, soldering, or woodworking. You may also be required to invest in personal hand tools and supplies, and you may need to make tools that are not available from suppliers.

If you are interested in working with electronic organs, you will need at least one year of electronics technical training to learn organ repair skills. Electronics training is available from community colleges and technical and vocational schools. The U.S. Armed Forces also offer excellent training in electronics, which you can apply to instrument work. Electronic organ technicians also may attend training courses offered by electronic organ manufacturers.

It is important to keep in mind that even those who take courses or attend school for their postsecondary training will need to spend years honing their skills.

A number of instrument repairers and tuners have completed some college work or have a bachelor's degree. Although no colleges award bachelor's degrees in instrument repair, people who major in some type of music performance may find this background adds to their understanding of the work.

Certification or Licensing

The Piano Technicians Guild helps its members improve their skills and keep up with developments in piano technology. Refresher courses and seminars in new developments are offered by local chapters, and courses offered by manufacturers are publicized in Guild publications. The guild also administers a series of tests that can lead to certification as a registered piano technician.

Other Requirements

Personal qualifications for people in this occupational group include keen hearing and eyesight, mechanical aptitude, and manual dexterity. You should be resourceful and able to learn on the job, because every instrument that needs repair is unique and requires individual care. You must also have the desire to learn throughout your professional life by studying trade magazines and manufacturers' service manuals related to new developments in the field. You can also improve your skills in training programs and at regional and national seminars. Instrument manufacturers often offer training in the repair of their particular products.

Other qualifications for this career relate to your instrument specialty. For example, if you want to work as a piano technician, you should be able to communicate clearly when talking about a piano's problems and when advising a customer. A pleasant manner and good appearance are important to instill confidence. While the physical strength required for moving a piano is not often needed, you may be required to bend or stand in awkward positions while working on the piano. If you are interested in working as a pipe organ technician, you will need the ability to follow blueprints and printed instructions to plan and execute repair or installation work. And any repairer and tuner who works in a store selling musical instruments should be comfortable working with the public.

EXPLORING

One of the best ways to explore this field is to take some type of musical instrument lessons. This experience will help you develop an ear for tonal quality and acquaint you with the care of your instrument. It will also put you in contact with those who work professionally with music. You may develop a contact with someone at the store where you have purchased or rented your instrument, and, naturally, you will get to know your music teacher. Ask these people what they know about the repair and tuning business. Your high school or local college music departments can also be excellent places for meeting those who work with instruments. Ask teachers in these departments whom they know working in instrument repair. You may be able to set up an informational interview with a repairer and tuner you find through these contacts. Ask the repairer about his or her education, how he or she got interested in the work, what he or she would recommend for someone considering the field, and any other questions you may have.

Part-time and summer jobs that are related closely to this occupation may be difficult to obtain because full-time trainees usually handle the routine tasks of a helper. Nevertheless, it is worth applying for such work at music stores and repair shops in case they do not use full-time trainees. General clerical jobs in stores that sell musical instruments may help familiarize you with the language of the field and may offer you the opportunity to observe skilled repairers at work.

EMPLOYERS

Approximately 6,100 people work as musical instrument repairers and tuners of all types in the United States. About one in six are self-employed and may operate out of their own homes. The majority of the rest work in repair shops and music stores and for manufacturers. Large cities with extensive professional music activity, both in the United States and in Europe, are the best places for employment. Musical centers such as Chicago, New York, London, and Vienna are the hubs of the repair business for stringed instruments, and any repairer who wishes a sufficient amount of work may have to relocate to one of these cities.

Some piano technicians work in factories where pianos are made. They may assemble and adjust pianos or inspect the finished instruments. Some technicians work in shops that rebuild pianos. Many piano repairers and tuners work in customers' homes.

Most of the few hundred pipe organ technicians in the United States are self-employed. These pipe organ technicians are primarily engaged in repairing and tuning existing organs. A small number are employed by organ manufacturers and are engaged in testing and installing new instruments. The great expense involved in manufacturing and installing a completely new pipe organ decreases demand and makes this type of work scarce.

STARTING OUT

Vocational schools and community colleges that offer instrument repair training can usually connect recent graduates with repair shops that have job openings. Those who enter the field through apprenticeships work at the local shop where they are receiving their training. Professional organizations may also have information on job openings.

ADVANCEMENT

Repairers and tuners may advance their skills by participating in special training programs. A few who work for large dealers or repair shops may move into supervisory positions. Some instrument repair technicians become instructors in music instrument repair programs at community colleges and technical institutes.

Another path to advancement is to open one's own musical repair shop and service. Before doing this, however, the worker should have adequate training to survive the strong competition that exists in the tuning and repair business. In many cases, repairers may need to continue working for another employer until they develop a clientele large enough to support a full-time business.

A few restorers of stringed instruments earn worldwide reputations for their exceptional skill. Their earnings and the caliber of their customers both rise significantly when they become well known. It takes a great deal of hard work and talent to achieve such professional standing, however, and this recognition only comes after years in the field. At any one time, there may be perhaps 10 restorers in the world who perform exceptional work, while another 100 or so are known for doing very good work. The work of these few craftspeople is always in great demand.

EARNINGS

Wages vary depending on geographic area and the worker's specialty, skill, and speed at making repairs. Full-time instrument repairers and tuners had a median income of $29,200 in 2006, according to the U.S. Department of Labor. The highest paid 10 percent earned $50,580 or more per year, and the lowest paid earned less than $16,230 annually. Some helpers work for the training they get and receive no pay. Repairers and tuners who are self-employed earn more than those who work for music stores or instrument manufacturers, but their income is generally less stable. Repairers who gain an international reputation for the quality of their work earn the highest income in this field.

Repairers and tuners working as employees of manufacturers or stores often receive some benefits, including health insurance, vacation days, and holiday and sick pay. Self-employed repairers and tuners must provide these for themselves.

WORK ENVIRONMENT

Repairers and tuners work in shops, homes, and instrument factories, surrounded by the tools and materials of their trade. The atmosphere is somewhat quiet but the pace is often busy. Since repairers and tuners are usually paid by the piece, they have to concentrate and work diligently on their repairs. Piano technicians and tuners generally perform their work in homes, schools, churches, and other places where pianos are located.

Instrument tuners and repairers may work more than 40 hours a week, especially during the fall and winter, when people spend more time indoors playing musical instruments. Self-employed tuners and repairers often work evenings and weekends, when it is more convenient to meet with customers.

As noted, many repairs demand extreme care and often long periods of time to complete. For large instruments, such as pianos and pipe organs, repairers and tuners may have to work in cramped locations for some length of time, bending, stretching, and using tools that require physical strength to handle. Tuning pianos and organs often requires many hours and can be tedious work.

The field at times may be very competitive, especially among the more prestigious repair shops for stringed instruments. Most people at the major repair shops know each other and vie for the same business. There is often a great deal of pressure from owners to fix their instruments as soon as possible, but a conscientious repairer cannot be rushed into doing a mediocre job. In spite of these drawbacks, repair work is almost always interesting, challenging, and rewarding. Repairers never do the same job twice, and each instrument comes with its own set of challenges. The work requires repairers to call on their ingenuity, skill, and personal pride every day.

OUTLOOK

Job opportunities for musical instrument repairers and tuners are expected to grow more slowly than the average for all occupations through 2014, according to the U.S. Department of Labor. This is a small, specialized field, and replacement needs will be the source of most jobs. Because training positions and school programs are relatively difficult to find, those with thorough training and education will have the best employment outlook.

It is a luxury for most owners to have their instruments tuned and repaired, and they tend to postpone these services when money is scarce. Tuners and repairers therefore may lose income during economic downturns. In addition, few trainees are hired at repair shops or music stores when business is slow.

FOR MORE INFORMATION

For information on organ and choral music fields, contact
American Guild of Organists
475 Riverside Drive, Suite 1260
New York, NY 10115-0055
Tel: 212-870-2310
Email: info@agohq.org
http://www.agohq.org

The GAL is an international organization of stringed-instrument makers and repairers. Visit the FAQ section of its Web site for information on building and repairing instruments and choosing a training program.

Guild of American Luthiers (GAL)
8222 South Park Avenue
Tacoma, WA 98408-5226
Tel: 253-472-7853
http://www.luth.org

For information about band instrument repair, contact
National Association of Professional Band Instrument Repair
   Technicians
PO Box 51
Normal, IL 61761-0051
Tel: 309-452-4257
http://www.napbirt.org

For information on certification, contact
Piano Technicians Guild
4444 Forest Avenue
Kansas City, KS 66106-3750
Tel: 913-432-9975
Email: ptg@ptg.org
http://www.ptg.org

Packaging Machinery Technicians

OVERVIEW

Packaging machinery technicians work with automated machinery that packages products into bottles, cans, bags, boxes, cartons, and other containers. The machines perform various operations, such as forming, filling, closing, labeling, and marking. The systems and technologies that packaging machinery technicians work with are diverse. Depending on the job, packaging machinery technicians may work with electrical, mechanical, hydraulic, or pneumatic systems. They also may work with computerized controllers, fiber-optic transmitters, robotic units, and vision systems.

HISTORY

Packaging has been used since ancient times, when people first wrapped food in materials to protect it or devised special carriers to transport items over long distances. One of the oldest packaging materials, glass, was used by Egyptians as early as 3000 B.C. Packaging as we know it, though, has its origins in the industrial revolution. Machinery was used for mass production of items, and manufacturers needed some way to package products and protect them during transport. Packages and containers were developed that not only kept goods from damage during shipment, but also helped to increase the shelf life of perishable items.

Initially, packaging was done by hand. Workers at manufacturing plants hand-packed products into paper boxes, steel cans, glass

QUICK FACTS

School Subjects
Mathematics
Technical/shop

Personal Skills
Mechanical/manipulative
Technical/scientific

Work Environment
Primarily indoors
Primarily multiple locations

Minimum Education Level
High school diploma

Salary Range
$20,000 to $41,050 to $70,000

Certification or Licensing
Voluntary

Outlook
More slowly than the average

DOT
638

GOE
05.03.02

NOC
7311

O*NET-SOC
49-9041.00, 49-9042.00

jars, or other containers as they were produced. As manufacturing processes and methods improved, equipment and machines were developed to provide quicker and less expensive ways to package products. Automated machinery was in use by the 19th century and was used not only to package products but also to create packaging materials. The first containers produced through automated machinery were glass containers created by Michael Owens in Toledo, Ohio, in 1903.

The use of new packaging materials, such as cellophane in the 1920s and aluminum cans in the early 1960s, required updated machinery to handle the new materials and to provide faster, more efficient production. Semiautomatic machines and eventually high-speed, fully automated machines were created to handle a wide variety of products, materials, and packaging operations. Today, packaging engineers, packaging machinery technicians, and other engineering professionals work to develop new equipment and techniques that are more time-, material-, and cost-efficient. Advanced technologies, such as robotics, are allowing for the creation of increasingly sophisticated packaging machinery.

THE JOB

Packaging machinery technicians work in packaging plants of various industries or in the plants of packaging machinery manufacturers. Their jobs entail building machines, installing and setting up equipment, training operators to use the equipment, maintaining equipment, troubleshooting, and repairing machines. Many of the machines today are computer-controlled and may include robotic or vision-guided applications.

Machinery builders, also called *assemblers*, assist engineers in the development and modification of new and existing machinery designs. They build different types of packaging machinery by following engineering blueprints, wiring schematics, pneumatic diagrams, and plant layouts. Beginning with a machine frame that has been welded in another department, they assemble electrical circuitry, mechanical components, and fabricated items that they may have made themselves in the plant's machine shop. They may also be responsible for bolting on additional elements of the machine to the frame. After the machinery is assembled, they perform a test run to make sure it is performing according to specifications.

Field service technicians, also called *field service representatives*, are employed by packaging machinery manufacturers. They do most of their work at the plants where the packaging machinery is being used. In some companies, *assemblers* may serve as field service technicians; in others, the field service representative is a technician other than the assembler. In either case, they install new machinery at customers' plants and train in-plant machine operators and maintenance personnel on its operation and maintenance.

When a new machine is delivered, the field service technicians level it and anchor it to the plant floor. Then, following engineering drawings, wiring plans, and plant layouts, they install the system's electrical and electromechanical components. They also regulate the controls and setup for the size, thickness, and type of material to be processed and ensure the correct sequence of processing stages. After installation, the technicians test-run the machinery and make any necessary adjustments. Then they teach machine operators the proper operating and maintenance procedures for that piece of equipment. The entire installation process, which may take a week, is carefully documented. Field service representatives may also help the plant's in-house mechanics troubleshoot equipment already in operation, including modifying equipment for greater efficiency and safety.

Automated packaging machine mechanics, also called *maintenance technicians*, perform scheduled preventive maintenance as well as diagnose machinery problems and make repairs. Preventive maintenance is done on a regular basis following the manufacturer's guidelines in the service manual. During routine maintenance, technicians change filters in vacuum pumps, grease fittings, change oil in gearboxes, and replace worn bushings, chains, and belts. When machines do break down, maintenance technicians must work quickly to fix them so that production can resume as soon as possible. The technician might be responsible for all the machinery in the plant, one or more packaging lines, or a single machine. In a small plant, a single technician may be responsible for all the duties required to keep a packaging line running, while in a large plant a team of technicians may divide the duties.

REQUIREMENTS

High School

Although a high school diploma is not required, it is preferred by most employers who hire packaging or engineering technicians. In high school, you should take geometry and vo-tech classes such as electrical shop, machine shop, and mechanical drawing. Computer classes, including computer-aided design, are also helpful. In addition to developing mechanical and electrical abilities, you should develop communication skills through English and writing classes.

Postsecondary Training

Many employers prefer to hire technicians who have completed a two-year technical training program. Completing a machinery training program or packaging machinery program can provide you with the necessary knowledge and technical skills for this type of work. Machinery training programs are available at community colleges, trade schools, and technical institutes throughout the country, but there are only a few technical colleges specializing in packaging machinery programs. These programs award either a degree or certificate in automated packaging machinery systems.

Packaging machinery programs generally last two years and include extensive hands-on training as well as classroom study. You will learn to use simple hand tools, such as hacksaws, drill presses, lathes, mills, and grinders. Other technical courses cover sheet metal and welding work, power transmission, electrical and mechanical systems, maintenance operations, industrial safety, and hazardous materials handling.

Classes in packaging operations include bag making, loading, and closing; case loading; blister packaging; palletizing, conveying, and accumulating; and labeling and bar coding. There are also classes in form fill, seal wrap, and carton machines as well as packaging quality control and package design and testing. Courses especially critical in an industry where technology is increasingly sophisticated are PLC (programmable logic control), CAD/CAM (computer-aided design and manufacturing), fiber optics, robotics, and servo controls.

Certification or Licensing

Although employers may not require certification, it can provide a competitive advantage when seeking employment. A voluntary certification program is available for engineering technicians through the National Institute for Certification in Engineering Technologies (NICET). Certification is available at various levels and in different specialty fields. Most programs require passing a written exam and possessing a certain amount of work experience. The Institute of Packaging Professionals offers the following voluntary certifications: certified professional in training (for professionals with less than six years of experience in packaging) and certified packaging professional (for professionals with at least six years of experience in packaging).

Union membership may be a requirement for some jobs, depending on union activity at a particular company. Unions are more likely found in large-scale national and international corporations. Field service technicians are usually not unionized. Maintenance technicians and assemblers may be organized by the International Brotherhood of Teamsters or the International Association of Machinists and Aerospace Workers. In addition, some technicians may be represented by the International Longshore and Warehouse Union.

Other Requirements

If you are interested in this field, you should have mechanical and electrical aptitudes, manual dexterity, and the ability to work under deadline pressure. In addition, you should have analytical and problem-solving skills. The ability to communicate effectively with people from varying backgrounds is especially important as packaging machinery technicians work closely with engineers, plant managers, customers, and machinery operators. You need to be able to listen to workers' problems as well as to explain things clearly. Packaging machinery technicians frequently have to provide written reports, so good writing skills are beneficial.

EXPLORING

You can test your interest in this type of work by engaging in activities that require mechanical and electrical skills, such as building a short-wave radio, taking appliances apart, and working on cars, motorcycles, and bicycles. Participating in science clubs and contests can also provide opportunities for working with electrical and mechanical equipment and building and repairing things. Taking vocational shop classes can also help you explore your interests and acquire useful skills.

Consider visiting a plant or manufacturing company to observe packaging operations and see packaging machinery technicians at work. Many plants provide school tours, and you may be able to arrange a visit through a school counselor or teacher. Reading trade publications can also familiarize you with the industry.

EMPLOYERS

Packaging machinery technicians are usually employed by companies that manufacture packaging machinery or by companies that package the products they produce. Packaging is one of the largest industries in the United States, so jobs are plentiful across the country, in small towns and large cities. Opportunities in the packaging field can be found in almost any company that produces and packages a product. Food, beverages, chemicals, cosmetics, electronics, pharmaceuticals, automotive parts, hardware, plastics, and almost any products one can think of need to be packaged before reaching the consumer market. Because of this diversity, jobs are not restricted to any product, geographic location, or plant size.

STARTING OUT

If you are enrolled in a technical program you may find job leads through your schools' office of career services. Many jobs in packaging are unadvertised—you can only find out about them through contacts with professionals in the industry. You can also learn about openings from teachers, school administrators, and industry contacts acquired during training.

You can apply directly to machinery manufacturing companies or companies with manufacturing departments. Local employment offices may list job openings. Sometimes companies hire part-time or summer help in other departments, such as the warehouse or shipping. These jobs may provide an opportunity to move into other areas of the company.

ADVANCEMENT

Technicians usually begin in entry-level positions and work as part of an engineering team. They may advance from a maintenance technician to an assembler, and then move up to a supervisory position in production operations or packaging machinery. They can also become *project managers* and *field service managers*.

Workers who show an interest in their work, who learn quickly, and have good technical skills can gradually take on more responsibilities and advance to higher positions. The ability to work as part of a team and communicate well with others, plus self-motivation and the ability to work well without a lot of supervision, are all helpful traits for advancement. People who have skills as a packaging machinery technician can usually transfer those skills to engineering technician positions in other industries.

Some packaging machinery technicians pursue additional education to qualify as an engineer and move into packaging engineering, electrical engineering, mechanical engineering, or industrial engineering positions. Other technicians pursue business, economics, and finance degrees and use these credentials to obtain positions in other areas of the manufacturing process, in business development, or in areas such as importing or exporting.

EARNINGS

Earnings vary with geographical area and the employee's skill level and specific duties and job responsibilities. Other variables that may affect salary include the size of the company and the type of industry, such as the food and beverage industry or the electronics industry. Technicians who work at companies with unions generally, but not always, earn higher salaries.

In general, technicians earn approximately $20,000 a year to start and with experience can increase their salaries to approximately $33,000. Seasoned workers with two-year degrees who work for large companies may earn between $50,000 and $70,000 a year, particularly those in field service jobs or in supervisory positions.

In 2006, median hourly earnings for industrial machinery mechanics were $19.74 (or $41,050 annually), according to the U.S. Department of Labor. Earnings ranged from $12.84 an hour (or $26,710 annually) to $29.85 or more per hour (or $62,080 or more annually).

Packaging machinery technicians who are certified by the Institute of Packaging Professionals earn higher salaries than technicians who are not certified. According to an IoPP survey, certified packaging professionals earned between 7 percent and 10 percent more than non-certified workers.

Benefits vary and depend upon company policy but generally include paid holidays, vacations, sick days, and medical and dental insurance. Some companies also offer tuition assistance programs, pension plans, profit sharing, and 401(k) plans.

WORK ENVIRONMENT

Packaging machinery technicians work in a variety of environments. They may work for a machinery manufacturer or in the manufacturing department of a plant or factory. Most plants are clean and well ventilated, although actual conditions vary based on the type of product manufactured and packaged. Certain types of industries and manufacturing methods can pose special problems. For example, plants involved in paperboard and paper manufacturing may have dust created from paper fibers. Workers in food plants may be exposed to strong smells from the food being processed, although most workers usually get accustomed to this. Pharmaceutical and electronic component manufacturers may require special conditions to ensure that the manufacturing environments are free from dirt, contamination, and static. Clean-air environments may be special rooms that are temperature- and moisture-controlled, and technicians may be required to wear special clothing or equipment when working in these rooms.

In general, most plants have no unusual hazards, although safety practices need to be followed when working on machinery and using tools. The work is generally not strenuous, although it does involve carrying small components and hand tools, and some bending and stretching.

Most packaging machinery technicians work 40 hours a week, although overtime may be required, especially during the installation of new machinery or when equipment malfunctions. Some technicians may be called in during the evening or on weekends to repair machinery that has shut down production operations. Installation and testing periods of new equipment can also be very time-intensive and stressful when problems develop. Troubleshooting, diagnosing problems, and repairing equipment may involve considerable time as well as trial-and-error testing until the correct solution is determined.

Technicians who work for machinery manufacturers may be required to travel to customers' plants to install new machinery or to service or maintain existing equipment. This may require overnight stays or travel to foreign locations.

OUTLOOK

The U.S. Department of Labor predicts slower-than-average employment growth through 2014 for packaging machinery technicians. However, with the growth of the packaging industry, which grosses more than $100 billion a year, a nationwide shortage of trained packaging technicians has developed over the last 20 years. There are far more openings than there are qualified applicants.

The packaging machinery industry is expected to continue its growth in the next decade. American-made packaging machinery has earned a worldwide reputation for high quality and is known for its outstanding control systems and electronics. Continued success in global competition will remain important to the packaging machinery industry's prosperity and employment outlook.

The introduction of computers, robotics, fiber optics, and vision systems into the industry has added new skill requirements and job opportunities for packaging machinery technicians. There is already widespread application of CAD/CAM technology. The use of computers in packaging machinery will continue to increase, with computers communicating with other computers on the status of operations and providing diagnostic maintenance information and production statistics. The role of robotics, fiber optics, and electronics will also continue to expand. To be prepared for the jobs of the future, packaging machinery students should seek training in the newest technologies.

With packaging one of the largest industries in the United States, jobs can be found across the country, in small towns and large cities, in small companies or multiplant international corporations. The jobs are not restricted to any one industry or geographical location—wherever there is industry, there is some kind of packaging going on.

FOR MORE INFORMATION

For information on certification and the packaging industry, contact

Institute of Packaging Professionals
1601 North Bond Street, Suite 101
Naperville, IL 60563-0114
Tel: 630-544-5050
Email: info@iopp.net
http://www.iopp.org

For information on certification, contact

National Institute for Certification in Engineering Technologies
1420 King Street
Alexandria, VA 22314-2794
Tel: 888-476-4238
http://www.nicet.org

For information on educational programs, contact

National Institute of Packaging, Handling, and Logistics
Engineers
177 Fairsom Court
Lewisburg, PA 17837-6844
Tel: 866-464-7453
Email: niphle@dejazzd.com
http://www.niphle.org

For industry information, contact
Packaging Machinery Manufacturers Institute
4350 North Fairfax Drive, Suite 600
Arlington, VA 22203-1632
Tel: 888-275-7664
Email: pmmiwebhelp@PMMI.org
http://www.pmmi.org

Index

Entries and page numbers in **bold** indicate major treatment of a topic.

A

AAMI (Association for the Advancement of Medical Instrumentation) 84, 87–88
accordion repairers 179
accordion tuners 179
Accrediting Commission of Career Schools and Colleges of Technology 60, 65
adjustors (elevator) 121
aeronautical technicians 5–16
  job description 6–9
  requirements 10–11
aeronautics, definition of 6
aerospace physiological technicians 7
aerospace technicians 5–16
  job description 6–9
  requirements 10–11
agricultural engineering technicians 19
agricultural equipment technician 17–25
  job description 18–20
  requirements 20–21
agricultural equipment test technicians 19
Air Commerce Act of 1926 27
air-conditioning technicians 38
aircraft industry, history of 6
aircraft launch and recovery technicians 7
aircraft mechanics 26–35
  job description 27–29
  requirements 29–31
aircraft powerplant mechanics 28
airframe mechanics 28
airlines, employment by 31
alternative fuel technicians (automotive) 58
American Boatbuilders and Repairers Association 165, 170
appliance service technicians 36–44
  job description 37–38
  requirements 38–40
appliance technicians 38

ASE. *See* National Institute for Automotive Service Excellence
Association for the Advancement of Medical Instrumentation (AAMI) 84, 87–88
Association of Diesel Specialists 109, 114
Association for Facilities Engineering 143, 146
automated packaging machine mechanics 189
automated people movers (APMs) 118
automation, in biomedical equipment 80
automobile, jobs created by 45–46
automobile collision repairers 45–54
  job description 46–48
  requirements 48–50
automobile-radiator mechanics 58
automobile service technicians 55–67
  job description 56–59
  requirements 59–61
Automotive Body Repair News (magazine) 50
automotive painters 47
aviation, timeline of 8–9
avionics technicians 7, 29, 98

B

Barnett Bicycle Institute 71, 73, 76
Bell, Alexander Graham 96
bench repairers (marine) 164
bicycle, history of 68–69, 72
bicycle mechanics 68–78
  job description 69–71, 77
  requirements 71–72
biomedical engineering technology 83
biomedical equipment technicians 79–88, 157
  job description 81–82
  requirements 83–84
Board of Examiners for Biomedical Equipment Technicians 84, 159
boat brokers 168
Boating Industry (magazine) 167